English A: Literature

FOR THE IB DIPLOMA

Hannah Tyson
Mark Beverley

OXFORD
UNIVERSITY PRESS

OXFORD
UNIVERSITY PRESS

Great Clarendon Street, Oxford OX2 6DP

Oxford University Press is a department of the University of Oxford.
It furthers the University's objective of excellence in research,
scholarship, and education by publishing worldwide in

Oxford New York

Auckland Cape Town Dar es Salaam Hong Kong Karachi
Kuala Lumpur Madrid Melbourne Mexico City Nairobi
New Delhi Shanghai Taipei Toronto

With offices in

Argentina Austria Brazil Chile Czech Republic France Greece
Guatemala Hungary Italy Japan Poland Portugal Singapore
South Korea Switzerland Thailand Turkey Ukraine Vietnam

Oxford is a registered trade mark of Oxford University Press
in the UK and in certain other countries

© Oxford University Press 2012

British Library Cataloguing in Publication Data

Data available

ISBN: 978-0-19-912970-6
10 9 8 7 6 5 4 3 2 1

Printed in Great Britain by Bell & Bain Ltd, Glasgow

Paper used in the production of this book is a natural, recyclable product made
from wood grown in sustainable forests. The manufacturing process conforms
to the environmental regulations of the country of origin

Acknowledgments

The publisher would like to thank the following for their kind permission to
reproduce photographs:

Cover: Sam Rothenstein/Michael Rothenstein; **P5:** Lewis, Percy Wyndham/
International War Museum; **P43:** © Pictorial Press Ltd/Alamy; **P49:** John
Klossner/The New Yorker Collection; **P65:** Getty Images; **P67:** Dudarev Mikhail;
P70: K. Kendall; **P70:** The Lovers, 1870 (Oil On Canvas), Szinyei Merse, Pal
(1845-1920)/Hungarian National Gallery, Budapest, Hungary/The Bridgeman
Art Library; **P76:** Carolthacker/Istock; **P79:** © Christopher Felver/Corbis; **P79:**
The Brechin Group INC; **P82:** Wim Claes/Shutterstock; **P102:** AAM Archives
Committee/Bodleian Library, University Of Oxford.; **P102:** Getty Images; **P102:**
Paul Weinberg/South Photographs/Africa Media Online; **P104:** Marilyn Kingwill/
Arenapal; **P104:** © Robbie Jack/Corbis; **P150:** Michael Joyce; **P151:** Ingrid
Ankerson; **P153:** Nick Montfort; **P157:** Serg64/Shutterstock; **P164:** Everett
Collection/Rex Features; **P164:** © AF Archive/Alamy; **P164:** Everett Collection/
Rex Features.

The author and publisher are grateful for permission to reprint extracts from
the following copyright material:

Edward Albee: *Who's Afraid of Virginia Woolf*, published by Jonathan Cape, reprinted by permission of The Random House Group Limited.

Gillian Clarke: 'The Field Mouse' from *Five Fields*, November 1998, reprinted by
permission of Carcanet Press Ltd.

Wendy Cope: 'An ABC of the BBC', reprinted by permission of United Agents on
behalf of Wendy Cope.

Githa Hariharan: *The Thousand Faces of Night*, copyright © 1996 by Githa Hariharan, reprinted by permission of Georges Borchardt, Inc., for the Author.

Brian Keenan: *An Evil Cradling*, published by Hutchinson, reprinted by permission
of The Random House Group Limited.

Louis MacNeice: 'Sunlight in the Garden' from *Collected Poems*, Faber & Faber,
reprinted by permission of David Higham.

Michael Ondaatje: *Running in the Family*, © Michael Ondaatje, reprinted by permission of Bloomsbury Publishing Plc. and W. W. Norton and Co.

George Orwell: *Down and Out in Paris and London* (Penguin Books 1940), copyright
© George Orwell, 1933, copyright © renewed by Sonia Pitt-Rivers © The Estate
of the Late Sonia Brownell Orwell, 1986, reprinted by permission of Houghton
Mifflin Harcourt Publishing Company, by permission of Bill Hamilton as the
Literary Executor of the Estate of the Late Sonia Brownell Orwell and by permis-
sion of Penguin Books Ltd.

George Orwell: 'A Hanging' from: *Essays*, with an introduction by Bernard Crick
(first published as *The Collected Essays, Journalism and Letters of George Orwell Vol's 1-4*
Martin Secker & Warburg 1968, this edition Penguin Books 2000) | *The Complete
Works of George Orwell* edited by Peter Davison, copyright © the Estate of the Late
Sonia Brownell Orwell, 1984, 'Introduction' copyright © Bernard Crick, 1994, reprinted by permission of The Random House Group Ltd. and Penguin Books Ltd.

Don Paterson: 'Waking with Russell' from *Landing Light*, copyright © 2005 by
Don Paterson, reprinted by permission of The Permissions Company, Inc., on
behalf of Graywolf Press www.graywolfpress.org.

Stephen Spender: 'The Express' from *New Collected Poems*, Faber & Faber UK ©
2004, reprinted by kind permission of the Estate of Stephen Spender.

John Steinbeck: *The Grapes of Wrath* (Penguin Books, 2001), copyright 1939 by
John Steinbeck, renewed © 1967 by John Steinbeck, reprinted by permission of
Penguin Books Ltd. and Viking Penguin, a division of Penguin Group (USA) Inc.

Tennessee Williams: *A Streetcar Named Desire*, copyright © 1947, 1953 by The
University of The South, reprinted by permission of Georges Borchardt, Inc. for
the Estate of Tennessee Williams and by permission of New Directions Publishing Corp.

Although we have made every effort to trace and contact all copyright holders
before publication this has not been possible in all cases. If notified, the publisher will rectify any errors or omissions at the earliest opportunity.

MIX
Paper from
responsible sources
FSC® C007785

Contents

Introduction

This book is designed to give students information, advice, and practice with the skills they need to complete each of the assessments required in Language A Literature.

It will be useful to students at both Higher and Standard Levels. In a number of cases the nature of the assessment is very similar at both levels; but in others, there are significant variations, which occur either in the nature of the assessment task or in the criteria used to mark them.

Although there are many ways to organize these materials, we have chosen to do so by the four "Parts" of the syllabus studied, since the "Parts" are most often studied as units during the course, although not always in the same order. As the Paper 1 assessment is not directly related to any one "Part", but addresses one of the essential skills for this course, it forms the initial section of the book.

Skills practised in one part of the book will almost certainly relate to those in some other sections, for example, the skills of written commentary, on a piece of literature needed in Paper 1 are also covered in the section on Part 2, where the commentary is delivered orally. Skills needed for Paper 2 (a literary essay) are developed through working toward the Written Assignment in Part 1. At times you will find similar aspects of the course, such as commentary, approached in more than one way. Just as different teachers will guide you somewhat individually to read and write as part of your English course, so the varying approaches here should broaden your skills and practice in this IB course.

Practice with reading literature and writing about it, the terms used in producing critical analysis, and practice with producing assessment tasks, as well as both understanding the assessment criteria and applying them are found throughout the book. Different groups of students will use the parts of the book in various sequences, based on the order in which the course is followed.

It is our hope that the many activities and examples found throughout the book will help students achieve clarity and build confidence in the successful completion of the course.

Thank you to the contributors Theodoros Chiotis, Max Jones, Patty Milligan, and Merion Taynton for their hard work and contributions towards Parts 1 and 4 of this book.

1 The skills of close reading

Throughout this book you will find continual reminders of the need to consider literary texts as works of art that have been carefully and deliberately constructed. In each part of the course, your attention will be drawn in different ways to the tools writers use in this creative process and much of your time will be spent identifying these tools as well as the effects they achieve. In many respects, this important premise is targeted particularly in the first of the course's two external examination papers, and so it is with this paper that we are going to begin.

In Paper 1, you are asked to demonstrate the ability to respond to poems, prose, or even dramatic texts that you will not have seen before. At Higher Level (HL) your examination answer is referred to as a 'Literary Commentary' and at Standard Level (SL) as a 'Guided Literary Analysis'. As we will see, the exam sits quite closely alongside the Part 2 Individual Oral Commentary (IOC) because both ask you to focus on the details of particular literary extracts, but a key point of difference is that in this first written paper you won't have any prior knowledge of the works chosen. This means that your preparation will focus on the acquisition and application of skills that can be applied to a range of different passages without knowledge of their context.

The aims of this chapter are:

1. To highlight the core skills and practices you will need to acquire for Paper 1.

2. To provide advice with constructive approaches to adopt in the examination.

3. To read examples of good practice.

Responding to something unseen

In the following introductory activities you are going to explore a range of ideas designed to give you confidence with responding to the art of literary writing when you come to it for the first time.

Activity

To begin with, let's explore a method for responding to an unseen work of art, and trace the journey from initial observation through to final evaluation. Because there are many points of similarity between literature and the visual arts in the way we read and make sense of them, let's begin with a picture.

Take some time to study the one you see below:

A Battery Shelled (1919), Wyndham Lewis.

Now follow the steps below as precisely as you can.

Step 1: Write a brief description of what you see in general in the picture.

Step 2: Write a brief description of particular details in the picture that you happen to notice. Think about why you notice them.

Step 3: How would you describe the way the various people, objects, and settings are presented? i.e. their colours, shapes, position, etc.

Step 4: How is your eye drawn around the picture? Trace the route your visual imagination takes by drawing a rough sketch of the painting and plotting its route on a piece of paper.

Step 5: What kinds of ideas do you think the picture is interested in?

Step 6: What do you think the artist's attitude is towards these subjects? Why?

Step 7: Do you think it is a good picture? Do you like it? Write down a few reasons that justify your reasoning.

The different kinds of thinking you have just undertaken, starting from the purely **observational** in steps 1 and 2, moving into the more **analytical** in steps 3 and 4, and through to the **interpretive** in steps 5 to 7, are going to come into play when you look at the Paper 1 extract.

Here is one student's response to the above task. Annotate her comments by identifying differences in the statements she makes (e.g. descriptive, analytical, interpretive), which reflect some of the stages outlined above.

Activity

Try completing this task again but with reference to a painting of *your* choosing. Select one that you have not seen before, and compare your response with others in your group. Did you all take the same 'reading journey' around the painting? Which particular details led you to your final interpretation and evaluation?

I can't say I like this picture because its subject and mood are rather bleak. It does strike me as very powerful, however. The subject is war and the different subjects within the picture are all depicted in a harsh, angular manner. In the foreground left of the picture there are three soldiers – perhaps officers – whom, I notice, are all looking in different directions, as if to indicate their detachment from each other and the carnage going on around them. Whilst to some extent their facial features are individualized, in contrast the figures in the background are all portrayed in a similar way. The formal similarity between these men and the destroyed building around them makes their actions seem mechanical and robotic, and they are shown to be vulnerable and broken, like the scenery around them. The painting seems to be making a comment, therefore, on the horror and brutality of the First World War – and, more particularly, highlights the industrialized nature of the killing that took place. It is quite shocking.

This brief activity captures the heart of what Paper 1 is all about. You have to show understanding of the content, form, and style of a piece of writing as well as demonstrate skills in independent thinking about its meaning and impact.

Activity

Looking at the painting on page 5 reminds us that the kinds of skills demanded by Paper 1 are ones that you will find developed throughout the range of texts studied on the course, but also in your general experience. And they can be acquired in reading, talking, and writing about any kind of literary text. On the next page are four different kinds of text types: a poem, an extract from a non-fiction article, a prose extract, and the lyrics from a song. Read them through carefully and jot down your impressions, trying to think about them in different ways, as we did with the picture. You could share thoughts with others, either through a class blog or simply by talking together.

- What kinds of things did you notice?
- How did your impressions compare with others?
- Did you like one text more than another?

Text 1

Waking with Russell

Whatever the difference is, it all began
the day we woke up face-to-face like lovers
and his four-day-old smile dawned on him again,
possessed him, till it would not fall or waver;
and I pitched back not my old hard-pressed grin
but his own smile, or one I'd rediscovered.
Dear son, I was *mezzo del' cammin*
and the true path was as lost to me as ever
when you cut in front and lit it as you ran.
See how the true gift never leaves the giver:
returned and redelivered, it rolled on
until the smile poured through us like a river.
How fine, I thought, this waking amongst men!
I kissed your mouth and pledged myself forever.

Don Paterson

(*mezzo del' cammin*: in the middle of life's path)

Text 2

Map-makers of Apartheid

It is late evening and the light is leaving Johannesburg North, fading out into the improbable vastness of Africa. As the darkness intensifies the security lights of houses along the road flicker into life. Behind the high walls, vicious dogs are on the prowl; revolvers are taken out of bedroom safes and tucked under pillows while each steel gate becomes a border.

Sometimes I stand in the garden after dark listening to the voices of Africa laughing, shouting, crying on the other side of the wall; they are voices of the warm dark, of maids, cooks and gardeners who live in the black world beyond the gates. Sooner or later the sirens of the police quick-response unit will ricochet through the dark and the assembled Rottweilers, Dobermans and German Shepherds will burst into unlovely barking. Somewhere out there, men will be hurtling towards a scene of violence and destruction while others struggle to feel secure inside the boundaries of their homes...

Fergal Keane

Text 3

Lullaby

The sun had gone down but the snow in the wind gave off its own light. It came in thick tufts like new wool – washed before the weaver spins it. Ayah reached out for it like her own babies had, and she smiled when she remembered how she had laughed at them. She was an old woman now, and her life had become memories. She sat down with her back against the wide cottonwood tree, feeling the rough bark on her back bones; she faced east and listened to the wind and snow sing a high-pitched Yeibechei song. Out of the wind she felt warmer, and she could watch the wide fluffy snow fill in her tracks, steadily, until the direction she had come from was gone. By the light of the snow she could see the dark outline of the big arroyo a few feet away. She was sitting on the edge of Cebolleta Creek, where in the springtime the thin cows would gaze on grass already chewed flat to the ground. In the wide deep creek bed where only a trickle of water flowed in the summer, the skinny cows would wander, looking for new grass along winding paths splashed with manure.

Leslie Marmon Silko

Text 4

Scattered Black and Whites

Been climbing trees, I've skinned my knees
My hands are black, the sun is going down
She scruffs my hair in the kitchen steam
She's listening to the dream I weaved today
Crosswords through the bathroom door
While someone sings the theme-tune to the news
And my sister buzzes through the room leaving perfume
in the air
And that's what triggered this.

I come back here from time to time
I shelter here some days.

A high-back chair. He sits and stares
A thousand yards and whistles marching-band
Kneeling by and speaking up
He reaches out and I take a massive hand.
Disjointed tales that flit between
Short trousers and a full dress uniform
And he talks of people ten years gone
Like I've known them all my life
Like scattered black 'n' whites?

I come back here from time to time
I shelter here some days.

Elbow

An important part of the process of responding to unseen material, therefore, is that your individual reactions to the text will mean something. Certain details will strike you more than others, and thinking about why this is so will lead you into making thoughtful, constructive responses.

The first key practice to adopt as you move through the two years of your literature course is to read as much as possible of different kinds of texts, and think about them in different ways. Doing so will greatly increase your sensitivity to features of language and style, as well as the different ways in which texts create their meaning.

Annotating

A second key practice is to get into the habit of annotating texts in detail. As stated above, any poem or prose extract will affect you in all kinds of ways when you look at it for the first time. Whether you are moved by it, challenged, made to think, made to laugh, shocked, confused, or inspired, the nature of your reaction will ultimately find a cause somewhere in the language, form, and meaning of the writing in front of you. Because of this, it is very important that the annotations you make reflect the variety of ways in which your reaction takes place. For example, look at the annotations below. Take time to study the symbols used as well as the written notes. What do they tell you about the response that the student had towards the poem and the way she interprets the point of the annotation process?

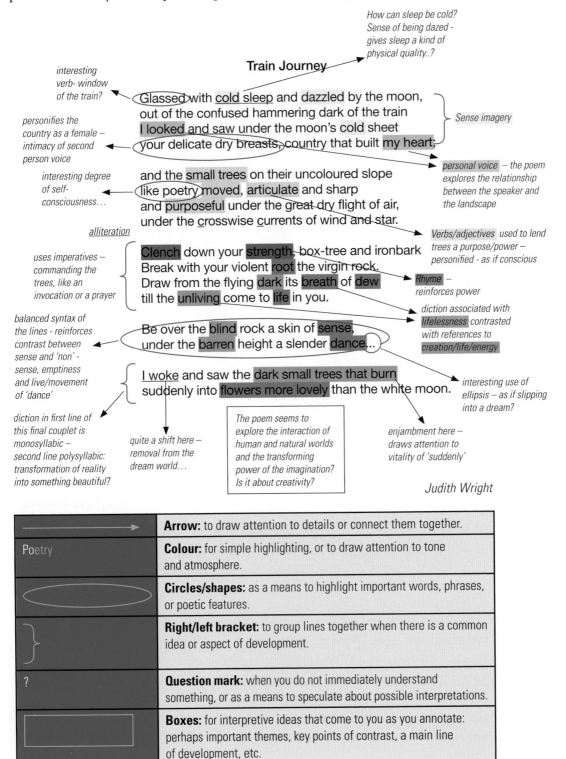

	Arrow: to draw attention to details or connect them together.
Poetry	**Colour:** for simple highlighting, or to draw attention to tone and atmosphere.
	Circles/shapes: as a means to highlight important words, phrases, or poetic features.
}	**Right/left bracket:** to group lines together when there is a common idea or aspect of development.
?	**Question mark:** when you do not immediately understand something, or as a means to speculate about possible interpretations.
	Boxes: for interpretive ideas that come to you as you annotate: perhaps important themes, key points of contrast, a main line of development, etc.

The annotation process is a record of your independent journey through the extract – from the moment you see it for the first time to the point at which you start to write your analysis. There are obviously parallels with the start of this chapter, when you looked at the painting in the first activity. The more you get into the habit of documenting your reactions and thinking about *why* the language and style encourages you to react in the way you do, the better. Indeed, teachers and examiners often comment on the fact that students who seem to do better in this component are ones who show evidence of 'active reading'. With careful and detailed annotation you will be reading the extract in the right kind of way, and as a result you will stand a much better chance of producing a successful piece of writing in the exam.

Focusing on the details

In other parts of the literature course you will spend considerable time talking about complete works – the way that action, themes, character, and so on develop through the work in its entirety. It is important to remember, however, that any complete literary work is only a sum of its parts. As we have just seen, the skills associated with identifying and exploring the impact of those parts is a crucial feature of Paper 1, the unseen commentary.

In the following units we are going to concentrate on the technical details, the tools that writers use to communicate their ideas. Each unit focuses on a different level or lens through which to look at the building blocks of poetry and prose. Our aim, as a result, will be to provide you with a range of angles from which to consider the way meaning in literary writing is constructed.

Hint

Some of the following activities ask you to explore literary tools in a fairly traditional, analytical way. However, an equally valid approach – and one that in many ways can be more successful as a means to sensitize yourself intuitively to the way writers use language for effect – is to write yourself. Maintaining a reading or writing journal is a highly valuable thing to do through these two years, and hopefully some of the writing activities below will be ones you can develop. Who knows? One day students of the future might well be exploring your writing as part of their IB programme!

Language and form

Imagine that a complete poem, or even a whole novel, was in front of you and that your eye was a camera that could zoom in on the smallest detail about which you could make some meaningful comment. What would that be? A sentence? A word? What about sound? Or indeed, what about the rhythms of poetry? Let's start there, with the sense of a simple beat, and test your ability to respond to its effects.

Hint

You can find more detailed reminders of the formal convention of rhythm and metre in poetry on the Internet.

Level 1: Focus on rhythm and sound

Activity

1. Hopefully you will be familiar with the terms 'stressed' and 'unstressed' syllables in a line of writing. Remind yourself of the way that patterns of stressed (/) and unstressed (⌣) beats are represented in poetry:

    ⌣ / ⌣ / ⌣ / ⌣ / ⌣ /

    If music be the food of love play on

    Try presenting the stressed and unstressed syllables of your name in the same way.

2. Where do you think the stressed and unstressed syllables occur in the lines of poetry below. Write the symbols above the lines.

Piping down the valleys wild Piping songs of pleasant glee -- from *Piping Down the Valleys Wild* by William Blake	
Now it is fog; I walk Contained within my coat -- from *Human Condition* by Thom Gunn	
Whose woods these are I think I know. His house is in the village though; -- from *Stopping by Woods on a Snowy Evening* by Robert Frost	
Bent double, like old beggars under sacks, Knock-kneed, coughing like hags, we cursed through sludge -- from *Dulce et Decorum Est* by Wilfred Owen	
Season of mists and mellow fruitfulness, Close bosom friend of the maturing sun -- from *To Autumn* by John Keats	

3. How many of the following terms, used to describe sound, do you know?
   - assonance/consonance
   - plosive/fricative
   - alliteration
   - onomatopoeia
   - full rhyme/half rhyme.

   See if you can identify examples of these techniques in the above examples and write a comment about their use in the right-hand column.

4. Think about the impact of sound and rhythm in the above lines. Which of the following statements would you apply to one or more of the extracts above?
   - The meter here creates a sense of momentum and the tone conveyed is light-hearted.
   - The rhythm in these lines is broken by the phrases in which two stressed syllables follow one another.
   - The assonance in these lines evokes a rich, sonorous mood, which reflects the poem's subject.

5. Add some more comments about the other effects of sound and rhythm in the right-hand column.

Level 2: Focus on diction

If we were to zoom out from rhythm and sound, the next meaningful level
we might reach is word choice or diction.

Activity

In the following prose extract, the words of one paragraph have been mixed up
and represented in alphabetical order. With the impact of sentence structure
being removed, what predictions can you make about the paragraph by simply
looking at the individual words?

> a a a a and and at at back because benighted black but candle catch cold colour danger darkness eyes eyes eyes fatten fear flames flash for from gleam green has he he him if if if is it knows lantern light like luminous mineral moonlight must night not of of on on only piercing pupils red reddish reflect run sequins shine spies stitched stock-still struck suddenly terrible that the the the the the the their then then they thickets those to traveller unnatural wolf's wolves yellowish you your

1. Jot down a few quick responses to these words. Which ones strike you the most?
2. Note down any examples of repeated words.
   Remove and organize words that fit into the following categories:
   - adjectives
   - verbs
   - nouns
   - adverbs
   - prepositions
   - articles.
3. Now look carefully at the writer's choice of words and discuss their meaning with a partner. You could talk about words that are denotative of particular things, as well as connotative of implied ideas and associations. What kind of story do you think this paragraph has been taken from?
4. Highlight the words that you feel are the most significant. Then complete a piece of writing on any subject, either a poem or prose extract, that incorporates your choice of words.
5. By looking at the original paragraph below, discuss to what extent your predictions about the work were accurate.

The Company of Wolves

At night, the eyes of the wolves shine like candle flames, yellowish, reddish, but that is because the pupils of their eyes fatten on darkness and catch the light from your lantern to flash it back at you – red for danger; if a wolf's eyes reflect only moonlight then they gleam a cold and unnatural green, a mineral, a piercing colour. If the benighted traveller spies those luminous, terrible sequins stitched suddenly on the black thickets, then he knows he must run, if fear has not struck him stock-still.

Angela Carter

Level 3: Focus on syntax

Moving our imaginative lens outwards once again, we might say we arrive
at a complete sentence. The rules of grammar and sentence structure are
of course extremely diverse and quite complex. The literature course does
not test understanding of linguistics in this sense, but a basic knowledge
of the ways sentences are typically put together can be helpful.

1. How would you describe the character of the three basic sentence types? See the *Remember* box to the right if you need a reminder of them.

2. Practise your understanding by writing a paragraph on any subject in which you incorporate all three.

3. Read through the following paragraph and look carefully at the different ways in which the sentences are structured.

Music and Silence

The lamp is lifted up. Held high, it burns more brightly, as though sustained by purer air, and the young man sees a shadow cast onto the wall. It is a long, slanting shadow and so he knows it is his own. It appears to have a deformity, a hump, occurring along its spine from below the shoulder-blades to just above the waist. But this is the shadow's trickery. The young man is Peter Claire, the lutenist, and the curvature on his back is his lute.

Rose Tremain

4. See if you can identify the different types of sentences and talk about their effect on the reader.

The three most basic types of sentence structure are as follows:

- **Simple:** this is a sentence with one main clause, consisting of a subject and a verb. For example: "*The following day we visited some castles.*"

- **Compound:** this is a sentence with two or more main clauses joined together by a conjunction such as: and, but, or, so, then, yet.

- For example: "*We skirted the walls but the main gate was locked and the custodian would not let us in.*"

- **Complex:** this is a sentence with one main clause and one or more dependent or subordinate clause.

  For example: "*After passing through the length of its buried catacomb-passages, we climbed the winding stairs of a tower and stood on the battlements, looking down over the al-Garb.*"

(Extracts from *In Xanadu* by William Dalrymple.)

Level 4: Focus on form and structure

The final component that we might say supports the foundations of any kind of writing has to do with the way words and sentences are ultimately formed into shapes.

1. Below is a sonnet by John Donne. It is printed in full but the lines have been presented in the wrong order. See if you can work out the correct order.

From rest and sleep, which but thy pictures be,
For those whom thou think'st thou dost overthrow,
And better than thy stroke; why swell'st thou then?
And dost with poison, war and sickness dwell;
And soonest our best men with thee do go,
Death, be not proud, though some have called thee
Much pleasure; then from thee much more must flow,
And death shall be no more. Death, thou shalt die.
One short sleep past, we wake eternally,
Thou art slave to fate, chance, kings, and desperate men,
Rest of their bones, and soul's delivery.
Mighty and dreadful, for thou are not so;
And poppy or charms can make us sleep as well
Die not, poor Death, nor yet canst thou kill me.

If you get stuck, search for the correct version of *Death, be not Proud* by John Donne here: www.online-literature.com

2. Talk about the way in which the following devices provide the sonnet with a sense of structure:
   - the rhyme scheme
   - use of rhythm
   - use of end-stopped and run-on lines
   - the grouping of lines into couplets/quatrains/sestet
   - punctuation
   - caesurae.
3. Can you put the argument presented by Donne into your own words?

Lines 1-4	
Lines 5-8	
Lines 9-12	
Lines 13-14	

So far, by and large, we have spent time looking at components that are integral to all kinds of writing. After all, newspaper articles, shopping lists, and instruction manuals also depend on sound, on words, and on syntax and structure to fulfil their objectives. Let's now turn our attention, however, to levels that are more explicitly literary.

Level 5: Focus on imagery

Activity

1. Read the following phrases and think about the meaning and impact of them. Write a poem or piece of prose in which you incorporate as many of them as possible:

the air hums with jets	its black eyes two sparks burning
the field lies bleeding	children dance in grass
bones brittle as mouse-ribs	wounding my land with stones

2. Read the poem from which the phrases come:

The Field Mouse

Summer, and the long grass is a snare drum.
The air hums with jets.
Down at the end of the meadow,
far from the radio's terrible news,
we cut the hay. All afternoon
its wave breaks before the tractor blade.
Over the hedge our neighbour travels his field
in a cloud of lime, drifting our land
with a chance gift of sweetness.

The child comes running through the killed flowers,
his hands a nest of quivering mouse,
its black eyes two sparks burning.
We know it will die and ought to finish it off.
It curls in agony big as itself
and the star goes out in its eye.
Summer in Europe, the field's hurt,
and the children kneel in long grass,
staring at what we have crushed.

Before day's done the field lies bleeding,
the dusk garden inhabited by the saved, voles,
frogs, a nest of mice. The wrong that woke
from a rumour of pain won't heal,
and we can't face the newspapers.
All night I dream the children dance in grass
their bones brittle as mouse-ribs, the air
stammering with gunfire, my neighbour turned
stranger, wounding my land with stones.

Gillian Clarke

3. What examples of different types of imagery can you find? e.g:
   - visual
   - tactile
   - kinesthetic
   - auditory.
4. Think about the impact of the imagery in the poem. Find evidence in the poem that could be used to support these statements of interpretation:
   - the poem relies on imagery to convey its mixture of both beauty and horror
   - imagery is used to convey the speaker's imaginative empathy with victims of war
   - the poem's imagery is an essential component in its portrayal of suffering and pain.

Level 6: Focus on metaphor

It is a certainty that throughout your course a considerable amount of time will be spent exploring the operation of non-literal or figurative language in the texts you study.

Activity

Write a brief definition and find an example of the terms below, each of which comes under the umbrella term of figurative language:

Simile	
Metaphor	

Metonomy	
Synecdoche	
Personification	
Symbolism	
Trope	

Metaphor is, of course, a particularly common term, and you will often find yourself exploring the various implications that metaphorical expressions generate. Along with tone, it is almost certain that you will refer to it at some point in your Paper 1 response.

Activity

1. Focus on a novel or play you are reading, or have recently read. Choose any character and by thinking about their appearance, personality traits, or development in the novel, identify what type of the following you think they would be:
   - car
   - item of clothing
   - item of food
   - place
   - time of year
   - type of weather
   - room.

2. Choose one or two and write a brief description of them in terms of this object. Try to focus on particular details as a means of highlighting particular character traits.

3. Explore the metaphorical associations and implications of the following:

> "I should have been a pair of ragged claws
> Scuttling across the floors of silent seas"
> -- from *The Love Song of J. Alfred Prufrock* by T. S. Eliot

> "Then it was June, and the sun shone more fiercely. The brown lines on the corn leaves widened and moved in on the central ribs. The weeds frayed and edged back towards their roots. The air was thin and the sky more pale; and every day the earth paled."
> -- from *The Grapes of Wrath* by John Steinbeck

> "Here are my bees
> Brazen, blurs on paper,
> Besotted; buzzwords, dancing
> Their flawless, airy maps."
> -- from *Bees* by Carol Ann Duffy

Level 7: Focus on voice

Whether you choose to write about the poem or the prose extract, you will spend at least some of your time exploring the voice of the speaker or narrator, and narrative voice is of course something that can emerge from all of the above literary tools. Let's complete three activities that focus on tone and point of view.

Tone

Activity

1. Think about three people you know well, whether friends or relatives, and write down a sentence that is typical of something they might say.
2. What kind of sentences have they spoken? For example:
   - imperative (command)
   - interrogative (question)
   - exclamatory (expressive of emotion)
   - declarative (statement).
3. Look carefully at each sentence and consider the way diction, syntax, figurative language, and so on have been used by them.
4. What is the cumulative effect of these devices? What kind of voices are they? Explore the ways in which tone is created.

Activity

Read through the following two extracts, from the beginning and the end of a chapter in a novel by the Australian novelist Tim Winton, and discuss the kind of voice generated. See if you can write two or three paragraphs that connect the two extracts, remaining as faithful as possible to the tone of the original.

> **That Eye, The Sky**
>
> **Extract 1:** In the reeds along the end of the creek, frogs churk and gulp and catch flies. The water is still and brown. By the end of the summer there'll probably be no water at all and there'll be roos and rabbits sniffing out pools all along here at dusk. Tadpoles scribble away across the surface. Birds tip-toe here and there like old ladies. There's tigersnakes about, but you just don't think about that. 'Can you see it?' I ask Fat...
>
> **Extract 2:** ...It wasn't such a good idea to come here. Everything is too sad.
>
> *Tim Winton*

Point of view

By point of view we do of course mean whether something is written in first, second, or third person, and how 'knowing' the voice is. Is the narrator fully aware of everything that is happening, and everything the characters are thinking or feeling? Or is the point of view limited in some way? Is the narrator close to the subject or more detached? Do we trust them implicitly, or does the narrative invite us to question their account? Are they, in fact, unreliable?

Activity

1. Read through the following extract and discuss its point of view.

> **The Life You Save May be Your Own**
>
> The old woman and her daughter were sitting on their porch when Mr. Shiflet came up their road for the first time. The old woman slid to the edge of her chair and leaned forward, shading her eyes from the piercing sunset with her hand. The daughter could not see in front of her and continued to play with her fingers. Although the old woman lived in this desolate spot with only her daughter and she had never seen Mr Shiflet before, she could tell, even from a distance, that he was a tramp and no one to be afraid of.
>
> *Flannery O' Connor*

2. Re-write the extract but change the point of view to first person. Think carefully about what you will need to change, or possibly add, as well as how to write in order for it to work.

3. Discuss the differences between the original and your version.

So far in this chapter we have concentrated almost entirely on aspects of language, form, and style. The reason for this, as you are reminded throughout this book, has to do with the course's emphasis on the art of literary writing. The final level, however, on which all texts work – whether or not they are 'literary' in nature – is, of course, in the way they present meaning to us. And inevitably, much of what you say, directly or indirectly, in the Paper 1 exam will be concerned with the content of the poem, prose, or drama extract.

Level 8: Focus on content

The term 'content', of course, refers to what the extract is about, as opposed to how its ideas are presented. Typically, you will find yourself talking about aspects that relate to the following areas:

1. The subject/s or topic/s being explored.
2. The action or events in the extract, i.e. what is actually happening.
3. Character and relationships between people.
4. The use of setting and creation of atmosphere.
5. Significant themes, motifs, or ideas, i.e. what is being suggested about any of the above.

Activity

Read through the paragraph below and then apply the five areas above to it. In the right-hand column of the table overleaf write down anything you think you might be able to say about the extract in terms of that particular feature of content.

> **Little Gods**
>
> Hours before dawn, on not quite the forty-seventh day of the way, a nineteen-year old girl was curled up in a too-small bed, looking like a doll that had been sold with the wrong cot. The room she slept in had been decorated for a baby – a stranger to her, long since grown and gone, along with those that cared for such things was being eaten by large pats of green mould. The girl's feet twitched, deep in a dog dream in which she ran fast, straight and light; a soft hum escaped her. It might turn into a throaty snore when she was older but now it was just a contented song of sleep.
>
> The bomb tore through this still night like birth, and landed like a foundling on a dark suburban doorstep. Every window in the street was blown out but only one house fell. It was so clean as to seem personal. The front two rooms were ejected straight out of the back, nothing but ash and splinters. The blast carved new corridors in seconds, sending slicing fragments of wood and glass hurtling along them. It cut a path straight to the attic, throwing floors and walls behind it. The girl was on top of a volcano; the building under her rushing to turn itself inside out. There was hardly any time; the scream of its arrival to the end of everything could be measured in a breath.
>
> *Anna Richards*

1: Subject	*The subject seems to be war – and perhaps the notions of childhood and time ...*
2: Action	*There is a large contrast between the 'contented song of sleep' in the first paragraph and the violence of the bomb blast in the second ...*
3: Character	
4: Setting/Atmosphere	
5: Themes/Ideas	

Perhaps inevitably you will find more to say about one of the five areas more than another. This may be because the extract is more interested in that particular aspect of content, or it may simply be because you were struck by that aspect more than another. An important skill in the examination, therefore, is to be selective with what you choose to write about. It is not possible to cover absolutely everything. You need to identify, analyse, and provide interpretation of the areas of the text from which you think it gains its meaning and impact.

Activity

Let's apply this important skill to two more passages.

1. Read through both passages carefully.

2. Select the features of content that you think are most important.

3. Explore the way/s in which element of language and style support these levels of meaning.

4. Choose the passage that you found more engaging and write down five reasons why.

Resistance

In the months afterwards all the women, at some point, said they'd known the men were leaving the valley. Just as William Jones used to forecast the weather by studying the sky or the formations of migrating birds, so the women said they'd been able to forecast the men's sudden departure. After all, they were their men, the husbands. No one could read them like they could. So no surprise if they should see what was coming. That's what the women said in the long silence afterwards.

But in truth none of them saw any change in the men's behaviour. None of them knew the men were leaving and in many ways this was the hardest part of what happened. Their husbands left in the night. Just days after news of the invasion came crackling through on Maggie's wireless, propped on a Bible on her kitchen table. The men, lit by a hunter's moon, met at William's milking shed and slipped out of the valley. Moving in single file they walked through the higher fields and up over the Hatterall ridge: an ellipsis of seven dark shapes decreasing over the hill's shoulder, shortening to a last full stop and then nothing, just the blank page of the empty slope. The women, meanwhile, slept soundly in their beds. It was only in the morning when a weak September sun shone into the valley that they realised what had happened.

Owen Shears

The Trees

The trees are coming into leaf
Like something almost being said;
The recent buds relax and spread,
Their greenness is a kind of grief.

Is it that they are born again
And we grow old? No, they die too.
Their yearly trick of looking new
Is written down in rings of grain.

Yes still the unresting castles thresh
In fullgrown thickness every May.
Last year is dead, they seem to say,
Begin afresh, afresh, afresh.

Philip Larkin

At the end of this unit, then, we return to the beginning. When you see something for the first time, you will be drawn to particular things, and be affected by details in a different way, potentially, to someone else. This is, ultimately, how literary texts are encouraged to be read, and why it is that we can come back to them time after time and continue to find new things within them.

Activity

To finish, read through the following poem carefully.

With the Shell of a Hermit Crab

This lovely little life whose toes
Touched the white sand from side to side,
How delicately no one knows,
Crept from his loneliness and died.

From deep waters long miles away
He wandered, looking for his name,
And all he found was you and me,
A quick life and a candle flame.

Today, you happen to be gone.
I sit here in the raging hell,
The city of the dead, alone,
Holding a little empty shell.

I peer into his tiny face.
It looms too huge for me to bear.
Two blocks away the sea gives place
To river. Both are everywhere.

I reach out and flick out the light.
Darkly I touch his fragile scars,
So far away, so delicate,
Stars in a wilderness of stars.

James Wright

1. Note down important aspects of content or style that strike you.
2. Remembering that it is crucial to avoid simply describing particular features in place of analysis and interpretation of them, copy the table below and add your own points about features of content and/or style with some brief comments about their significance on the right. You could consider:

   - The 'impact' of the feature you have identified.
   - The relationship between content and style.
   - The connection between this particular detail and the whole work.
   - Always provide evidence to support your ideas.

   Some examples have been provided to start you off:

Features of content/style	Significance
Presentation of the crab	• sense of fragility/vulnerability: 'little life', 'delicately', 'a quick life and a candle flame'
Relationship between speaker and the crab	• intimacy, sense of shared experience - 'lovely', 'all he found was you and me', I sit here ... holding a little empty shell' • contrasts recognition of 'tiny face' with 'too huge for me to bear' - sense of being overwhelmed
Informal, 'speaking' voice	• Mixes 1st and 2nd person • Formal stanza length, informal line structure - mix of end stopped and enjambment
Extensive use of metaphor	• contrasts beauty and suffering - 'stars in a wilderness of stars', 'the raging hell'...

Preparing for the exam

Experience shows that students who set about preparation for sitting the Paper 1 examination in a methodical, structured manner are likely to do better than those who move into the writing quite quickly. What follows is a suggested 'reading practice' that might help you to this end. It should be stated that this structured method is of course not the *only* way, but might serve at least as a starting point from which to then fine tune your skills and practices as you rehearse them.

Activity

As we have seen earlier in this chapter, meaning in literary texts emerges from a range of different components, from the sounds of particular words through to the social contexts in which texts are written and read. As a means to alert you to the range of levels through which your particular poem

Remember

In the final exam Higher Level (HL) students have 2 hours and Standard Level (SL) students 1 ½. Furthermore, the response written by HL students is referred to as a 'Literary Commentary', wherein students must show an ability to structure their ideas more independently in the form of an essay. SL students, on the other hand, are asked to complete what is referred to as a 'Guided Literary Analysis' because they have two guiding questions, one on aspects of content and the other style. As a means to help SL students focus their ideas, these questions must be answered either explicitly or implicitly in the course of their analysis, although the piece of writing must remain continuous.

or extract seems to gain its effects, let's imagine that we are in the exam, faced with a choice of two passages. Try to read and re-read the passages with a focus each time on a different aspect, in the manner suggested below. In addition to the comments made already by one student, see if you can add some ideas of your own.

The Sunlight on the Garden

The sunlight on the garden
Hardens and grows cold,
We cannot cage the minute
Within its nets of gold,
When all is told
We cannot beg for pardon.

Our freedom as free lances
Advances towards its end;
The earth compels, upon it
Sonnets and birds descend;
And soon, my friend,
We shall have no time for dances.

The sky was good for flying
Defying the church bells
And every evil iron
Siren and what it tells:
The earth compels,
We are dying, Egypt, dying

And not expecting pardon,
Hardened in heart anew,
But glad to have sat under
Thunder and rain with you,
And grateful too
For sunlight in the garden.

Louis MacNeice

Running in the Family

The bars across the windows did not always work. When bats would invade the house at dusk, the beautiful long-haired girls would rush to the corner of rooms and hide their heads under dresses. The bats suddenly drifting like dark squadrons through the house - for never more than two minutes - arcing into the halls over the uncleared dining room table and out along the verandah where the parents would be sitting trying to capture the cricket scores on the BBC with a shortwave radio.

Wildlife stormed or crept into homes this way. The snake entered through the bathroom drain for remnants of water or, finding the porch doors open, came in like a king and moved in a straight line through the living room, dining room, the kitchen and servant's quarters, and out the back, as if taking the most civilized short cut to another street in town. Others moved in permanently; birds nested above the fans, the silverfish slid into steamer trunks and photograph albums - eating their way through portraits and wedding pictures. What images of family life they consumed in their minute jaws and took into their bodies no thicker than the pages they ate.

And the animals also on the periphery of rooms and porches, their sounds forever in your ear. During our visit to the jungle, while we slept on the verandah at 3 a.m., night would be suddenly alive with disturbed peacocks. A casual movement from one of them roosting in the trees would waken them all and, so fussing, sounding like branches full of cats, they would weep loud into the night.

One evening I kept the tape recorder beside my bed and wakened by them once more out of a deep sleep automatically pressed the machine on to record them. Now, and here, Canadian February, I write this in the kitchen and play that section of cassette to hear not just peacocks but all the noises of the night behind them - inaudible because they were always there like breath. In this silent room (with its own unheard hum of fridge, fluorescent light) there are these frogs as loud as river, gruntings, the whistle of other birds brash and sleepy, but in that night so modest behind the peacocks they were unfocused by the brain - nothing more than darkness, all those sweet loud younger brothers of the night.

Michael Ondaatje

Aspect 1: Respond to layout before reading anything:

- What can you say about the presentation of the text on the page?
- Are there stanzas or paragraphs? If so, how many, and of what kind?
- Is there anything noticeable in terms of punctuation?
- Does the text appear to use the white space around it in any meaningful way?

The Sunlight on the Garden	Running in the Family
• 4 stanzas of even length • 4th line in each stanza is shorter • fairly formal structure?	• clear division into paragraphs • relatively even length

Aspect 2: Read for first impressions. Note down anything that strikes you on a first reading e.g.:

- What seems to be going on?
- Which words or sections strike you initially?
- What questions do you have?

The Sunlight on the Garden	Running in the Family
• opening and closing lines almost the same • who is the 'friend'? • mournful, melancholic tone	• evocative, atmospheric description of night • moves into present tense in final paragraph

Aspect 3: Read for the events, key actions and/or subjects e.g.:

- What seems to be going on in the extract?
- Paraphrase the different sections.
- What are the main concerns or ideas being explored?

The Sunlight on the Garden	Running in the Family
• literal focus on a garden and nature • figurative concerns with time, loss and death - of a loved one?	• memory of past - colonial(?) experience • focuses in 1st para on the invasion of the bats, then animal movements, then sounds and finally moves into present tense - strong sense of development

Aspect 4: Read for the basics – language and form:

- What can you say about diction, syntax, and grammar?
- Is there an appeal to rhythm and/or sound?
- How is the extract organized?

The Sunlight on the Garden	Running in the Family
• irregular iambic/trochaic metre – trimeter, with dimeter in 4th line - gentle, lyrical rhythm - but natural • strong use of sound - various rhyming patterns e.g. 'sky' and 'flying' (internal), frequent use of assonance and some alliteration e.g. 'cannot cage' - reinforces melodic feel • diction is simple but rich, evocative - reflective of narrator's honesty	• quite long, descriptive sentences with multiple clauses - to create detailed sense of place • informal syntax in places e.g. use of hyphens - sense of a speaking voice? • diction that refers to physical (sound and movement), sensory presence e.g. 'drifting', 'weep loud', 'silent room'

Aspect 5: Read for figurative language:

- Identify any use of metaphor, imagery, and symbolism.
- How do figurative expressions contribute to the content?

The Sunlight on the Garden	Running in the Family
• extensive use of metaphorical expression, e.g. 'grows cold', 'as free lances', 'earth compels', 'hardened in heart' - sense of emotive, expressive voice • sense imagery resonates - visual and textual - occasionally synesthetic e.g. 'sunlight...hardens' • particular strands of imagery/metaphor e.g. imprisonment/restraint e.g. 'cage' and 'nets'	• plenty of metaphorical description - especially of the various animals, e.g. 'wildlife stormed', 'like dark squadrons', 'brothers of the night' - conveys sense of the animal world as something in itself 'alive', with character - almost human • reinforces passage's concern with bringing the memory, the place (and the past) into the present

Aspect 6: Read for speaking/narrative voice and tone:

- What kind of narrative voice is generated?
- What is the narrative perspective?
- What is the narrator's attitude towards his or her subject?

The Sunlight on the Garden	Running in the Family
• maintains a fairly objective, descriptive distance through the metre and abstract, metaphorical language • at the same time, uses personal pronouns to generate sense of intimacy - 'we', 'you' • thoughtful, reflective but mournful tone - 'We are dying, Egypt, dying'	• informal/colloquial voice - recounts memory in an anecdotal, almost 'chatty' manner - 'Now, and here, Canadian February, I write this in the kitchen...' • sense of nostalgia in his presentation of details as well as the admission of the cassette recording • conveys distance from the subject through time, but imaginatively intimate as he writes about it

Aspect 7: Read for content:

- What 'meaning' can you find in the passage?
- To what extent is the author interested in character and relationships, setting or key actions in the extract?
- What thematic concerns are present?
- What does the author seem to be 'saying'?

The Sunlight on the Garden	Running in the Family
• relationship between speaker and anonymous 'friend' - lover? who is no longer there • the garden as a motif for beauty and memory, as well as loss	• the relationship between human and natural worlds - animal kingdom seems more 'present' than the human one - it has life, colour, intelligence • the action of recording the noises is reflected in the writing of the extract itself - he brings the past alive

Aspect 8: Read for significance.

Find a way to tie your ideas together:

- What is the most important idea to emerge in the extract?
- Are there any contrasts or oppositions?
- What is contradictory, paradoxical, or ambiguous?
- Does the passage show a sense of important development?
- In what way is the passage designed to affect or influence the reader?

The Sunlight on the Garden	Running in the Family
• use of metaphor to transform the pain of loss into something beautiful • creates a dream-like atmosphere, reflective of the shadowy nature of memory	• makes use of the contrast between human worlds - 'BBC', 'fluorescent light' etc. and the active, living force of nature • is interested in the process of recapturing the past - reflected also in the development of the passage

Organizing your ideas

At this stage, after the various 'readings' that you have made and, hopefully, with a range of completed annotations, you are nearly ready to begin planning your answer.

As stated earlier, if you are a SL student, then you will be expected to answer two questions in your Paper 1 response. Remember, however, that you must produce a continuous piece of writing, and so your answers to the questions should emerge naturally as your analysis progresses. Furthermore, the questions are there for guidance and should not prevent you from making points that do not relate directly to them.

As a HL student, however, you are expected to develop your ideas more independently, and to achieve the higher grades for Criterion C, you will need to be at least 'effective' and ideally 'persuasive' in the way you structure them.

Ultimately, however, whether Standard or Higher Level, you will need to demonstrate an ability to organize your ideas, and the two most common ways are as follows:

- a 'linear' approach, which more or less explores the development of the poem or prose extract in sequence
- a 'conceptual' or 'topical' approach, which breaks the extract down into component parts, for example, targeting a different aspect of content and/or style identified above as a paragraph topic.

Providing an argument

The best responses to Paper 1 are organized in such a way as to develop a particular line of interpretation, evaluation, or 'reading'. One way of doing this is to foreground one of the main areas of significance that you considered in the final suggested 'reading strategy' above: for example the most important idea to emerge, a key opposition or contrast, or a point about the way the extract develops. This is a bit like fixing up a washing line from which to hang the rest of your main points in order to provide a sense of focus and direction for them.

Activity

Have an initial discussion with a partner how you would set about structuring a commentary on the prose extract above.

Next, in the left-hand column below you will see how the student who made the notes above has organized her commentary on the poem. Answer the following questions:

- What has she chosen to include in her introduction? Do you think it is effective?
- What kind of structure has she chosen to adopt? Discuss whether you think it works.
- From the notes she made above, what key ideas has she chosen to focus on? What does selecting ideas in this way indicate to the examiner?
- What do you think of her conclusion?
- In what sense has she provided an argument, or 'reading'?

Do the same for your prose extract. Write your topic statements out and compare with other people in the class. Or, if you use the Outline view in Microsoft Word, it will be easy to move your paragraph topics around in order to identify the most effective means of organizing and developing points.

Commentary on *The Sunlight on the Garden*	Commentary on *Running in the Family*
Introduction In this poem, Louis MacNeice focuses on 'sunlight' and a literal garden through which to explore concerns with the past, the nature of loss and the passing of time. He makes extensive use of figurative, natural imagery and sound to create a lyrical, but quite melancholic mood, but this is redeemed in the final stanza when the speaker appears to be more accepting of the problem of change.	

Commentary on *The Sunlight on the Garden*	Commentary on *Running in the Family*
The opening of the poem contrasts the beauty of the garden with the impact of time.	
In stanza two the theme of the inevitability of time is brought to bear on the notion of freedom.	
Imagery in the third stanza introduces the notion of things having passed and there is recognition of the finality of death.	
The poem concludes with a shift in tone, however, as the speaker emphasizes love as a means to overcome the problem of time.	
The poem's use of sound and rhythm is key to its atmospheric quality and the sense of a 'natural' speaking voice.	
Conclusion Language and form are therefore essential to this poem. Whilst it is concerned, ultimately, with loss and suffering as inevitable consequences of the problem of time and death, MacNeice makes use of figurative imagery and musical elements of sound and rhythm to highlight the transformative power of the imagination. In this way, love is shown to be something that can be preserved and, in a sense, the problem of time something that can be overcome.	

Introductions and Conclusions

Finally, before we look at some responses in full, let's focus more explicitly on ways in which you can begin and end your Paper 1 answer.

Activity

1. With a partner discuss what you think could or should be included in an introduction. You might consider such things as:
   - showing that you understand the **subject** of the poem or prose extract
   - identifying what you think are the **most important features** of content, language, and style
   - providing the examiner with an indication of the **direction** your analysis is going to go in, i.e. try to present an argument or thesis.
2. Read through the following *introductory* paragraphs, each written by a different student but in response to the same poem.

> *The poem 'In the Rear-View Mirror' by Robert Shaw explores the common experience of having to say goodbye to people you are close to. The speaker of the poem suggests that this experience is inevitable in life, as we keep having to say goodbye to our loved ones. The poet creates a sense of nostalgia by using mirrors both literally and figuratively and makes use of the structure of the poem to say something about the inevitability of time passing and the present always moving into the past.*

> *'In the Rear-View Mirror' by Robert Shaw is a poem about a car journey away from a familiar place into the unknown, through which a more metaphorical journey is implied. In response to the possibility of an empty, unknown future, the speaker seems concerned with the importance of memory and the security we often find in preserving the past. The poem's intimate, informal voice draws the reader into the poem so that, alongside the speaker, we are also invited to think about the relationship between absence and presence.*

3. Consider the different ways in which they fulfil the suggestions made above about the role/s of an introduction.

4. Now read these *concluding* paragraphs from the same students:

> *Overall, 'In the Rear-View Mirror' by Robert Shaw effectively portrays the importance of the past and the role of memory as a figurative journey through life, represented by a mundane car journey. To me, the greatest significance of the poem is the message that memories can affect feelings of both loss and nostalgia and in this sense can be both positive and negative. We want to remember people and events but sometimes experience pain in that they are no longer with us. In this way, the final effect of the poem for me is quite ambiguous.*

> *In conclusion, this poem explores the power of memory. Whilst the first section of the poem portrays a sense of loss, the second provides a degree of balance through ideas of return. Metaphors to do with distance and journeys are used throughout, ultimately pointing out the whereas actual experience diminishes, memory is unlimited and in that way, timeless.*

There is clearly no correct or incorrect way to conclude your Paper 1 analysis, but it is usually a good idea to avoid simply restating what you have already said. You could consider:

- identifying what you think is the most interesting thing to have emerged from your exploration of the poem or extract.
- identifying the stylistic feature that you think is the most important. i.e. from where does the poem or extract gain its main strength or power?
- making some comment on the key aspects of human or natural experience that you see in the poem or extract, i.e. in what sense does it connect with 'real life'?
- identifying a key point of 'message' to have emerged from the poem or extract (if you feel that one exists).

Discuss whether you think the conclusions above fulfil some or all of these ideas.

The most important thing, perhaps, is to demonstrate to the examiner a sense of **being in control**, that you have a reading of the poem or extract that you want to persuade us the validity of. As a means to demonstrate this, try the following activity.

Activity

Below is a prose extract and a student response to it. The first and last paragraph have been removed. See if you can write the introduction and conclusion and then compare with others in your class.

The Thousand Faces of Night

The room was full of people, young black men and women, even a few children. As her apprehension grew into a sudden shyness, Devi reassured herself that this was just like India—the throng of voices competing with the loud, blaring music, the high-pitched voices of excited children in the background.

They spoke to each other, over the music, in a shorthand that fascinated Devi, but she could not bring herself to play impostor and speak like them.

The more serious conversations, carried out in little huddles in various corners of the room, were about being black in white America. Devi leaned forward to listen to an intense young woman with a spectacular head of a hundred little plaits. Her frizzy, snake-like braids were held in place with blue and green beads at regular intervals.

"So this nurse—all polite and freezing cold—I had paid for the hospital room, see—said, 'I'll take the baby to the nursery for the night, you get some rest alone.' She didn't want me to be disturbed by my baby. 'Disturbed!' I screamed into her icy face. 'When are you people going to learn that black love is black wealth?'"

Devi saw the principle of the thing, she admired this beautiful spitfire who was so sure of her rights, and of the inevitable chorus of confirmation she would draw out of her audience. But Devi also found she had less and less to say, and she spent the entire evening quiet, watching. The music throbbed in her head, and she listened to snatches of conversation, words that drifted by and that she recognized, but separate, fragmented, like words in a foreign language she had recently learnt, but still could not put together to make sense.

Devi sat surrounded by people, in increasing isolation, terrified of drawing attention to herself, but aching for any means to do just that.

Hours later, her eyes watering in the smoke-filled room, she remembered she had brought the host an Indian gift, a wall hanging of cotton cloth, hand-printed with vegetable dye. The host held it up for them all to see, and they looked at the blue, baby-faced man on the cloth, bare-chested and crowned with a peacock feather, dancing as he played the flute. For the first time, the image struck Devi as almost grotesque: a grown man, practically naked, wearing a perpetual baby-mask.

"That's Krishna, the dark god who loved milk, butter and women," said Devi.

"They couldn't bear to have a black god, so they made him blue, huh?" said the intent young woman Devi had earlier admired. She smiled, but her voice was edged with contempt.

Devi laughed with the rest of them, but she knew she had brought the wrong gift. A brass goddess holding a lamp could have been used as an ethnic ashtray. Or safer still, a bottle of wine. It would have been less original, but it would not have set her apart from the others with such finality.

Githa Hariharan

Student response (without the introduction and conclusion):

The emotional journey that Devi undergoes is emphasized by the continuous change of feelings and emotional states that take place within her. Initially the situation is chaotic as she finds herself " in a room…full of people" and her "shyness" is evident as she tries to convince herself "that this is just like India". As the passage develops however, she realizes that she is not part of this culture and everything about it seems unfamiliar. The "words…drifted by", "separate", "fragmented" which reflect her internal emotions of confusion and uncertainty as she is unable to make sense of the situation around her. Devi's "increasing isolation" is shown as she cannot "draw attention to herself" as she is overpowered by the dominant black culture characterised by "loud voices" and "music". By the end of the extract Devi's separation becomes permanent as she "sets" herself "apart from the other". Therefore her emotional development is paralleled by a development in her relationship with the people surrounding her as well as dramatizing the contrast between the dominating black culture and her inability to fit in as she remains in a paradoxical situation "surrounded by people" yet "in increasing isolation".

A particularly powerful element through which this cultural hierarchy is established is through the use of dialogue, as the black woman's voice predominates. Devi seems to remain passive as she hears all their "conversations" about "being black in white America". This is ironic as they themselves are effectively outsiders in a white culture but yet they are unable to accept Devi as she is different to them. Devi is fascinated by this "intense young woman" who embodies the black culture with her "spectacular head of a hundred plaits". Everything that she says has an aggressive undertone, when she describes the "nurse" with the "polite and freezing" manners and her "icy face". The sense of coldness is juxtaposed with the "black love" which the woman refers to as being "black wealth" showing how proud she is of her own roots and cultures. Even when Devi offers them her gift, the woman reads it as an attack and immediately mocks Devi by stating that "they couldn't bear to have a black god, so they made him blue, huh?" The use of the personal pronoun "they", further emphasized the sense of separation between Devi and the other people as she is not a part of them. This also shows that the woman is aware of the wider social context and prejudices surrounding her but she is still able to be "sure of her rights" and speak up, whilst Devi in opposition remains "quiet" and is merely a passive observer.

The notion of loneliness and isolation is further explored through the presentation of cultural identity. Devi initially recalls her own country as a means of reassuring herself but by the end she is embarrassed by it. She leans "forward", she "listens" and throughout the passage she identifies the woman as something "spectacular", something exotic with her "frizzy, snake-like braids". On a literal level she is able to "admire this beautiful spitfire" but on a more metaphorical level, it reflects her longing to be accepted and her suffering because of her inability to integrate. She feels like an "impostor" and she realizes that she cannot pretend to be something that she is not. The climax of this cultural tension is reached when she presents the "Indian gift" to the "host", effectively sharing a small part of her own culture with them and she suddenly exposes herself. Her own perspective changes and for the first time she sees the "blue, baby-faced man on the cloth, bare-chested and crowned with a peacock feather" become a "grotesque figure" of a "grown man, practically naked wearing a perpetual baby mask". This transformation parallels the development in Devi's feelings as she is herself trying to put up a "mask" and be someone that she is not, by the end of the passage she is ashamed of her own identity as her desire to integrate intensifies. The mask is "perpetual" it is everlasting; this adjective also builds up to the concluding sentence which establishes the finality of her separation within this community.

Marking a student commentary

Let's now assess the way all of the above is ultimately going to be assessed in the final exam. Take some time to familiarize yourself with the assessment criteria in your coursebook and think carefully about the ways in which you think an examiner might reward work according to the different bands.

We'll begin with a Standard Level answer. Remember that at SL you will be asked to incorporate answers to two Guiding Questions and so you might like to consider the ways in which this student has managed to present his answers in addition to making note of what the examiner has to say about the quality of analysis.

The poem about which this student decided to write is as follows:

The Express

After the first powerful, plain manifesto
The black statement of pistons, without more fuss
But gliding like a queen, she leaves the station.
Without bowing and with restrained unconcern
She passes the houses which humbly crowd outside,

The gasworks, and at last the heavy page
Of death, printed by gravestones in the cemetery.
Beyond the town, there lies the open country
Where, gathering speed, she acquires mystery,
The luminous self-possession of ships on ocean.

It is now she begins to sing—at first quite low
Then loud, and at last with a jazzy madness—
The song of her whistle screaming at curves,
Of deafening tunnels, brakes, innumerable bolts.
And always light, aerial, underneath,

Retreats the elate metre of her wheels.
Streaming through metal landscapes on her lines,
She plunges new eras of white happiness,
Where speed throws up strange shapes, broad curves
And parallels clean like trajectories from guns.

At last, further than Edinburgh or Rome,
Beyond the crest of the world, she reaches night
Where only a low stream-line brightness
Of phosphorus on the tossing hills is light.
Ah, like a comet through flame, she moves entranced,

Wrapt in her music no bird song, no, nor bough
Breaking with honey buds, shall ever equal.

Stephen Spender

Guiding Questions:

1. How does Spender's selection of particular words and phrases help us understand his appreciation for his subject?

2. To what extent would you say that the poem develops some of the speaker's thoughts and feelings?

Student answer

In the poem, 'The Express' by Stephen Spender, the poet constructs an elaborate, mystical scene about a steam locomotive and its travels from the city and throughout the countryside. Spender's tone in the poem can be best characterized as one of admiration and great celebration for the train.

Spender's unique appreciation for the train is established and made clear to the reader by his brilliant choices of grammatical forms, figurative language, sensuous imagery and the overall structure of the poem itself. One interesting element to note is that the subject of the poem, a train, is never identified directly in the poem itself. The actual word 'train' never appears. However, the reader is able to identify the train due to the writer's implementation of certain grammatical forms, nouns in this case, that are usually identified with the steam locomotive. The title of the poem, The Express, is the initial hint of the train; however the subject is clearly identified as a train after reading the words 'station'; in line 3, 'her whistle' in line 13, 'her wheels' in line 16 and finally 'steaming' in line 17. These specific nouns are commonly identified with the train, and thus the reader can easily identify the train and begin to construct a mental image of the poet's scene in the poem.

Another technique utilized by Spender, which quickly becomes apparent to the reader is his anthropomorphizing of the train and his identification of the train as a female. The train is referred to as 'she' and the train, a man-made machine in reality, performs human actions. The train 'glides like a queen' in line 3 'without bowing', 'begins to sing' in line 11, 'moves entranced' in line 25 and finally is 'wrapt in her music' in line 26. The effect of this choice both in style and words has drastic effects on the tone of the poem. By giving the train a feminine identity rather than the masculine, Spender establishes a rare precedent. Usually the train symbolizes the growth of industry and the expansion of power and wealth, elements in society commonly identified with the efforts of males in power – not females. Thus, by establishing the train as a female the reader is able to view the train from a different perspective. In this poem no longer is the train a symbol of power and greed, but rather a symbol of elegance, beauty and comfort. Likening the train to an attractive woman with a mind of her own allows the reader to more easily appreciate this unique view of the train; the train is not viewed by the reader as an inanimate machine, which is the case in reality. Thus, by contrasting such a different image of the train and emphasizing its grace and beauty, the admiration and celebration that Spender holds for the train is very apparent.

One other technique that Spender utilizes extensively in the poem to establish his unique appreciation for the train, as well as the physical scene within the poem, is his use of sensuous, vivid imagery. Spender incorporates a wealth of soft, beautiful imagery into the poem. Figurative language such as similes, oxymorons and contrasts are included. The train 'gliding like a queen' in line 3 and the train moves 'like a comet through flame' in line 25 are two examples of similes and potent examples of Spender's attempts to describe the sheer beauty and mystery of the train. Spender's word choices in these two instances are contrasting to a degree; a queen would not usually be described as a comet on fire. His contrasting descriptions draw a very complex, but extravagant image of the train. The oxymoron 'jazzy madness' describing the train's singing in line 12 is another instance in the poem where Spender's description of the poem is highly intricate,

---

Is the word 'unique' necessary here?

Are nouns best described as 'grammatical forms'? The student could be more concise here. It is also two thirds through the paragraph before we get to any direct quotations.

Try to avoid phrases like this; another common one is 'it allows the reader to…'. These phrases imply that we read poetry with a particular agenda in mind, rather than let the words take us in new and sometimes surprising directions.

This doesn't really say very much. What exactly is the 'image' being described? There is room for more analytical depth here.

This is a good topic statement: it identifies clearly the subject of the paragraph and makes a valid point of literary analysis

Good use of embedded quotations.

The student extracts *significance* from the point of *analysis:* this is an important thing to remember.

The student needs to be careful here, there is a danger of speculation.

This is a good point, but s/he needs to show how and where it is shown. There is plenty of material to use in support of the idea – s/he doesn't need to rely on something that may or may not be 'usual' in life.

Good, another clear topic statement.

Again, it is not a good idea to describe anything as 'usual'. Arguably describing anything as a 'comet on fire' is not usual unless describing a comet.

This point is not explained clearly.

and thus the reader cannot easily picture the image the poet is trying to establish. However, descriptions of the train such as 'light' and 'aerial' in line 15, 'luminous' in line 10 and 'brightness' and 'light' in lines 23 and 24 are not ambiguous in the slightest. They display a picture of a train as positive and comforting. Thus, in the end, Spender achieves by smart word choice and vivid imagery in constructing a gloriously beautiful and elegant depiction of the train. His admiration and celebration of the train is very clear.

> Good point.

> This concluding statement just restates something that has already been said. Ideally, a paragraph and the essay should develop and move forwards.

Furthermore, with regards to Spender's use of vivid imagery in the poem, he incorporates rough, bleak imagery that is clearly contrasting to the soft, attractive imagery of the poem. References to industry such as 'pistons' I line 2, 'gasworks' in line 5 and 'metal landscape' in line 17 are included, as well as other gloomy imagery such as 'death' and 'gravestones' in line 7. Such industry is usually associated with the male segment of the human population, the inclusion of references to industry and death early in the poem, and the fact that the feminine train quickly leaves these masculine and gloomy images behind, makes it clear to the reader that the train is not associated with these images. 'She' enters the 'open country' and in so doing it becomes evident that the train, in the eyes of Spender, is an elegant and free entity. This stark contrast between rough, soft, bleak and beautiful imagery gives the poem an interesting complexity to admire; Spender's complex images of the train contrast, but it is apparent that he loves the image of the train for that complexity.

> This point is a good one, but the syntax of the sentence is clumsy.

> Avoid speculation.

> Good point.

> Unlike the conclusion of the previous paragraph – this one develops an idea.

One final feature of the poem noteworthy for discussion is the acceleration and intensification of expression as the poem progresses. The poem almost mirrors the movement of an actual train; it starts at the station slow, but as it progresses it quickens its pace and the sound of the train intensifies. The poem similarly has an intensification of figurative language and grammatical forms. In the opening of the poem, the train slowly 'leaves the station'. The train moves forward 'gathering speed' and 'acquires mystery.' The train begins 'screaming' and by the end of the poem 'she' travels 'beyond the crest of the world.' Spender incorporates the exclamation 'Ah' in line 25, and in his last statement in the poem he states the 'song' of the train has no 'equal'. This choice in style, as well as the choice to write the poem in free verse, and so removing a regular meter and thus all expectations from the reader, creates this apparent intensification. The effect is a fun, compelling poem to read and enjoy.

> Another good, clearly defined point.

> There is some impressive sensitivity to language and style here.

Examiner's comments

There are many things to admire in this Guided Literary Analysis. The student engages productively with the poem, showing good understanding of the main ideas and is able to refer to a range of supporting details in an appropriate and thoughtful way. S/he could have said more about the presentation of the train as a kind of mythical, larger than life entity, although the student identifies some interesting contrasts and the way the poem develops. The tendency towards speculation about 'life' as opposed to art is in part unhelpful, although picking up on the gender issue nevertheless provides some interesting points of interpretation. Equally, there are a range of perceptive points on language and style; the student manages to offer comment on diction, imagery and other kinds of figurative language, although it is a pity s/he didn't say more about the poem's structure and syntax. The analysis is well organized and paragraph topics are clearly delineated; language is clear and generally accurate – though could perhaps be a little more precise in places. Finally, the student answers both questions quite effectively in the scope of the analysis, at the same time as managing to go beyond the implications of the questions and demonstrate some further independent thinking.

Criterion A: Understanding and interpretation 4

Criterion B: Appreciation of the writer's choices 4

Criterion C: Organization 4

Criterion D: Language 4

Did you think the examiner was fair? From the comments and final marks awarded you should be starting to understand the skills the final examination is asking you to demonstrate.

Let's put that to the test. Below you will find two Paper 1 answers, the first a SL Guided Literary Analysis in response to a prose extract, and the second a HL Literary Commentary in response to a poem.

1. Read the responses through carefully, making note as you go along of things that strike you as examples of either good or bad practice.

2. Afterwards, answer the questions that follow, and talk about your responses with others in the class.

3. With careful reference to the official criteria, award these students with a mark that you deem appropriate.

4. What advice would you give these students to help them improve? Either annotate the answers with coments, as if you were the examiner, or provide a generic response at the end that highlights the things they have done well, and what they could do to get a better mark.

5. Compare your comments and marks with the ones provided by the examiner at the end of this chapter.

Standard Level guided literary analysis: prose

Markheim

First one and then another, with every variety of pace and voice - one deep as the bell from a cathedral turret, another ringing on its treble notes the prelude of a waltz - the clocks began to strike the hour of three in the afternoon.

The sudden outbreak of so many tongues in that dumb chamber staggered him. He began to bestir himself, going to and fro with the candle, beleaguered by moving shadows, and startled to the soul by chance reflections. In many rich mirrors, some of home designs, some from Venice or Amsterdam, he saw his face repeated and repeated, as if were an army of spies; his own eyes met and detected him; and the sound of his own steps, lightly as they fell, vexed the surrounding quiet. And still, as he continued to fill his pockets, his mind accused him with a sickening iteration, of the thousand faults of his design. He should have chosen a more quiet hour; he should have prepared an alibi; he should not have used a knife; he should have been more cautious, and only bound and gagged the dealer, and not killed him; he should have been more bold, and killed the servant also; he should have done all things otherwise: poignant regrets, weary, incessant toiling of the mind to change what was unchangeable, to plan what was now useless, to be the architect of the irrevocable past. Meanwhile, and behind all this activity, brute terrors, like the scurrying of rats in a deserted attic, filled the more remote chambers of his brain with riot; the hand of the constable would fall heavy on his shoulder, and his nerves would jerk like a hooked fish; or he beheld, in galloping defile, the dock, the prison, the gallows, and the black coffin.

Terror of the people in the street sat down before his mind like a besieging army. It was impossible, he thought, but that some rumour of the struggle must have reached their ears and set on edge their curiosity; and now, in all the neighbouring houses, he divined them sitting motionless and with uplifted ear - solitary people, condemned to spend Christmas dwelling alone on memories of the past, and now startingly recalled from that tender exercise; happy family parties, struck into silence round the table, the mother still with raised finger: every degree and age and humour, but all, by their own hearths, prying and hearkening and weaving the rope that was to hang him. Sometimes it seemed to him he could not move too softly; the clink of the tall Bohemian goblets rang out loudly like a bell; and alarmed by the bigness of the ticking, he was tempted to stop the clocks. And then, again, with a swift transition of his terrors, the very silence of the place appeared a source of peril, and a thing to strike and freeze the passer-by; and he would step more boldly, and bustle aloud among the contents of the shop, and imitate, with elaborate bravado, the movements of a busy man at ease in his own house.

But he was now so pulled about by different alarms that, while one portion of his mind was still alert and cunning, another trembled on the brink of lunacy. One hallucination in particular took a strong hold on his credulity. The neighbour hearkening with white face beside his window, the passer-by arrested by a horrible surmise on the pavement - these could at worst suspect, they could not know; through the brick walls and shuttered windows only sounds could penetrate. But here, within the house, was he alone? He knew he was; he had watched the servant set forth sweet-hearting, in her poor best, "out for the day" written in every ribbon and smile. Yes, he was alone, of course; and yet, in the bulk of empty house above him, he could surely hear a stir of delicate footing - he was surely conscious, inexplicably conscious of some presence. Ay, surely; to every room and corner of the house his imagination followed it; and now it was a faceless thing, and yet had eyes to see with; and again it was a shadow of himself; and yet again behold the image of the dead dealer, reinspired with cunning and hatred.

At times, with a strong effort, he would glance at the open door which still seemed to repel his eyes. The house was tall, the skylight small and dirty, the day blind with fog; and the light that filtered down to the ground story was exceedingly faint, and showed dimly on the threshold of the shop. And yet, in that strip of doubtful brightness, did there not hang wavering a shadow?

Robert Louis Stevenson

Guiding Questions:

1. Explore the presentation of the central character.

2. Discuss the way the passage is structured for particular effect.

Student answer

In this passage from Markheim, Robert Louis Stevenson explores the internal conflict of a burglar who debates over his enterprise of stealing from an antique's shop. The use of powerful imagery and personification by the author not only provides the reader with an effective description of the location where the action takes place, but also works effectively as a form of characterization, since the atmosphere ultimately reflects the main character's psychological state.

The passage starts with a long, descriptive sentence whose complicated syntax postpones the revelation of the subject matter to its end; this creates a sense of uncertainty before he realizes that the 'sudden outbreak' in question is nothing more than several clocks ringing the hour of three. The description of the setting continues, and other elements of the scenario are introduced, such as the mirrors of various origins and the poor lighting of the antique shop. But similar to the initial clocks, what interests me most in these descriptions is the effect that the objects have on the main character. The descriptions are not written in an impartial light, and in fact the reader can sense the state of mind in which Markheim is found by precisely paying attention to the tone of the observations made by the omniscient third person narrator.

Markheim is disconcerted by the situation in which he gets himself, and his discomfort and erratic state of mind are reflected in the presentation of his surroundings. One way Stevenson effectively manages to achieve the translation of his character's mind into the physical setting is through the use of personification. Not only are objects personified, but their descriptions seem to come from a schizophrenic mind that feels persecuted by seemingly non-threatening things, and that helps to remind the reader of the emotional pressure under which Markheim is found. For examples, the clocks have 'tongues' and 'voices' that range from deep to treble, Markheim's eyes 'detected' him with accusatory fierceness, the sound of his feet 'vexed' the silence, and moving shadows 'beleaguered' him. Imagery like this occurs throughout the entire passage, and is present until the end, when the open door 'seemed to repel [Markheim's] eyes' just as if it knew this man was doing something wrong. In a sense, by attributing human actions to inanimate objects, Stevenson reinforces the alertness and paranoia experienced by his character, whose agitated mind assumes all objects in his surroundings to have a recriminatory attitude towards him, which in turn only serves to reveal the character's own feelings of guilt.

The establishment of this 'recriminatory attitude' is greatly aided by the use of imagery that alludes to violence and war, forms of aggression that reflect Markheim's questionable integrity. Terrors invade the character's mind like a 'besieging army' and he is haunted by the ghost of the dead dealer, as well as the metonymic images that he beholds in 'galloping defile', starting at the moment where he could be caught, and culminating at his death in the reference to 'black coffin'. Markheim's fertile imagination also embarks on higher flights, and he pictures how his nerves 'would jerk like a hooked fish' at the thought of being arrested, or how the people at family parties were 'weaving the rope that was to hang him.' These strong images strengthen the notion of fear, culpability, and unease experienced by Markheim, and the result is that the reader develops sympathy for him, whose 'poignant regrets' and 'incessant toiling of the mind' attest to his human nature and lack of experience in such criminal activities.

Lastly, the structure of the passage also contributes to conveying the main character's utter discomfort and paranoia with the situation. The story does not follow a continuous and organized train of thought, and instead it progresses in a rather jumbling, erratic way. Markheim's mind jumps from his terror of people around Christmas tables with uplifted ears to a mysterious 'delicate footing' in the second floor, following a truly desperate stream of consciousness as the different chambers of his brain seem to have multiple 'activities' simultaneously taking place. This shifting storytelling also achieves a realistic quality, and does not only make the entire scene more credible, but also Markheim becomes more relatable to the reader, especially when he ponders what to do with the irritating ticking noise of the clocks, and the consequent silence that would result from stopping them: 'He would step more boldly, and bustle aloud among the contents of the shop, and imitate, with elaborate bravado, the movements of a busy man at ease in his own house.'

Stevenson reaches the climax of his character hallucination, and he 'trembles on the brink of lunacy', with the creation of a possible and mysterious 'faceless thing' that could in fact be observing, and consequently incriminating Markheim with its anonymous testimony. The character, until then absorbed in his thoughts and skewed observations, is suddenly 'inexplicably conscious' of the presence of someone else in the 'bulk of empty house above him', someone that could not be the servant since she, as Stevenson says in the witty and socially-charged 'out for the day written in very ribbon and smile' was not there. But just as the reader is about to be fully convinced this is another product of the character's paranoid imagination, there are indications that Markheim may in fact be right: a shadow wavers 'in the strip of doubtful brightness' that filtered under the door. With this new twist of suspense, the passage ends with an unresolved mystery, so, after all, was Markheim in fact completely alone? The answer to this question only the devil knows.

Higher Level literary commentary: poem

The Wasps' Nest

Two aerial tigers,
Striped in ebony and gold
And resonantly, savagely a-hum,
Have lately come
To my mail-box's metal hold
And thought
With paper and with mud
Therein to build
Their insubstantial and their only home.
Neither the sore displeasure
Of the U.S. Mail
Nor all my threats and warnings
Will avail
To turn them from their hummed devotions.
And I think
They know my strength,
Can gauge
The danger of their work:
And yet they seem
Too deeply and too fiercely occupied
To bother to attend.

Perhaps they sense
I'll never deal the blow,
For, though I am not in nor of them,
Still I think I know
What it is like to live
In an alien and gigantic universe, a stranger,
Building the fragile citadels of love
On the edge of danger.

James L Rosenberg

Student answer

'The Wasps' Nest' by James L Rosenberg initially appears to deal with an undesired nest of wasps located in the narrator's mailbox. The uneven syntax of the poem and the clipped line length convey a disjointed, broken rhythm as he explores the tension in his relationship with the insects. Power becomes a dominant concern, and along with simple diction and vivid imagery, the poem's free-verse structure provides a means for him to convey an intimate, sceptical tone. By the end of the poem, however, there is a dramatic development in the speaker's attitude; he comes to understand their mutual sense of being 'alien' in a 'gigantic universe'. As a result of this, in the final lines, Rosenberg is able to convey a message that we need empathy and understanding in order to survive in this unforgiving world.

Throughout the poem Rosenberg describes a setting that seems characterised by danger and threat, in which human and animal creatures exist in a fraught relationship with each other. He uses the adverb 'savagely' to describe the arrival of the wasps in his mailbox and comments on the 'sore displeasure of the U.S. Mail'. The word 'mail' is perhaps a play on the word 'male', hinting that the tension between human and animal is a largely masculine one. In this initial section of the poem rhyme and line length draw attention to the vulnerability of the wasps. In contrast to the 'metal hold' of the mailbox, their home is built 'with paper and mud' and is described as 'insubstantial and their only home.' This is one of the longest lines in the poem and coupled with the fact that it comes at the end of the poem's first sentence, reinforces their precarious position.

In spite of this sense of danger, the wasps are portrayed as focused and determined - oblivious to the position they are in. Rosenberg repeats the onomatopoeic word 'hum' in line 14 - this time to describe their 'hummed devotions', and the use of 'devotions' conveys an almost religious sense of commitment to their task. This stands in ironic contrast, of course, to the danger we know they are in. The speaker says that he suspects 'they know my strength' and reminds us that 'one blow could crush them.' And yet they continue regardless. At this point the poem seems concerned with the survival instinct and the determination that exists in nature to persist against the odds.

Rosenberg emphasizes the mutual tension between the speaker and the wasps with the use of pronouns. He sets 'my', 'I' and 'their' or 'they're' as a means to distinguish between them and reinforce their opposition. The sense of conflict is further emphasized through his comment that 'One blow could crush them / And their nest; and I am not their friend.' The half rhyme in the couplet here accentuates the power he feels, and his sense of emotional distance from them - further reinforcing the danger in which the wasps are placed. In this respect the wasps' actions seem almost futile as the speaker is clearly in a position of power and control, able to destroy them as and when he likes.

However, at this point in the poem there is a transition. The speaker makes clear his distinction from the wasps with the statement 'I am not in nor of them', literally identifying the fact that they are of different species. And yet his sense of difference from them is precisely what causes him to 'never deal the blow'. He expresses an understanding of them. This understanding is reflected in the change of tone; previously the narrator was concerned with 'threats and warnings', whereas towards the end of the poem he is far more understanding. He says that 'I think I know what it is like to live / In an alien and gigantic universe.' In some respects this shift has been foreshadowed in a subtle way from the beginning. Describing them with the metaphorical description 'aerial tigers' in the first line conveys a degree of admiration, perhaps even awe, and this is exaggerated with the reference to 'ebony and gold' in his portrayal of their stripes. These colours suggest beauty more than they do evil. Rosenberg uses equally positive diction towards the end to indicate that the wasps' existence is not futile; he describes their homes as 'fragile citadels of love'. The metaphorical term 'citadel' lends them a kind of strength- in contrast to their 'insubstantial ... only home' of line 9. In this way, although remaining 'on the edge of danger', the wasps determination reminds the speaker of his own attitude towards love as a kind of power.

The free verse structure of Rosenberg's poem presents an informal speaking voice trying to make sense of issues to do with power, the relationship we have with nature and a sense of alienation from the world. In a way a common thread that runs throughout is one of paradox; the wasps are vulnerable and yet - like 'tigers' - powerful. In reverse, the speaker is able to 'deal the blow' but knows what it means to 'live ... a stranger.' As the lines are both end stopped and run on, so the diction and imagery in the poem weaves through these contradictory ideas to conclude that fragility and strength are indivisible from each other, and essential components to our experience of love. I find this an intriguing and compelling idea.

Questions to guide your comments and marks:

1. **Focus on Criterion A: Understanding and interpretation**

   - Does the student demonstrate accurate understanding of the content of the poem?

   - Are points always supported with detailed reference back to the text?

   - Has s/he provided points of interpretation as well as points of analysis?

   - Do you find the interpretation put forward by the student persuasive?

2. **Focus on Criterion B: Appreciation of the writer's choices**

   - Does the student display identify a range of features of language, form, and style?

   - Does s/he explore the way in which these techniques convey meaning and have an impact or effect?

   - Is there as much sensitivity to matters or technique and style as there is content?

3. **Focus on Criterion C: Organization**
   - Does the response show evidence of organization in the form of paragraphs?
   - Has the SL student answered the guiding questions?
   - Are ideas developed in a meaningful way e.g. through a central line of argument or thesis?

4. **Focus on Criterion D: Language**
   - Do you think the commentary is generally accurately written?
   - Do you think the commentary is written in an appropriate register?
   - Does the student employ a variety of sentence structures and vocabulary that suggests confidence with the task?
   - Are ideas connected – both between sentences and between paragraphs?
   - Is the language of the essay clear?

Examiner's Marks
Standard Level guided literary analysis

Criterion A: Understanding and interpretation 4

The candidate demonstrates good understanding of the extract, exploring aspects such as the presentation of character and setting, action and theme, and the relationships between them. Points of interpretation are generally convincing, although in places there is room for more detailed reference back to the text. Both the guiding questions, one on characterization and one on structure, are prominently addressed in the commentary.

Criterion B: Appreciation of the writer's choices 4

The candidate demonstrates sensitivity to aspects such as word choice, syntax, imagery, and some aspects of metaphor, as well as some ways in which these features support the meaning. There is a need for more consideration of components such as narrative voice and tone. At times there is tendency towards description in place of detailed analysis of the impact of literary features.

Criterion C: Organization 4

For the most part ideas are organized coherently in paragraphs and there is a sense of overall control. The candidate takes aspects of setting, character, and structure as focal topics for the paragraphs, although there are elements of repetition and the analysis does not perhaps develop as logically it might.

Criterion D: Language 5

The language is in places quite articulate, though not consistently so. The candidate employs a variety of diction and syntax and generally maintains an appropriate register.

Higher Level literary commentary

Criterion A: Understanding and interpretation 5

The candidate explores a range of ideas in the poem, including the presentation of the speaker, the wasps, and setting as well as thematic concerns to do with power, security, and love. The reading is clear, consistent, and persuasive, reflective of confidence about the material and a sense of independent engagement.

Criterion B: Appreciation of the writer's choices 4

The candidate demonstrates very good understanding of a range of literary features and their effects. Diction, imagery, pronouns, metaphor and aspects of ironic voice are identified and explored. There is more to say about the significance of form and structure, although the candidate is alive to the shifts in tone and the development of the poem's language.

Criterion C: Organization 4

The commentary is effectively organized, each paragraph being devoted to one central idea. Although a line of argument is clearly declared, the structure doesn't quite do justice to it, and there are one or two moments of repetition, or where the logic goes slightly awry.

Criterion D: Language 5

The candidate writes clearly and effectively. Confidence in word choice and syntax is demonstrated consistently, and although the language is not overly sophisticated, the essay is accurate, concise, and cogent.

Part 1: Works in translation

In the study of this part of the syllabus, you are likely to run into some questions about what you are facing when working closely with writing that started out in another language.

The following passages are both from a story written by Argentine author Jorge Luis Borges.

"I recall him (though I have no right to speak that sacred verb – only one man on earth did, and that man is dead) holding a dark passionflower in his hand, seeing it as it had never been seen, even had it been stared at from the first light of dawn to the last light of evening for an entire lifetime."

-- from *Funes, His Memory* by Jorge Luis Borges (trans. Andrew Hurley)

"I remember him (I scarcely have the right to use this ghostly verb; only one man on earth deserved the right, and he is dead), I remember him with a dark passionflower in his hand, looking at it as no one has ever looked at such a flower, though they might look from the twilight of day until the twilight of night, for a whole life long."

-- from *Funes, the Memorious* by Jorge Luis Borges (trans. Anthony Kerrigan)

You have probably already noticed that the two translated passages are fundamentally the same in their meaning and intent, though they differ greatly in their content.

Activity

In the spaces below, list three differences in the two passages that caught your eye as you read:

1.

2.

3.

How do these differences affect your experience of each text? Do you like one excerpt more than the other? Is one more effective than the other? How does something as seemingly simple as a translator's word choice have an effect on the translated work?

You can see that the exploration of literature in translation is one that calls for a close and detailed study, and one that raises many interesting issues, from literary aspects to the importance of the culture that exists behind the work you study. Ultimately, you will come away from your study of the texts in this section with an enhanced appreciation of the role that culture can play in literature. Through your discussions and written work, you will also develop the following skills:

1. You will be able to understand and discuss the **content and qualities** of the works that make them worth studying as literature.

2. You will be able to work independently as you both explore the **cultural background** of the works and connect your own background to the works.

3. You will be able to understand the role and importance of **cultural and contextual elements** in the works.

Hint

Although you may be working here with writing that you might be able to read in its original language, your discussions, and particularly your written work to be submitted to the examiner, must address the text as it appears in the Language A.

An examiner is chosen for his or her expertise in a particular language A, and is not expected to handle written or spoken work in its original form, but as it is translated into your Language A.

Your main objective in this part of the course is to produce a final piece of critical analysis called the Written Assignment. It counts for 25% of your overall score in the course, and will be marked externally by an outside examiner (not your teacher). However, you won't be working toward this final product on your own. You will have the guidance and assistance of not only your teacher, but your classmates as well. The Written Assignment is actually the final part of a process made up of many elements: class discussion, personal reflection, and literary analysis. This graphic illustrates the progression you will make through different assignments as you study each work.

1. INTERACTIVE ORAL

⬇

2. REFLECTIVE STATEMENT

⬇

3. SUPERVISED WRITING

⬇

4. WRITTEN ASSIGNMENT

Stage 1: The Interactive Oral

For this part of the course, class discussions are going to be a vital part of your learning process as well as a great help to you as you begin working toward the final Written Assignment. You will be given the responsibility, alone as part of a larger plan or with a group, for initiating a discussion about the culture and context of at least one work. Your teacher may assign you a broad topic to investigate and "report" on to the rest of the class, or you may be given the freedom to choose your own topic.

Activity

Think of a work of literature that you have read or studied in the last year, and use that text to complete the responses below. These are the kinds of issues you should address in your Interactive Oral.

The time and place in which your text is set are important because...

The hardest part of the work to connect to your own life is...

The easiest part of this work to connect to your own life is...

One way that the issues and events of this work connect to your own place and time is...

One of the most interesting literary techniques or devices used by the author of this work is...

If you have been assigned to present an Interactive Oral about the culture and context of a work, where should you begin? If your teacher does not give you a specific topic to investigate, you will have to generate one on your own. Using *Effi Briest* as a model, let's see what options might be worth exploring. Start with a basic statement about the novel: "*Effi Briest* was written by German author Theodor Fontane in 1894." Using that sentence as your starting point, what are some of the topics you could research that might help you and your classmates gain a better understanding of the novel?

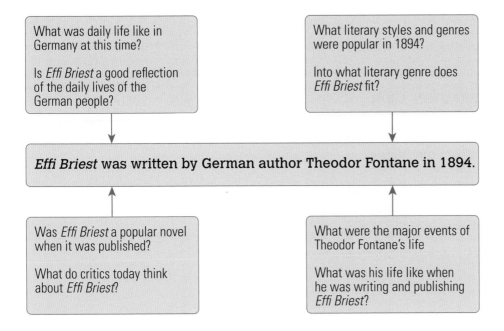

What was daily life like in Germany at this time?

Is *Effi Briest* a good reflection of the daily lives of the German people?

What literary styles and genres were popular in 1894?

Into what literary genre does *Effi Briest* fit?

Effi Briest was written by German author Theodor Fontane in 1894.

Was *Effi Briest* a popular novel when it was published?

What do critics today think about *Effi Briest*?

What were the major events of Theodor Fontane's life

What was his life like when he was writing and publishing *Effi Briest*?

Activity

Using a text of literary merit that you and your classmates have read in the last two years, try to create three good "starter" questions that you could use to begin an exploration of the culture and context of the text. These may be questions about the culture depicted in the text, the life and times of the author, or even certain literary aspects of the text that you still remember (for example, a surprising ending or an unconventional structure.)

Title:

Question 1:

Question 2:

Question 3:

As you can see, it is easy to brainstorm topics that you can then use in your Interactive Oral. The Internet makes it easy to look at old newspaper stories or to research literary criticism about an author or time period, so your preparation can be not only interesting but efficient.

Activity

Here are some basic questions you can ask that may lead you to a topic that you will enjoy investigating and relating to your classmates:

- What are the major events in the life of the author?
- What is the historical and cultural background of the author or of the events in the work?
- What were the critical reactions to the work? Why is this work "famous"?
- What other works is this work often compared to, and why?

Speaking and listening

You can see that there are important aspects to both sides of presenting aspects of oral work.

THE INTERACTIVE ORAL

HOW TO BE A GOOD PRESENTER:

- Prepare sufficiently and have your material ready to go when your presentation starts.
- Give your presentation a clear structure so that your classmates can follow it easily.
- Speak clearly and spell any difficult names or terms that are important to your presentation.
- Speak slowly and be considerate of classmates who ask you to repeat any information.
- Link your presentation to the text as often as possible.
- Create a handout, outline, or slide presentation to share with classmates.
- Try to come up with one or two discussion questions that can lead to further class discussion.

HOW TO BE A GOOD LISTENER:

- Take notes during the presentation, making sure to mark any information that seems confusing or might need more clarification.
- Try to constantly take the information and create your own connections between the presentation and the work you are studying.
- Ask questions or raise other possible areas of investigation related to the presentation.
- Be an active participant in any discussions that arise from the presentation.
- As you write, mark or highlight any information that is especially useful and may be worth noting on your Reflective Statement later.

Activity

As you put together a presentation for an Interactive Oral, highlight the key terms and ideas that you think are essential for your classmates to note during your presentation. At the end of your part of the Interactive Oral, quickly survey your classmates to see how many of them wrote down or made note of the terms and ideas that you consider crucial. If some are missing, ask what you could have done to make them stand out in your presentation.

To prepare for your Interactive Oral your teacher may ask you to work in groups to find appropriate research questions. Look at this worksheet about preparing an Interacive Oral on *Ficciones* by Jorge Luis Borges. What follows is only one approach to arranging the Interactive Oral. Your teacher may have one or more different ways of arranging for the work on culture and context to be delivered by students.

Literature in translation: *Ficciones* by Jorge Luis Borges

Part 1: The Interactive Oral

The first step toward the creation of your Written Assignment for IB English is called the Interactive Oral. Don't be put off by the name- this is exactly the kind of discussion we have for all of the works that we read over the course of the year. If you have been selected to be a "discussion starter" for our look at the Borges stories, your job is simple: you must help the class place the stories we read into a "big picture" that we will call culture and context. In other words, we should be able to not only appreciate the literary features of these stories, but also understand why the stories are significant in terms of the culture that they represent and the overall context – historical and literary – into which they "fit".

To begin, let's start with a basic statement about the stories we are covering in class:

These short pieces of fiction were all written by Jorge Luis Borges and published in a collection titles *Ficciones*.

How can we use that statement as a sort of launching pad for our research into the culture and context of the stories? Today in class, we will brainstorm and see what kinds of questions are raised by the statement above. Try to generate at least three questions for each of the following items:

- Fiction

- Jorge Luis Borges

- *Ficciones*

After we finish brainstorming, those of you who are assigned to this text will need to come up with a research question that you will investigate. After I approve your topic, you as an individual will need to prepare a short presentation – no more than five minutes or so – for the class that will both give us useful information *and* start a discussion that will be helpful as we attempt to understand these stories. Your presentation can be a simple oral report, or you may want to create a handout or even a brief slide show for us to use as we follow along. The format is entirely up to you. Remember that your main goal is to tie your findings back into our study of these short stories.

Here is a possible outline or handout that you or another student could create, based on this assignment:

Handout for Interactive Oral discussion starter: Jorge Luis Borges

Research question: what is the background of *Ficciones* and what influence has it had on other authors and works?

The background of *Ficciones*

- *Ficciones* is actually a combination of two other short story collections by Jorge Luis Borges. One is called the *The Garden of Forking Paths* and it was published in 1941. The other is called *Artifices* and it was published in 1944.
- The two collections were combined and a few more stories were included when the official version of *Ficciones* was published in 1956.
- The stories were originally written in Spanish, but they were translated and published in English for the first time in 1962.
- Jorge Luis Borges also wrote poetry and essays, but he never wrote any long fiction. He is most famous for his short stories.

The influence of *Ficciones*

- There is actually an adjective to describe literature that shows the influence of Borges: *Borgesian*.
- The stories in *Ficciones* often involve alternate realities and questioning the nature of how time works. This can be seen in many science-fiction stories that are written today.
- Borges also blurred the line between illusion and reality, so the reader is never sure if what is taking place is real or imaginary. This is similar to modern-day stories that involve ideas like virtual reality.

Discussion topics for Interactive Oral

- What are some stories in *Ficciones* in which Borges makes us question what is real and what is not? How does he create this kind of confusion in the reader?
- Many of the stories in *Ficciones* seem frustrating to us because they are not always easy to understand unless we read them very closely. How does that affect our enjoyment of these stories?
- In Theory of Knowledge class, we watched the movie *Inception* during our unit on Sense Perception. That movie's writer, Christopher Nolan, has said that the film was influenced by the Borges stories "The Secret Miracle" and "The Circular Ruins". What are some ways that we can see the influence of these two stories on the plot of *Inception*?

Activity

Visit the website and click on the link for [insert link here]. These are two Interactive Oral presentations about the stories of Jorge Luis Borges. One deals with literary elements of "The Shape of the Sword" while the other examines the cultural background of the story "The South." Even if you have not read the stories, listen to the presentations and assess their value in enhancing the overall understanding of the stories. Do the presenting students seem confident in their presentations? Do other students seem to be engaged in the discussion? What advice, if any, would you give to the presenting students?

Activity

One way that your teacher might involve several members of your class in an Interactive Oral is by asking you to contribute to a "dictionary" of sorts. Using a text that you and your classmates have read in the last two years, generate a list of five terms (or concepts or references) that would be useful to a new reader in understanding the text as a whole. (What are some of the things that you wish you had known before beginning to read the work?)

Stage 2: The Reflective Statement

At the end of each Interactive Oral (and remember, an Interactive Oral may be made up of several people introducing or explaining relevant topics), you will be asked to write a Reflective Statement. This piece of writing should be 300 to 400 words in length, and it requires you to write down your own thoughts and insights about the Interactive Oral that just took place. You are simply answering one question: **how was your understanding of cultural and contextual considerations of the work developed through the Interactive Oral?** That may sound a bit complicated, but it's not. Think of it this way:

- How did class discussions about the background of the work help you understand the work better (or get more out of it)?

- What did you learn about the style or techniques of the author? What facts about the author's background helped you understand the work better?

- What connections did the work have to your own background, or to other works you have read or other topics you have studied?

- What techniques or literary devices in the work were interesting to you and why?

As you craft your Reflective Statement, keep the following hints in mind:

- Make sure to address one or more of the questions above.

- While you can be somewhat informal and can write in first person, don't forget that this is still a piece of writing that will be assessed externally. It is meant to be an immediate reflection, not a researched and heavily edited piece of writing. Your teacher will establish a time frame for its submission and it will be kept on file.

- Think of the Reflective Statement as a kind of "before and after" experiment. What do you know and understand after the Interactive Oral that you did not understand before it? If you were studying *Effi Briest*, for example, you may have gained an idea about the historical and cultural context behind Effi and her husband, an officer in the German military. It is much easier to understand the behaviours and beliefs of Effi's husband after learning about that aspect of the novel's background, and that is exactly what you would write about in your Reflective Statement.

Remember

1. Take notes during the Interactive Oral.
2. Stay focused on the ways in which your understanding grew thanks to the Interactive Oral.
3. Remember to show a before and after change in your understanding.
4. Count your words! An easy strategy is to stop after each pargraph and do a quick word count. At the very least you should stop at the bottom of your first page and count the words. Whether you handwrite or type your reflective statement, make sure you never exceed 400 words.

Activity

Using a novel, play, poem, or short story that you have read as a part of your studies in the last two years, think of one way in which the culture or events depicted in the book connected with an experience from your own life. How might that connection help you understand or appreciate the work more fully?

Here are three sample Reflective Statements, all covering different works. The first two have been marked (the highest mark is a score of three) and include an examiner's comments. The third sample has not been marked, but it did receive the full three marks. Note down at least three attributes of the Reflective Statement that made it worthy of full marks, in your opinion.

Student sample 1

Reflective Statement on *Leo Africanus* by Amin Maalouf

This book is based on the life of a 14th century traveller and biographer, Leo the African. He doesn't get the name Leo until late in the book, and he is known as Hasan from the beginning. It is divided into 4 books, one for Granada, which is in Spain, one for Fez in Morocco, one for Cairo in Egypt, and one for Rome, which is in Italy. Each book is divided into chapters, ranging from 6 to 18, making the Book of Fez the longest and, to me, the most interesting. In the presentation we learned that there is a lot of work going on right now into exploring the person, known as Leo the Africanus and that there is a lot of controversy about him. We don't get much sense of controversy from Maalouf's book but it is interesting that it is going on in the background while we are studying it.

The book as a whole both has and does not have a lot of togetherness, as the presenters have pointed out. There are many interesting individual adventures that Leo has, especially after he meets up with Harun the Ferret who is an adventurous and clever person. He knows Harun almost throughout the whole of his life, and this adds interest to the story. Between them, Harun and Hassan cook up a lot of good adventures, some of which are not really believable but enjoyable to read, nevertheless.

I particularly like the Book of Fez because so many different things happen in it I get a sense of what Morocco is like. There is all the controversy about Mariam's marriage, and the travels with Hasan's uncle, and his love affair with Hiba. Toward the end, Harun gets married to a woman called Hiba, so a lot happens to our hero in this section and it's fairly easy to understand, unlike what happens in Rome later in the book. This part seemed more important for the presenters, though it was not for me.

This book has changed me by making me thinking about four places I was not familiar with, and it was good to do that through a novel, where you get a sense of what real people were experiencing in this period. (361 words)

Examiner's comments

In a rather diffuse and rambling Reflective Statement, this candidate touches on what she has heard in the Interactive Oral. Although the scholarly controversy about the identity of Leo, the novel's coherence or lack thereof, and the attention that the presenters have given to the latter section of the work are all touched upon, the candidate does not make much of them, nor show that they have had a developmental impact on her own responses and preferences about the novel. Clearly, she is aware of the context but the sense of that seems superficial.

Mark: 1

Student sample 2

Reflective Statement on the Interactive Oral presenting the geographical setting of *Broken April*.

I found it useful to be reminded of the way the writer plays with the city versus the mountain landscape through the portrayal of the "city" people (Bessian and Diana) and the mountain people, (Gjorg and his family) and the really creepy place that he goes to pay the blood feud money. I never really got a strong sense of what the city was like except that it seemed that Bessian and Diana came from a fairly wealthy group of people. Diana's marriage almost seem "arranged" to me.

The high mountain country seems very morbid and dark. When Gjorg is on his way to pay the blood feud, he runs into a lot of ruins and remains of other people's lives. I think this ties into the earlier parts in his village. I was surprised that we didn't have Gyorg running into a few more bloody shirts from other occurrences of the blood feud. As we learned, the blood feuds continue even until today, even though there have been efforts to stop them.

At least Gyorg seems like an "insider" as he walks along the roads and gives the reader a lot of background about the laws of hospitality and the way the blood feud is connected to that. On the other hand, when Bessian and Diana are journeying into the highlands in the carriage, they seem both amazed (Bessian) and depressed (Diana), and outsiders. One can understand how both could happen because Bessian obviously has a romantic idea about the high mountains so they look mysterious and "accursed", in an intriguing way. When Diana looks out the windows, she sees a "wasteland", and it is "mute and frozen". Both of the people seem to spend a lot of time looking out at the landscape. It seems to impact the mood inside the carriage.

I certainly got the same feeling about the geographical setting as Diana. The novel mostly takes place in gloomy weather, the interiors of the buildings seem as cold as the landscape outside. The roads are rough, and when we are walking (with Gyorg) we feel the landscape in a different way then when we see it from inside the carriage. All in all, geography seems to matter a lot to the mood of this novel, but it certainly isn't one that encourages me to visit Albania. (391 words)

Examiner's comments

The significant weakness of this Reflective Statement is the random quality of the observations, many of which are impressionistic reports of what the candidate recalls from the novel, and not all having to do with the geographical setting of the work. The statement is more reactive than reflective and the scope is wide. "Development of thinking" about the novel's context is limited, though there are certainly allusions to culture. One does not sense that the candidate took very much advantage of the details the Interactive Oral provided about Albania, its regions and particularly the facts about features of topography, distance, altitude, climate, and weather that have an impact on how Kadare chose to embed his characters in the story and are much more clearly seen in other Reflective Statements from this school.

Mark: 2

Student sample 3

Reflective Statement on *A Chronicle of a Death Foretold*

I was really glad that the second Interactive Oral on our translated works went further into the issue of honour in Latin American cultures. It was useful that John pointed out, first, that "Latin American Culture" is in itself an over-simplified label and that the Colombian context of this novel is not that of the Argentinean culture of Borges. Honour is one thing in a Colombian village, but the honour among the gauchos of Borges is not quite the same.

Honour in this Colombian novel became, in this presentation, much more clearly connected for me to the terms "marianismo" and "machismo" that we heard a little about in the first presentation on *Chronicle of a Death Foretold*. It's worth seeing that while Angela's mother is deeply connected to family honour, to the older ideas of women being like the Virgin Mary, and the need for everyone in the family to protect the honour of their women, Angela doesn't really buy into those ideas completely. She and her friends know ways to fake virginity, which itself says something about how much (or how little) they are impacted by the previous generation's ideas. They don't seem particularly worried about honour even though that's what leads to Santiago's death. Looking at these details is a reminder that honour is also tied to a particular context and contains some ambiguity.

And I found it useful to see that even the "machismo" (supposedly) of Angela's brothers was really undermined by the author (is this irony?) even though the ending was a very bloody and very macho event in defense of honour. I can see that all these terms can be used a bit too loosely, as Melody showed with her three statements including the terms, all of which could be questioned and misinterpreted. I'm seeing that I will need to be careful about using these terms, if I use them at all, when I write my essay.
(322 words)

Activity

This Reflective Statement received full marks from the examiner. Why did this Reflective Statement get full marks? What are three ways in which it fulfilled the requirements of an effective Reflective Statement?

Stage 3: Supervised Writing

So far, your examination of the works in the *Works in translation* section of the syllabus has been largely focused on the culture and context of the works. You should be in a strong position to either explicitly or implicitly include this learning in your Written Assignment, which is the second element of the process marked externally. However, while the cultural material is a crucial and often fascinating area of study, you will now be asked to look more closely at the literary aspects of a work. In fact, your final Written Assessment will be about a literary topic – culture and context may still come into play, but literary analysis is at the heart of this part of the course. You won't have to come up with this topic on your own, however. For this part, your teacher will give you three or four prompts or questions about the work, and you will be asked to pick one of those prompts and write a critical response during a class period. You will be able to refer to your texts and notes. You won't be able to see the prompts in advance so you will have to do a bit of quick thinking. The Supervised Writing should take between forty and fifty minutes – in essence, it is a timed essay. Of course, it doesn't have to be as formal as an essay you would work on at home, but it will be as formally structured than the Reflective Statements that you have already written. Try not to spend much of your time agonizing over an introduction or conclusion to your writing; instead, focus on giving the best response that you can – one that shows your understanding of the work as well as your ability to analyse literature. Thinking about a text 'on your feet' this way is a skill that will serve you well in other assessments of the course.

The real reason that the Supervised Writing is so important is because it will serve as a "rough draft" of sorts for your final Written Assignment. In fact, your Written Assignment ought to be related in some meaningful way to the topic you choose for your Supervised Writing. So as you look at the list of prompts that your teacher gives you, don't just think of the immediate situation – try to pick a topic that will be interesting to you later as you develop it into a full-fledged literary essay. Because your teacher will be creating the prompts for the Supervised Writing, there are no guaranteed models that you can follow for this part of the course. However, keep in mind that the questions will allow you to shape them into your own more focused topics for the Written Assignment. Here are four possible prompts for *Effi Briest*:

1. How does Theodor Fontane use work, professions, and/or work environments to add depth and interest to the characters in *Effi Briest*?

2. How far does setting serve to reinforce or emphasize meanings or themes in *Effi Briest*?

3. How does Theodor Fontane present issues of freedom and imprisonment in *Effi Briest*?

4. What is the importance of the minor characters in *Effi Briest*?

Activity

Try to come up with one question that you think would be a suitable prompt for a Supervised Writing on the last major work that you and your classmates read together. Remember that it needs to ask about a literary topic, and should be broad enough to elicit a variety of responses. It also needs to lead to a more focused topic if it is chosen by a student. It's not an easy task!

Compare your question with those of your classmates. Are some more appropriate than others? Could you easily answer some of the questions posed by your classmates? Can they answer yours?

Here is another set of prompts for a Supervised Writing, this time covering the stories of Jorge Luis Borges. Looking at those questions and the ones above, you can see that they leave you a lot of room to explore the topics as you choose (for example, you get to pick the minor character or characters to focus on in question four above). More importantly, they give you space to come up with your own topic for the final Written Assignment – and it is unlikely that one of your classmates will come up with exactly the same approach to a topic, given that much freedom to choose. Should great similarities occur in the Written Assignment on a given prompt – which is not unlikely – the examiner will still be looking for your individual voice in making your argument and choosing your supporting evidence.

Examples of Prompts

1. The stories of Jorge Luis Borges often seem to focus on intriguing situations or thought experiments; his treatment of characters seems to be a secondary focus. In what ways does Borges create sympathetic or relatable characters in his fiction, and what effect does that have on the reader's overall experience of the text?

2. How does Borges incorporate the worlds of fantasy or dreams or imagination into his fiction, and what effect is produced by his use of those devices?

3. Describe the ways in which Borges incorporates symbols and metaphors (circles, labyrinths, mirrors, etc.) into his fiction and the effect that is achieved through his use of those devices.

4. Discuss the opening and closing scenes, sections, or sentences of a story or stories by Borges and the way(s) in which those moments affect the reader's experience of those fictions.

Activity

1. First make a list of literary aspects of one of the works you have studied. In other sections of this book (those on Paper 1, and Parts Two and Three) you will find many of these literary aspects, features, and conventions. Choose several that you think are important to the work and write three Supervised Writing prompts that would give a good direction for a literary essay. Try these out on a partner, and revise them, if you need to make them clearer. Enter them in the "List of student-generated prompts" in the class blog.

2. Choose one of your own prompts or those of a classmate, and write for 50 minutes, setting out your first approach to developing that prompt. Give your supervised writing to another classmate and have him/her respond to it using these three criteria:
   - Does the writing have a clear focus?
   - Do you see an appropriate and believable connection between the approach and the text?
   - Is there enough material in the text to provide detail and examples of the angle the writer is trying to prove?

Stage 4: The Written Assignment

Take a quick look back at all of the work you have already done with the text you are studying:

1. In addition to classroom exercises and standard discussions, you have also participated in an Interactive Oral and explored the cultural and contextual background of the work.

2. You have written about your own learning experiences and increased understanding in a Reflective Statement.

3. Finally, you have responded to a Supervised Writing prompt that required you to quickly synthesize your knowledge of the text.

The final step in the process is a natural extension of all three of these previous activities: the Written Assignment.

The Written Assignment is a formal essay between 1200 and 1500 words in length that focuses on a literary aspect of the work you are studying. However, you have already done much of the preliminary work for this assignment, because your essay will be based in some way on your response for the Supervised Writing. The first thing you should do before starting your Written Assignment is to look over the rubric that will used to mark it.

Criterion	What to ask yourself about your own Written Assignment...	Marks Possible
A. Reflective Statement	Did you write about your new or improved understanding of the work that came from the Interactive Oral? Did you directly connect the Interactive Oral to the text and show a change in your view of the work?	3
B. Knowledge and understanding	Have you shown a true understanding of the work from a literary point of view? Have you included appropriate details and/or quotations from the text to support your assertions? Have you offered an insight into the work instead of just re-telling the story?	6

C. Appreciation of the writer's choices	Have you examined the literary devices or techniques used by the author and connected those devices to effects or meanings in the work? Have you shown your appreciation of the way in which the author uses metaphors, symbols, structure, imagery, diction, and other literary devices to achieve a definite purpose in the text?	6
D. Organization and development	Have you organized your writing in a logical and effective way? Have you worked the quotations or relevant details from the text smoothly into your writing? Do your quotations from the text help your argument?	5
E. Language	Have you used formal language, appropriate to this kind of assignment? Do you use the correct literary terms in your discussion? Have you avoided repetition?	5
TOTAL		25

Other hints for the Written Assignment:

1. **Narrow your focus:** if you discussed three characters in your Supervised Writing, perhaps you might narrow your focus on one of those characters for your Written Assignment. Maybe you talked about an author's use of symbolism in a work – now you can narrow your focus to a discussion of that symbol's use in only one part of the work.

2. **Consult your teacher:** even if you feel confident about your topic, you should discuss it with your teacher to make sure that it is suitable and that you will be able to write enough words about it (it may turn out, of course, that your topic is too big for only 1500 words – in that case, your teacher will be able to help you narrow your focus to a suitable range).

3. **Write a first draft:** your teacher cannot mark on the draft itself, but he or she can talk to you about the progress and direction of the paper, or your teacher may choose to give you feedback in written form on a separate sheet of paper. Once you have this feedback, in whatever form it may take, you must complete the final draft of your essay without any further assistance from anyone.

> ### Activity
>
> Go back to a question you created for a Supervised Writing earlier in this section. How could that question be turned into a thesis or the basis for a literary argument in a Written Assignment? (Hint: If you have trouble making this transition, that may mean you need to go back and rethink your initial Supervised Writing question.)
>
> Write out a brief response, making clear just what it is you plan to argue about the work, based on your work with a Supervised Writing prompt.

Detail and effect

One of the most successful strategies in producing a Written Assignment is to explore just *how* the writer creates the impact of a successful piece of literary art. Candidates can do this by precisely citing details and their effects to build the argument.

The Metamorphosis by Franz Kafka is a popular work in IB classes and will serve as a good work for exemplifying this strategy. The student in this case has selected the topic: "How Kafka has effectively presented a dramatic tension between the outer and the inner reality of Gregor Samsa in this novella of transformation." As you can see the student

has advantaged herself already by focusing on technique: *how* the two realities, man and insect, are kept in a tension throughout the novella.

For a truly successful essay on this topic, the candidate will want to demonstrate, through detail, the degree to which Kafka has managed to keep the two realities in an intriguing tension for the reader, who is never allowed to settle into either situation: Gregor has simply become a kind of thinking bug, or here is a man who believes himself to be transformed into an insect but continues to think as a man. For a strong essay, the candidate will show not only **details** from the text which support this idea, but will also make a proposal about the **effect** of each detail in maintaining this tension between Gregor portrayed as a man and as an insect.

Activity

Below are four examples of some of the details the student has decided to use to support her argument. In the first case we have given you both the details and the *effect statement* the student has written. See if, for the subsequent three examples, you can write an "effect statement", keeping in mind the line of argument the candidate has decided upon: presenting the tension of inner and outer reality.

"Why didn't his sister join the others? … Well, why was she crying? … Because he wouldn't get up and let the chief clerk in, because he was in danger of losing his job, and because the chief would begin dunning his parents again for the old debts?" (p96)

With this set of five rhetorical questions, Kafka has confirmed for us that Gregor is still thinking of himself as a viable wage-earner. We also see that he is capable of moving beyond his own situation of change into the realm of empathy, of thinking about others, something that certainly distinguishes him from an insect. Here Kafka is reinforcing the delicate balance of Gregor the man, Gregor the bug by giving him a moral sense about these issues.

As we first encounter Gregor in the opening paragraph, we meet the revelation that "he found himself transformed in his bed into a gigantic insect. His back is "armor-plated," he finds he has a "domelike brown belly," and "numerous legs."

What is the effect of these details?

In the evening, Gregor wakes and is drawn to the door into the hall by the smell of food. He discovers "a basin filled with fresh milk … ". He dips his head into it, but finds he cannot eat because his left side is tender, but also because "he did not like the milk either, although milk has been his favorite drink…". He crawls away, "almost with repulsion". (p105)

How might these details be used to advance the argument about the tension between man and bug?

At a later point in the story his sister, Grete, considers whether it is best to leave Gregor's room with its present furniture or if it might be better to remove it to give him more freedom to crawl around. Gregor has a conflicted reaction to this proposal. However he finally decides that "he could not dispense with the good influence of the furniture on his state of mind … even if the furniture did hamper him in his senseless crawling around and around … ". (p117)

How do these details about a very commonplace reality, furniture, develop some of the conflicts that Gregor is experiencing about his transformation?

This exercise is only a brief sample of an effective way to proceed in constructing a literary argument. Remember that assertions are unconvincing without supporting details, and details are best developed by making a proposal about the effect they have on advancing your argument. Note: You will find some further aids to writing a good essay in Chapter 4 on part 3 of the course.

-- extracts from *The Metamorphosis* by Franz Kafka

Let's look at the assignments one student might have completed in her class study of *Effi Briest*. Notice the connections between all of the assignments.

1. The Interactive Oral

The student participated in three Interactive Orals for this novel. In one, she presented her findings about characteristics and activities of seaside resort towns in Germany in the late nineteenth and early twentieth century. In the course of *Effi Briest*, some of the characters move to a fictional town called Kessin, which is based on these real-life resort towns. The student presented the daily routines and typical activities of the year-round residents of those towns and asked her classmates if that particular backdrop made it easier to understand some of the choices made by the characters in the novel. The discussion also covered what life is like today for people who live full-time in areas where tourism is a large part of the economy. Other Interactive Orals by her classmates covered the areas of realism in literature, the life and accomplishments of Kaiser Wilhelm and Otto von Bismarck (two central figures in the period of German history where the novel takes place), and the other works of author Theodor Fontane.

2. The Reflective Statement

The student wrote one of her reflective statements about the literary movement known as realism, which had been the subject of another Interactive Oral. Because realism often involves the detailed depiction of "everyday" or mundane activities, the passages in *Effi Briest* that detailed the main character's domestic routines or long walks along the beach suddenly made a great deal more sense. The student's Reflective Statement pointed out that before the Interactive Oral, those scenes had seemed meaningless to her and she had wondered why they were included in the novel at all.

3. Supervised Writing

The student's teacher gave the class four prompts to choose from as part of the Supervised Writing. The student chose question 2: "How far does setting serve to reinforce or emphasize meanings or themes in *Effi Briest*?" She wrote about two of the settings in the novel – the seaside town of Kessin and the dreary house where the main character lives with her husband and child. For both, she connected the settings to feelings of boredom or imprisonment, making sure to connect the device of setting to an overall effect in the novel.

4. The Written Assignment

After discussing some options with her teacher, the student decided to write about the descriptions of living quarters, specifically bedrooms, in *Effi Briest*. In the essay, the student connected the language that Fontane uses to describe those rooms with the feelings of entrapment and oppression experienced by the main character. Thus, the literary device of setting was explicitly connected to its effect – the creation of an atmosphere of oppression and imprisonment. The essay contained several quotes from the text of the novel and stayed focused on a single topic, making it a likely candidate for high marks.

Now that you have a good sense of the process leading to the Written Assignment, we are ready to look at an example of the two final steps, Supervised Writing and the Written Assignment. These are based on the Albanian novel, *Broken April*, which explores an insider and outsider view of the blood feuds which take place in the high mountainous territory of the country. Gyorg is charged with carrying out a a revenge murder; Bessian and Diana are journeying into Gyorg's territory as a honeymoon trip. Kadare plays the two perspectives off each other to provide some complex views of the country and the culture.

1. First read the prompt and the piece of Supervised Writing. How far do you see the candidate responding to the prompt? Do you think that the written piece provides some promising directions for an essay?

2. Read the essay, and going back to the chart of questions on the criteria found earlier in the chapter (p50–51), change the pronouns in the questions to "he" or "she," and with a partner or as part of a group, determine how you would answer them.

3. Look at the assessment criteria in your course book and assign marks for each, based on your reading of this essay.

   Criterion B:____

   Criterion C:____

   Criterion D:____

   Criterion E:____

4. Finally, read the marks and comments by the examiner and see how far you can agree with them.

Supervised Writing prompt: What use does Kadare make of the setting of the natural world in his novel, *Broken April*?

50-minute response to the prompt

In *Broken April*, Kadare uses the natural landscape to effectively distinguish characters' relationships and emotions. To begin with, there is the distinct contrast of the lowlands and the highlands. Kadare uses characters from the two regions to oppose and question one another. The divide is deeper than ethnic origin; their conflicting opinions are only imposed more due to the 'outsider' stigma attached to Bessian and Diana. This incorporation of region and landscape as indicators of bias and emotion builds up as the novel continues. Weather and the characters' descriptions of the setting, often give the reader insight and reveal or develop the motives and conflicts within the character. Many times, the settings described are highly symbolic, and dramatic to the point of excessive.

The first chapter begins with Gjorg waiting for Zef, a rifle slung over his shoulder. He describes "daylight fading," which casts the scene with a gloomy light. Gjorg goes on to repeatedly describe the icy snow with "wild pomegranates scattered through the brush-covered space on both sides of the road." For someone lying in wait to murder another, this image of red and white is highly significant. As he waits Gjorg remarks that "he had only a vague animosity for the wild pomegranates and the patches of snow." Sin or anger, buried like pomegranates in the snow—Kadare wants the reader to be acutely aware of Gjorg's internal struggle. After he kills Zef, he notices that the patches of snow "were still there, scattered witnesses." He sees the patches as remnants of his innocence. The landscape is used to reflect his new guilt.

The imagery employed when Bessian and Diana first arrive in the highlands is also significant. The two are unfamiliar and naïve in their expectations regarding the highlands. As their carriage approaches the highlands, Diana notes the "heavy layer of mist." Bessian tries to point out the "Accursed Mountains," but Diana cannot see through the fog. She goes on to describe the talk among her fashionable friends in the lowlands about Bessian's plan for a honeymoon in this part of Albania. Her friends find it very odd to choose such a place. The couple themselves are very innocent and naïve about life in the highlands—reflected in the fog and the mist. Diana begins to see the place as menacing and a "wasteland." She would like to pour her memories of home "out upon the endless waste." Already the reader sees the depression that the world of the highlands gives Diana. Bessian is still in admiration of a church he sees, and the kullas that he points out. Yet, despite their different emotional reactions, Kadare builds the two as outsiders, separate from the natural landscape so crucial to the natives of the highlands.

The essay that follows has developed out of the work done in the Supervised Writing, expanding on the way the natural landscape has been used in the novel.

The Functionality of Landscape and Setting in *Broken April*

In *Broken April*, Ismail Kadare uses descriptions of setting and landscape to effectively distinguish characters' evolving attitudes towards the blood feuds and one another. He utilizes landscape as a device to display the tension surrounding the Kanun, and to differentiate between participants and onlookers in the novel. Gjorg, as a character directly involved in a blood feud, is consistently described in the context of the harsh highland terrain, entirely vulnerable and under the control of something greater than himself. Conversely, Bessian and Diana are emotionally and psychologically detached from the archaic lifestyle of the Albanian northerners. Thus, Kadare creates landscapes that reflect this removal, frequently describing the foggy climate and indistinct landmarks.

In the opening of the novel, Gjorg's personal connection with blood feuds and the Kanun is reflected in Kadare's intense descriptions of the landscape. As he lies amidst shrubbery, waiting to enact his revenge on Zef Kryeqyqe, Kadare creates a setting that is indicative of Gjorg's attitude and emotional state. With the "daylight fading" (p.7), Gjorg crouches in the bushes. This half-lit setting is contrasted by the stark image of "wild pomegranates scattered through the brush-covered space on both sides of the road" (p.7). The pomegranates are a repeated motif in this scene, and Kadare implies that their presence is reflective of Gjorg's apprehensive state. He has not yet killed Zef Krycqyqe, but the impending act looms over him, imminent and predetermined. Red is a colour often symbolic of bloodshed, passion, or hatred. The red of the pomegranates against the innocence and purity represented by snow create an intriguing juxtaposition representative of the transgression and innocence of Gjorg's youth. As the act that drives the rest of the plot approaches, Gjorg remarks that he has "only a vague animosity for the wild pomegranates and the patches of snow, and sometimes he told himself that were it not for them, he would have given up his vigil long ago." (p.8). After Gjorg shoots Kryeqyqe, the pomegranates vanish from the scene's imagery, and Kadare displays Gjorg's loss of virtue, remarking that "patches of snow were still there, scattered witnesses" (p.10). In contrast with the aforementioned fading light, the day is now "dying" (p.10), yet another descriptor indicative of Gjorg's transformation. This is the first scene in the novel, and it can be noted that Kadare uses the symbolism of the pomegranates in the snow and the time of day to introduce the convention of the landscape and setting as indicators of mood and characters' emotions.

Gjorg's journey to the Kulla of Orosh is another scene in the beginning of the novel that is representative of Kadare's use of setting to distinguish a character's personal struggle. He walks along a deserted road, noting that "for miles the landscape was empty" (p.52). The vision of emptiness and desolation that surrounds Gjorg is significant as he walks, alone, to pay the blood tax after killing Zef. Kadare creates a setting that is dull and callous. The landscape is reflective of Gjorg's emotional numbness after carrying out his dictated duty to the Kanun. As he treks along the barren path, Gjorg notices that "the emptiness of the road on either side seemed emptier still because of the shrubby growth that had sprung up there as if with an evil intention" (p.53). Subtle attributions like the evil of the shrubbery, combined with the repetition of the emptiness of the road Gjorg travels on work to evoke the apprehension and loneliness that Gjorg feels throughout the chapter, as he contemplates his abruptly broken April. Towards the end of the journey, Gjorg looks for the elusive Kulla of Orosh, remarking that "from the time of his childhood he had heard about the princely castle that had guarded for centuries men's adherence to the Code, but he did not know what it looked like, or anything more about it." (p.53–54). Gjorg's internal struggle lies between his dutiful abidance of the Kanun's blood feud laws and his individual remorse for the bloodshed he has perpetuated. His fantastic devotion to the abovementioned princely castle, a physical institution of the Code, is diminished by his inability to actually locate it. When at last he sees the structure in the distance, Gjorg comments on the path, finding that "it gave the impression that the road climbed up in switchbacks, and that his changing point of view made the building change continually." (p.54). As Gjorg's princely castle comes into view, he is forced to reconcile with his imagination, and the "changing point of view" perhaps has more to do with this realization than the sharp turns in the road. Kadare's manipulation of landscape and setting in this sequence are insightful into Gjorg's internal struggle as an active participant in the ancient traditions of the highlands. When *Broken April* commences, Bessian and Diana Vorpsi are urbane newlyweds, onlookers to the northern culture, peoples, and ideals of the highlands. Kadare accentuates their distance from the reality of the region in his removed and indistinct descriptions of the landscape and setting. They each struggle with their new surroundings, and this emotional and ethical distress is reflected in Kadare's presentation of their environment. The first significant scene that distinguishes the couple as outsiders is the Vorpsi's first carriage ride in the highlands. The atmosphere is distant and unclear, with a "heavy layer of mist" (p.62) settled on what Bessian coins the "Accursed Mountains" (p.62). The initial response to the landscape is that it is a "wasteland" (p.67), devoid of anything noteworthy. These preliminary judgments effectively create a distinction between the couple and Gjorg. Kadare wants it to be apparent that Bessian and Diana are removed enough from highland lifestyle that they can make rapid assertions, despite the foggy uncertainty of the surrounding scenery.

Following the first carriage ride, Bessian and Diana begin to experience some self-realization as they experience more of the highlands. Within this self-realization there is also a division forming between the two characters. Although Kadare presents the two as outsiders, and uses their surroundings to accentuate their displacement, they begin to evolve into different brands of onlookers. Diana is emotionally involved, while Bessian remains scholarly in his approach to the culture. These evolutions are reflected in the setting as the couple spends the night in an inn before continuing on their tour in the carriage yet again. In the wee hours of the morning, Diana finds that she cannot sleep. She notices on the dark wall of the bedroom that there is "a patch of dim light. For a long moment, as if spellbound, she stared at the grayish patch... Outdoors, as it seemed, day was breaking." (p.90) With Bessian asleep, Diana's vision of the patch of light is symbolic of her individual reasoning process. She begins to connect to the northern sunlight at daybreak- something more tangibly meaningful and enjoyable than the elusive fog that consistently surrounds her when she is with her companion. She notes that "in the depressing darkness of the room, that shred of dawn was like a message of salvation" (p.90). However, this pure warmth is negative when it attempts to breach the comfort of the Vorpsi's isolated carriage. Grey daylight is described as having "found its way only sparingly into the carriage, and in addition the velvet upholstery absorbed part of it, deepening the gloom" (p.91). The significance of the sunlight is altered from Diana's chamber to Bessian's private carriage, implicating the separation of Diana's attitude from that of her husband.

In the second half of the novel, Kadare describes a natural landscape that is much less emotionally relevant to Gjorg, reflecting Gjorg's own disconnect with the approaching lift of his 30-day bessa as he tries to rationalize his current state. As Gjorg walks along a rural road on the seventeenth of April, the day his bessa will be lifted, Kadare writes "he raised his head in order to find the sun; the clouds, high in the sky, covered it over, but one could tell its position" (p.203). The elusivity of the sunlight is reflective of Gjorg's resignation to his fate- he is no longer tormented; rather, he is contemplative. The road is described as being "strewn with reddish glints" (p.203) and later "drowning in the light" (204). Unlike previous scenes, Gjorg is at peace, and his view of the landscape reflects his state.

By the end of the novel, Bessian and Diana are acutely aware of their increasingly dissimilar approaches towards the highlands. Kadare's descriptions of the landscape begin to reveal their differing perspectives. During one of their final carriage rides, Bessian remarks that the landscape has grown "familiar to him" (p.170), despite its frequent obscurities. As they are leaving, "a white, mysterious mist came down upon them, like a curtain lowered on the play just ended" (p.215). Closing as it had commenced, Kadare culminates the tale by illustrating once again the supreme disconnect that remains as the newlyweds leave the highlands.

In conclusion, it can be derived from the text that Kadare uses descriptions of setting and landscape to distinguish the ethical and emotional divide of Gjorg and the newlyweds in regards to highland culture.

Works Cited

Kadare, lsmail [translated by New Amsterdam Books]. *Broken April*. New Amsterdam Books, 1990. Chicago, Illinois. Print.

Marks and Comments for Written Assignment on *Broken April*

Criterion B: Knowledge and understanding 4

The candidate seems to have both good knowledge and understanding of the bifurcated viewpoints of the major characters, Gyorg who is involved in executing the blood feud and paying the blood tax, and Bessian and Diana who are coming from an urban, lowland setting. The assertions need to be, at places, more amply supported by detail, and also would profit from greater clarity. For example, in the fifth paragraph where "rapid assertions" needs fuller description. This weakness holds true of other places in the essay, and impacts how fully understanding is demonstrated.

Criterion C: Appreciation of the writer's choices 4

The opening paragraph immediately frames the essay from the angle of Kadare's choices as he uses setting to show evolution in attitudes and the difference between highland and lowland characters. Setting is the consistent focus and how it serves the author's purposes in the novel is reasonably explored. There is certainly evidence of insight about the way Kadare employs landscape symbolically and as a motif to further authorial purposes.

Criterion D: Organization and development 3

The candidate proceeds in a form of organization that looks alternately at Gyorg and then at Bessian and Diana, as characters being illuminated by reference to landscape. Examples from the novel are very smoothly integrated. At points the analysis needs development; the fluency of the argument is somewhat choppy, moving between the pair and the solo character without much real transition. The conclusion fails to bring the observations to a sufficiently rounded closure.

Criterion E: Language 5

The language used by the candidate to convey her ideas is correct, articulate and often sophisticated. It meets the all the aspects of the level 5 criterion.

The following is a practice essay for a Written Assignment based on a work other than those the candidate studied for Part 1. Here the teacher is working to help students develop good strategies and good writing practice for their actual Written Assignment. Although a teacher would never provide this kind of close commentary on an assignment to be submitted for External Assessment, you may be able to pick up some good hints for your own success.

Activity

Read through the essay and then compose a short message to the student, suggesting how he could remedy some of the problems the teacher has noted. Be very specific. You may also find some strengths and weaknesses the teacher has not noted. Include those in your message.

Supervised Writing prompt: In what ways and how effectively does Chekhov address human disappointment in his stories?

Written Assignment: Chekhov: disillusionment and its consequences

As the old adage says, "The grass is always greener on the other side." It seems that some people—despite their situation—are always looking for something that they perceive to be better than what they already have. In "The Peasants" written by Anton Chekhov, wanting for what one does not have is an ever present trend. The story begins with a family, Nikolay, Olga, and daughter Sasha who live a comfortable life in Moscow until Nikolay falls ill and is no longer able to work. However, as Nikolay and Olga become disillusioned with their present situation, they romanticize of a new environment only to discover the harsh realities they overlooked while in their previous environment. Disillusionment drives Nikolay and Olga to perpetually move from the Moscow to the countryside (and back) as they romanticize what they do not have. The primary driving force behind Nikolay and Olga's migration from the city to the country is rooted in disillusionment.

> These kind of 'adage' openings tend toward cliché. It is best to avoid them.

> Is 'perpetually' an accurate description?

> What are they disillusioned with?

The root of the disillusionment that Nikolay and Olga face derives from their romanticized view of the country that leads them to move there. Nikolay had a comfortable job at the Slav Fair in Moscow as a waiter before becoming ill. After their money ran out, he decided to take his family back to the village in which he grew up, Zhukovo.

> Why did their money run out?

"He [Nikolay] had always remembered his old home from childhood as a cheerful, bright, cozy, comfortable place, but now, as he entered the hut, he was actually scared when he saw how dark, crowded, and filthy it was in there. Olga, his wife, and his daughter, Sasha, who had travelled back with him, stared in utter bewilderment at the huge, neglected stove (it took up nearly half the hut), black with soot and flies—so many flies! It was tilting to one side, the wall-beams were all askew, and the hut seemed about to collapse any minute… This was *real* poverty!"[1]

> A lengthy quote from the original text needs some commentary – perhaps note the difference in the memory and reality?

1 Chekhov, Anton Pavlovich. "The Peasants." *The Lady with the Little Dog and Other Stories, 1896–1904*. New York: Penguin, 2002. 22. Print.

As Nikolai and his family discovered, country life was not the way they imagined it to be. Their initial disillusionment grew as time passed and they were unhappy with their living conditions. At first Nikolai and his family thought living in the country would be quaint. Despite their idealized view it was not long before Nikolai "realized he had made a mistake coming here, ill as he was, without any money and his family into the bargain—a real blunder!" (24). As it turns out, the countryside was not all that Nikolay expected it to be. As critic Lev Shestov says, "Tchekov was the poet of hopelessness. Stubbornly, sadly, monotonously, during all the years of his literary activity, nearly a quarter of a century long, Tchekov was doing one thing alone: by one means or another he was killing human hopes. Herein, I hold, lies the essence of his creation."[2] It seems as if this feeling of hopelessness that Shestov describes holds true for the characters in "The Peasants."

As Olga becomes disillusioned with the life she is leading in the countryside, she begins to romanticize life in Moscow once again. Her husband Nikolai has finally passed away after his long struggle with illness, leaving Olga with no attachment to his family in the countryside. Despite the fact that Nikolays' family no longer wished that she stay with them, she longs to escape the town of Zhukovo and go somewhere else. Olgas' desire to leave is clearly expressed by the passage "…and tears poured down her face; a passionate longing to go far, far away, as far as the eyes could see, even to the ends of the earth, made her gasp for breath. But they had already decided to send her back to Moscow as a chambermaid" (54). While Olga left Moscow for the country expecting a quaint and peaceful existence in the country, she instead faced poverty and heavy hardships. As the decision is made for her to return to Moscow, she agrees to leave. Her disillusionment with the countryside as a result of seeing the harsh realities of peasant life was a driving factor in her decision. Olga yearned to escape the realities of Zhukovo, and the family's decision to send her to Moscow facilitated her desire. Both the idealized version of life in Moscow, and the disillusionment with her experiences in the country led Olga to return to Moscow.

After Sasha and Olga had been living in Moscow for some time, they once again grow, disillusioned with the city and wish to return to life in the country. In Moscow, Olga manages to find places to sleep here and there while Sasha is living with Kladiva Abramovna; a middle-aged prostitute. Olga is overworked to the point that she no longer is able to go to church. The living conditions that she finds herself in are not ideal, and Sasha is growing up sleeping on the floor next to a prostitute. For both Olga and Sasha returning to Moscow was different than how they had imagined. Their living conditions were once again so poor that it becomes clear that Olga grows disillusioned once again with city-life in Moscow. Olga receives a letter from Marya (an in-law in Zhukovo) with a laundry list of complaints regarding poverty, the misery of their lives in the country. However, as Olga reads the letter, despite all the complaining she feels that "for some reason these crooked lines, where every letter resembled a cripple, held a special, hidden charm, and besides those greetings and complaints she also read of the warm clear days in the country now, of quiet fragrant evenings when you hear the church clock striking the hour on the other side of the river. She could visualize the village cemetery where her husband lay. The green leaves breathed peace and one envied the dead…" (p.60).

2 Shestov, Lev. "NCW—What the Critics Say About Anton Chekhov." *Your Home Page Goes Here*. Web. 11 Feb. 2011. <http://mockingbird.creighton.edu/ncw/chekcrit.htm>.

Margin annotations:

Some details of this would be useful here.

Clear up your use of present or present perfect tense to achieve top marks.

This general observation has been made several times.

Again, please develop and elaborate on this quotation. Readers need to understand why this critical view has been included.

Improve the citation.

Elaborate on what the 'harsh realities' are.

Needs a better transition to indicate the passing of time.

Confusion of verb tenses.

It is as if Olga does not remember the suffering and misery she experienced when she lived in the country and sees a romanticized view of an alternate location because she cannot bear to live in Moscow any longer because she is once again disillusioned with her living conditions. Olga has gone full circle with her journey from the Moscow to the country and back. The cycle is perpetuated by disillusionment and unhappiness with her living conditions, and a romanticized view of somewhere else.

> This whole paragraph is primarily re-description and paraphrase.

No matter where Olga or Nikolay may be, they are unhappy with their environment. The disillusionment that they face drives them to glorify life in a different environment. Once they are prompted to move, they find only the harsh realities of life in this new place, and none of the romantic imagery that they wished to find. As the cycle of disillusionment for Olga perpetuates, she finds herself constantly fluctuating between hating the city and romanticizing the natural beauty of the countryside, and struggling to make ends meet in Zhukovo and wishing for a better life in the city. Unhappiness is inescapable for Olga. No matter how she tries, she cannot help but be disillusioned with her current living conditions. Disillusionment drives the cycle of movement from the city to the country and back. Chekhov has offered us a reflection on disillusionment in this story, and portrayed it very effectively.

> This essay has not been strongly executed. It's largely unarguable rehearsal of content without a great deal of interest for the reader. In order to improve it, you'd have to find a more sharply defined position for an argument. You just meet the bottom word count at 1206 words; there is surely more room for development. To say Chekhov has "portrayed [disillusionment] effectively" would be a good starting point for a better essay which explores just how he did that.

Activity

1. Read the following essay and make two lists: in one note the aspects of the essay that you think are positive and in the other, places where you think the writer could have made improvements. Discuss these as a whole class or with a small group or partner.

2. Read the examiner's questions listed at the end of the essay and discuss how you would answer them.

Supervised Writing Prompt: How does Garcia Marquez use imagery to enhance the effective delivery of *A Chronicle of a Death Foretold?*

Written Assignment for Part 1, Literature in Translation

The Role of Imagery as Foreshadowing in Garcia Marquez's *A Chronicle of a Death Foretold*.

Gabriel Garcia Marquez employs specific types of imagery for different purposes in his novel, *A Chronicle of a Death Foretold,* Garcia Marquez's novel tells the story of an Arab man names Santiago Nasar who is murdered for allegedly taking the virginity of a young woman names Angela Vicario. Animal imagery, as opposed to other forms of imagery, is arguably the most important type of imagery used in the first chapter to foreshadow Santiago's murder. Within the first chapter of the novel, animal imagery expresses the way in which Santiago was murdered, where and why he was murdered, and his masculine and sexual personality which eventually led to his demise.

One of the strongest animal images in the first chapter of *A Chronicle of a Death Foretold* is the rabbit. Although the rabbit only appears in one scene,

Hint

Remember always to provide a citation to other works you have used.

- Your primary text is the one you have written about in the assignment. Be sure to include the translator.
- Your secondary text(s) are those critical or factual resources you have used.
- The IB does not specify a particular system of citation, but you should use one system consistently.

its impact weighs heavily on the reader due to the explicit descriptions. In the middle of the first chapter, the narrator interviews Victoria Guzman, chef of Santiago's household. Victoria "recalled without affection" the morning of Santiago's murder when she "had been quartering three rabbits for lunch, surrounded by panting dogs." (Garcia Marquez, 9) As her daughter Divina served Santiago his coffee and liquor, Santiago did not "take his eyes off the two women disemboweling the rabbits on the stove." The next time Divina passed, Santiago grabbed her and said that "the time has come for [her] to be tamed." To defend her daughter, Victoria "showed him the bloody knife" and cried "Let go of her, white man … you won't have a drink of that water as long as I'm alive." Even though she explains that Santiago was "just like his father … a shit," "she couldn't avoid a wave of fright as she remembered Santiago Nasar's horror when she pulled out the insides of a rabbit by the roots and fed the steaming guts to the dogs." When Santiago tells here "not to be savage," "she went on feeding the dogs with the insides of other rabbits, just to embitter [his] breakfast." The knife she uses and how she uses it is explained in detail. Victoria explains the relations Santiago's family has had with her own in a negative light, and while protecting her daughter from Santiago's reach she shakes the bloodied knife towards Santiago. Santiago is killed later that morning for allegedly taking away another girl's virginity before she married, dishonoring her family.

In this scene, killing the rabbit is symbolic for killing that which is sexually active and fertile, since rabbits are known for their large litters, short pregnancies, and ability to reproduce at a remarkably young age. Garcia Marquez also explains how the rabbit is cut up from the belly, which portrays a clearer idea of killing for sexual reasons since sexual activity commonly takes place in such a position and the region in which it is cut is closer to the reproductive organs. Garcia Marquez's description of Victoria shaking the knife at Santiago foreshadows the weapon used for his demise, covered in the blood of a sexually active symbol. After Victoria is done quartering the rabbit, she throws the scraps on the floor for the dogs to eat. Dogs are often portrayed in literature negatively, especially when something is being discarded to them. Victoria explains that she fed the innards to the dogs to embitter Santiago's breakfast. Throwing the innards for the sexually active symbol of Santiago to the dogs shows the disdain the community felt towards Santiago. The dogs, the knife used to butcher the rabbit and the rabbit itself are used to symbolize the reasons for his murder, the way in which he would be murdered later that morning, and perhaps even the discontent that the community felt with Santiago.

On the first pages of the novel, Garcia Marquez uses imagery to describe how Santiago often has pleasant dreams where he imagines misting rain, but "when he awoke [on the day of his murder] he felt completely spattered with bird shit." (Garcia Marquez, 1) While this can be said to foreshadow a bad event, it sets the mood of the day more than anything else. The bird, in this context, is not used to foreshadow death in any way since it is not described with deathly qualities. While in the beginning the bird and its environment are used to set the mood, Garcia Marquez later used a bird to foreshadow Santiago's murder by using the buzzard. Garcia Marquez used this scavenger bird by depicting him sitting on the "peaked tin roof" of the "former warehouse," keeping "watch over the garbage on the docks." (Garcia Marquez, 10). His house overlooks the docks where Santiago would later be murdered. Garcia Marquez purposely went out of his way to describe the scavenger bird in order to foreshadow the location of Santiago's murder. While there is a connection between the type of bird and the location, the bird feces on Santiago in the beginning does not symbolize his demise.

Unlike the rabbits, dogs or buzzard, roosters reoccur throughout the first chapter of this novel. The rooster is a symbol of masculinity, known for his crow to proclaim territory and willingness to fight. In the chapter, Divine explains how Santiago would violate her "whenever he caught her in some corner of house …grabbing [her] whole pussy," but while she normally retaliates or acts in a surprised manner, "on that day she felt the urge to cry." (Garcia Marquez, 13)

Afterward, Garcia Marquez describes how the boat with the bishop ceases tooting, and how the roosters began crowing. Divina says that there "was such a great uproar that she couldn't believe there were so many roosters in town," and that she "thought there [were more roosters] coming on the bishop's boat." (Garcia Marquez, 14) The rooster and their crowing portray the victory that the masculine figure, Santiago, felt when Divina stopped resisting, like the boat ceasing to honk. This hyper-masculine aspect is later further developed. Garcia Marquez explains how "one could see the crates of well-flattened roosters they were bearing as a gift for the bishop" all around the docks. (Garcia Marquez, 16). The roosters here symbolize how Santiago would later be killed on the docks for reasons relating to masculinity and power. Throughout the first chapter, the rooster is used to display Santiago's masculinity and pride. The flattened roosters on the dock are an example of an image used to depict Santiago's personality, his alleged crime and foreshadow his murder.

Pigs are generally perceived as dirty, greedy, and "lower class" animals. In the first chapter, there are many references to pigs. A woman named Margot says that "if [she'd] have known, [she] would have taken him home with [her] even if it means [she] had to hog-tie Santiago" to prevent him from going to the dock if she knew that he was going to be murdered. (Garcia Marquez, 20). It is interesting that she used the expression "hog-tied" since it generally has a negative connotation. It is stated earlier in the novel that many of the people of the village knew of Santiago's fate. I think her reference to hog-tying is meant to give the image that although she claims not to have known about his murder prior to the event, virtually everyone in town was actually aware. A bit earlier in the chapter, on p. 18, the narrator talks about the number of hogs that were to be killed at a particular feast in the public square. It seems as though the townspeople rejoice over the elimination of an image of dirt and greed. Santiago, similarly, is perceived as dirty, and he is killed in a public area for many to see. The hog foreshadows not only the setting in which he is murdered but the public feeling and knowledge about his murder and their willingness to prevent it.

In conclusion, imagery in *A Chronicle of a Death Foretold* is key for foreshadowing Santiago's murder. Although all imagery is important, they do not all serve the same purpose. Some serve to convey emotion, while others serve to express types of relationships. Garcia Marquez consistently uses animal imagery throughout the first chapter to foreshadow Santiago's death by selecting animals that live off the dead such as buzzards, isolating animals that embody the reasons for his death such as the rabbit and the rooster and portraying social; awareness of his murder with the hog. Animal imagery is clearly the most important type of imagery because of the way it adds to the story of the novel, depicting not only what happens to Santiago, but the feelings about what Santiago did and about his murder. Animal imagery is crucial in *A Chronicle of a Death Foretold* because it characterizes Santiago Nasar and helps the reader to better understand and imagine Santiago's murder.

(1488 words)

Works cited

Garcia Marquez, Gabriel. *A Chronicle of a Death Foretold*. Translated by Gregory Rabassa. New York: Vintage Books, 1983

Activity

Answer these questions which an examiner would raise about this essay:

1. Is there a literary focus to the essay, a sense of authorial choices?
2. Does the candidate reveal that s/he knows the novel well and understands it?
3. Are the facts that are included about the novel accurate?
4. Is there a clear line of argument in the essay?
5. Has the candidate made detailed reference to the text?
6. Have the details been relevant to supporting the argument?
7. Does the candidate reveal that s/he is conscious of the writer making choices and producing effects in his writing?
8. Does the essay have a clear structure, making good use of paragraphs and transitions between them?
9. Are the conventions of writing a formal essay followed in citing the text, including quoted material, observing the rules of spelling, punctuation and grammar, appropriate verb tense, and sentence structure?

Activity

The examiner has awarded the mark of 3 for the Reflective Statement of this candidate and awarded a total mark of 19 out of 25. Looking at the criteria in your course book see if you can determine how the marks might have been distributed.

Part 2: Detailed study

- What does this part of the syllabus include for me to read and analyse?
- What are the goals in Part 2 and how can I do really well with them?
- How will my success in studying these literary works be assessed?

In this part of your Literature syllabus, if you are a Higher Level (HL) student, you will read three works. They could be from any three different kinds (genres) of works, but one must be poetry. If you are Standard Level (SL) student you will study two works, one of which could be poetry, and the other a different genre.

In order to have examples to work with, first we are going to look at some poetry by Margaret Atwood, a Canadian poet and novelist. You might study different poetry, but some of the same features will apply.

The other two works that both levels of students might study are *Hamlet* by Shakespeare and *Down and Out in Paris and London* by George Orwell, which features his own experiences of trying to survive working at menial jobs in Paris and as a tramp in London and on the road. We will also use these works as examples throughout the chapter.

How we will work in this unit

It is important to be able to trade ideas in written or oral form with your classmates during the IB programme. As with other parts of this book, your teacher may ask you, and others, to contribute to a class resource pool or blog for the following activities, as well as working in your own book.

The art of words – "word-art"

It's probably worth exploring a little more how studying these or any other works will make you appreciate word-art and give you some skills you can use now or later.

Activity

Contribute some thoughts about one of the following to class resource pool or blog:

- How putting together words can create something that can be called **art** (you will need to define what you mean by "art"). Don't be too narrow in your thinking; you've been exposed to a lot of word-art in your life: where did you find it and how does it work to affect you?

- How the **skills** you could pick up by closely reading words could be applied to one of the following professions: engineering, law, diplomacy, long distance truck or lorry driving, publishing, flying jet planes, engineering, computer programming, medicine, or one not mentioned here.

In the introduction to this IB course, the creators have provided a paragraph that is packed with ideas about how they envision what you can learn by immersing yourself in this work.

"The course is built on the assumption that literature is concerned with our conceptions, interpretations and experiences of the world. The study of literature can therefore be seen as an exploration of the ways it represents the complex pursuits, anxieties, joys and fears to which human beings are exposed in the daily business of living. It enables an exploration of one of the most enduring fields of human creativity, and provides opportunities for encouraging

independent,

original,

critical,

and clear thinking.

It also promotes [a respect] for the imagination …."

(from Language A: literature guide © International Baccalaureate Organization 2011)

Activity

Look at the preceding paragraph, and following the free word arrangement of the last five lines (which were originally written in the style of the first six lines) reshape all of the content in the manner of a poem, highlighting, enlarging, or minimizing, using the possibilities of fonts, etc. the words or phrases that are most meaningful to you. You may want to refer back to this statement of purpose from time to time; your personalized version may be the most meaningful and help to guide your efforts. The aim of this activity is to raise your awareness of how spacing and arrangement can affect the way we view and understand words. The visual aspects of a text have more impact on the way we 'receive' words than we may always realize.

Assessment: a summary of how it works in Part 2

After they have read, discussed, and probably also written about the works in Part 2, Higher Level candidates will be asked to prepare and deliver, orally, a comment of about eight minutes in a one-to-one situation with their teacher. The comment or "commentary" is about a poem you have studied in this part of the syllabus. The teacher will then ask some follow-up questions about your comments, for two or three minutes. This part of the assessment is called the **Individual Oral Commentary**.

After this part, the teacher has ten minutes to converse with you about **one** of the other two works you have studied. There will be questions (from the teacher) and answers (from you). This can turn into quite an interesting interchange or conversation. This part of the assessment is called the **Discussion**. All in all, the whole assessment will take twenty minutes.

Standard Level candidates have only one exercise: commenting on a passage from one of the two works they have studied. They will be doing only the **Individual Oral Commentary**. This assessment takes ten minutes in all, an eight-minute "solo" from you with two minutes of follow-up questions from the teacher.

We will develop your ideas about this assessment more fully later in the unit. You can see that becoming very comfortable with expressing your thoughts about literature "out loud" is a skill you will want to practise as much as you can. Taking part in class discussions and learning to listen to what others say (as your teacher will do in the follow-up questions and the discussion) are good ways to practise.

Activity

Read the following poem, preferably more than once.

The Journey

One day you finally knew
what you had to do, and began,
though the voices around you
kept shouting
their bad advice – though
the whole house began
to tremble
and you felt the old tug at
your ankles. "Mend my
life!"
each voice cried. But
you didn't stop.
You knew what you had to do,
though the wind pried with its
stiff fingers
at the very foundations,
though their melancholy
was terrible.
It was already late enough,
and a wild night, and the
road full of fallen branches
and stones.
But little by little,
as you left their voices behind,
the stars began to burn through
the sheets of clouds, and there
was a new voice which you
slowly
recognized as your own,

that kept you company
as you strode deeper and deeper
into the world, determined to do
the only thing you could do –
determined to save
the only life you could save.

Mary Oliver

Taking some differently coloured highlighters, mark the places in the poem where any of the following appear:

- personal pronouns (words like "I", "you" and "your" or "we")
- words referring to the natural world
- verbs.

Some people are helped in seeing particular features of a written text, particularly poems, by marking elements in different colours to create a visual pattern of connections. You can do more of this if you find it helpful. You can also use it when you're doing your twenty minutes of preparation for you Individual Oral Commentary.

In this case, see if any of the patterns you have marked give you some insight into the way Mary Oliver is working here to create the impact of her thoughts.

Activity

Looking closely at the poem, make some notes on the following.

1. Personal pronoun use suggests:

2. Words referring to the natural world indicate:

3. Verbs suggest:

The important outcome, of course, is whether looking at these patterns helps you to understand the what and the how of the poem: the meaning of the poem and how the poet manages to convey these with some impact, either of beauty or perhaps of truth. Even the visual arrangement, where the words appear in a line on the page can affect your response.

Overleaf is the original version, not the adapted one above, of Mary Oliver's poem.

The Journey

One day you finally knew
what you had to do, and began,
though the voices around you
kept shouting
their bad advice—
though the whole house
began to tremble
and you felt the old tug
at your ankles.
"Mend my life!"
each voice cried.
But you didn't stop.
You knew what you had to do,
though the wind pried
with its stiff fingers
at the very foundations,
though their melancholy
was terrible.
It was already late
enough, and a wild night,
and the road full of fallen
branches and stones.
But little by little,
as you left their voices behind,
the stars began to burn
through the sheets of clouds,
and there was a new voice
which you slowly
recognized as your own,
that kept you company
as you strode deeper and deeper
into the world,
determined to do
the only thing you could do—
determined to save
the only life you could save.

Mary Oliver

Activity

Your final activity on "word-art" is to look at both versions of the poem *The Journey* and consider two things:

1. Does the different visual arrangement of the poem, and the accompaniment of a photograph change the way you respond to the poem?

2. How did marking the poem with colours affect your understanding or appreciation of the way the poem is put together?

Literary terminology

There are many, many terms that come into play when trying to engage critically with a text – meaning talking about how the text is working to produce some effects on its readers.

At the very least, there are about ten terms basically needed so that we can practise good critical analysis. Equipped with some of these terms, we can move with confidence into convincing conversation about the works we are studying. You will find others that will suit your work in the chapter on Paper 1, as well as in the chapter on Part 3.

The first of these terms is really a trio which works together. The terms are **Voice or Speaker, Address** or **Addressee Tone**.

These are elements that frame the **discourse** you are reading, that is, the written words the author has put together. The **voice** is the **speaker**; that voice is **addressing** someone (or everyone) who is reading or hearing the words, or possibly the material of the poem. The reader or receiver is the **addressee**. The relation between the voice and the addressee produces the **tone** of the writing.

Hint

You know about **tone.** You create it and you hear it from others everyday.

If you are speaking to someone with respect or admiration (or they may be speaking to you), you discern it through the tone.

If you are declaring your undying love, you can do it sincerely or ironically. Tone here would be called devoted, admiring, or ironic.

If you are "talking down" or "putting someone down" you can do it through content or tone, or both. Tone could be described as scornful or dismissive, or even aggressive.

A neutral tone is a third and common option: speaking to another as an equal in order to inform, tell a story, conduct business. But the neutral tone is seldom uncoloured by either positive or negative modulations. Tone is a subtle and shifting aspect of human speech.

Activity

What kinds of tone would you imagine being used in the interchange in these images?

Activity

See if you can determine the tone of the following bits of literature. Remember that tone is usually named in emotional terms describing the attitude the speaker holds to the material or the audience. "Informational" or "expository" or "communicative" is not a precise description of tone; "admiring," "hesitant", "ironic", "defensive", "humble", or "arrogant" are words that describe tone.

Down and Out in Paris and London

"If you set yourself to it, you can live the same life, rich or poor. You can still keep with your books and your ideas. You just got to say to yourself, 'I'm a free man in *here*'" – he tapped his forehead – "and you're all right."

George Orwell

The Deaths of the Other Children

Did I spend all those years
building up this edifice
my composite
self, this crumbling hovel?

My arms, my eyes, my grieving
words, my disintegrated children

Margaret Atwood

Hamlet

Let four captains
Bear Hamlet like a soldier to the stage.
For he was likely, had he been put on,
To have proved most royal. And for his passage,
The soldiers' music and the rite of war
Speak loudly for him.

William Shakespeare

Activity

Using some works that you are currently studying, find some examples of various tones. Post three examples to the class blog, identifying what you think the tone is. Also respond to one other person's posting, either agreeing with their description or offering an alternative one.

A second crucial literary feature is **metaphor**. The way humans communicate is often enhanced by comparison, analogy. If we want to make something clear or vivid or beautiful, we often do it by comparing one thing to another. And so written words intending to be vivid as well as beautiful often employ comparisons that are designated metaphors.

One way of looking at metaphor is to apply the label to comparisons that are implied, opposite to similes where the comparison is indicated by the use of "as" or "like." In a more sophisticated sense, the one you are acquiring now, metaphor is an underlying and pervasive tool of literary works. When a poet (and Plato, who wanted them excluded from the city, would include the novelists and the dramatists as "poets") wants to heighten the way he conveys his meaning, he travels the path of metaphor. And we love it, since it pulls many things into the shaping of the words.

Sometimes people talk about metaphors by separating what the writer is trying to heighten by analogy and the entity that is being used to heighten it in order to get some precision about what's going on. And sometimes two particular terms are used for the two parts: **tenor** and **vehicle**.

Metaphors describe one object or action in terms of another. The object being described is called the **tenor**. The term **vehicle** is the term used to describe the means by which the object, action, or being is more vividly conveyed.

Look at these examples and the accompanying explanations of the tenor and vehicles in each one:

Yes! in the sea of life enisled, ... We mortal millions live alone. -- from *To Marguerite* by Matthew Arnold	The tenor (the object being spoken about) is us, humanity. The vehicle (the object we resemble and are being described in terms of) is an island. "Enisled" in the word that makes the comparison.
A Sonnet is a moment's monument ... -- from *The Sonnet* by D.G. Rossetti	Tenor: sonnet. Vehicle: a monument (i.e. a tangible structure, such as a statue).
Not, I'll not, carrion comfort, Despair, not feast on thee ... -- from *Carrion Comfort* by Gerard Manley Hopkins	There are two metaphors here. (1) Tenor: the abstract emotion despair. Vehicle: a dead carcass. (2) Tenor: the "I", the speaker. Vehicle: a bird of prey or an animal (like a hyena) that feeds on carrion.
I taste a liquor never brewed ... Inebriate of Air – am I – ... -- from *I taste a liquor never brewed* by Emily Dickinson	The vehicle is immediately obvious – liquor, an alcoholic drink. We know that this is a metaphorical and not literal description as it has "never *[been]* brewed". However, it's only when we get farther along in the poem that we discover more about what experience is intoxicating the speaker – the tenor. Then we find that the tenor might be summed up as nature, or her joy in nature. An interesting point here is the metaphor can convey experience which would otherwise be hard to name.
I shall never get you put together entirely Pieced, glued, and properly jointed. -- from *The Colossus* by Sylvia Plath	The vehicle is a statue, announced in the poem's title, "The Colossus". The tenor, we discover gradually, is some enormous, dominating, but obscure, presence which she has to labour to recover and understand and which is named finally as her father.

Adapted from Seamus Cooney, http://homepages.wmich.edu/~cooneys/tchg/lit/adv/analysis.html

Essentially, the tenor or subject of the metaphor is the thing or person or emotion that the writer tried to convey as vividly and memorably as possible. The vehicle or carrier is the analogous or comparable set of words used to achieve that impact. One other thing to remember is that a metaphor can have multiple vehicles. Look at the third example above, and these lines from Stephen Spender's poem, *Not Palaces*:

"Eye, gazelle, delicate wanderer,

Drinker of horizon's fluid line."

Notice the three ways of making us thinking about the commonplace but wonderful reality of the eye through three vehicles in the 'gazelle', 'delicate wanderer', and 'drinker of horizon's fluid line'.

Thinking about metaphors

Here is what one IB student wrote about her understanding of metaphor.

When I was younger, I thought of metaphor as a distinct, easily crafted but essentially meaningless phrase — one is another. His face was a sunflower in the early morning sunlight; it is a nice enough image, pleasing to the ear, yet too easily constructed to have any meaning. But lately my understanding of the metaphor has evolved into something clearer. The real depth of a metaphor happens off the page, I thought. There are bad metaphors and there are good metaphors, and they appear very similar — maybe they're even the same. But a good metaphor has contained within its two parts an insight which elevates the subject; a good metaphor is much more than aesthetically pleasing. If, when I had written the above metaphor, I had been thinking of a sunflower's particular character — the supple texture of the petals, or the way a sunflower turns to face the light — and by referencing the sunflower, I had conferred on the subject's sleep-creased face the texture of the sunflower's petals, or on his actions the behavior of a sunflower — then perhaps it would be a good metaphor.

In her simple description, the boy is the tenor, the sunflower is the vehicle; she also realizes how much richer she could make that metaphor by developing the vehicle.

Activity

Contribute to the class resource pool or blog a paragraph in which you find a good way of describing metaphor, as you understand it.

Activity

See if you can separate the *tenor* and the *vehicle* in the following lines. The first two are from the play, *Hamlet*; the second two are from prose other than fiction, *Running in the Family,* which is a memoir or autobiography; the third pair are from the poems of Margaret Atwood; and the final one is from *Down and Out in Paris and London* by George Orwell.

"I have heard of your paintings too, well enough. God hath given you one face and you make yourselves another."
-- from *Hamlet* by William Shakespeare

"There's letters sealed, and my two school-fellows,
Whom I will trust as I will adders fanged,
They bear the mandate."
-- from *Hamlet* by William Shakespeare

"The garden a few feet away is suddenly under the fist of a downpour."
-- from *Running in the Family* by Michael Ondaatje

"In the heart of this 250-year-old fort we will trade anecdotes and faint memories, trying to swell them with the order of dates and asides, interlocking them all as if assembling the hull of a ship."
-- from *Running in the Family* by Michael Ondaatje

"The moving water will not show me my reflection
The rocks ignore. I am a word
In a foreign language"
-- from *Disembarking at Quebec* by Margaret Atwood

> "His feet slid on the bank, the currents took him;
> He swirled with ice and trees in the swollen water
> And plunged into distant regions, his head a bathysphere;"
> -- from *Death of a Young Son by Drowning* by Margaret Atwood
>
> "It was a very narrow street – a ravine of tall, leprous houses"
> -- from *Down and Out in Paris and London* by George Orwell

Armed with a little knowledge of two major features of literary art that will help you approach an oral commentary with some confidence, you should be able to look at particular poems, in this case written by Margaret Atwood and Sylvia Plath, in a way that you will help you approach poets you will prepare for your Individual Oral Commentary. Why? Because tone and metaphor are some of the most significant features of poetry, and indeed of all literary art.

Genre

Since we have just involved ourselves in looking at bits of three different forms of artistic writing, drama, poetry, and prose other than fiction, it is time to directly address the reality that "literature," like music, has different **forms** or **types**. Muscially, we have sonatas, rap, jazz, blues. You certainly are aware that there are differences between novels and poems. If you randomly pick up a book of poetry in a library, once you open it, you recognize that it's not a novel. Why? Partly because of the way that it looks. You aren't likely to call *The Road not Taken* or *Ode to a Grecian Urn* a novel or a play.

On the other hand, because they both have a tendency to tell stories, or a **narrative**, students writing or speaking in examinations often call every work of literature a "novel." You want to avoid this very common error.

The International Baccalaureate Language A Literature program distinguishes 4 literary types or forms. The common name for all of these types or forms is **genre**. In this program at Higher Level, you study at least one work from each of the four following genres; at Standard Level you will study three of the four.

- Drama
- Poetry
- Novels and/or Short Stories
- Prose other than novel or short story. Sometimes the term "prose other than fiction" is used to describe this category.

If you're paying really close attention, you will probably raise a question about the last two genre labels: why not just call them fiction and non-fiction?

The reason things are labeled this way is that there are elements of "making things up" and "reporting actual events" in both categories. Frequently, a writer's first novel very closely resembles his or her own life; in autobiographies or memoirs, there is always likely to be some fictionalization as the writer tries to create events of long ago. Memory is an imperfect record-keeper.

Activity

Just to get your mental gears working on this matter of genre, see how well you can identify the genre of the following works:

1. *The Merchant of Venice*
2. *The Golden Compass*
3. *The Cremation of Sam McGee*
4. *Ender's Game*
5. *Romeo and Juliet*
6. *The Canterbury Tales*
7. *Obama: From Promise to Power*
8. *Outliers*
9. *Mending Wall*
10. *Freakonomics*

Activity

Titles don't always indicate genre, but you probably did get about half of these right. What are some of the signals that may have helped you? You may want to contribute any hints that you have, or maybe some other titles you know of that either conceal or reveal their genre, to the class resource pool or blog.

Denotation and connotation

Now that we've looked at a large matter, let's look at a pair of minute matters that can make all the difference when you are performing (since oral work is often exactly that: a performance) the assessment for this part of your syllabus: words.

One of the more subtle things about words that can matter quite a lot when you are trying to read literature closely and accurately is the way words take on different meanings in different contexts, how they acquire nuances and special significance over time. To recognize and appreciate the difference between the literal meaning of a word or its **denotation**, and its **connotation**, the meaning words acquire through actual usage can be very important. When you are looking closely at the 20–30 lines or so you will be asked to discuss in your Individual Oral Commentary, these distinctions can matter.

Michael Adams says some good things about this matter of denotation and connotation:

The Writer's Mind

Denotation is the dictionary meaning of a word. The association surrounding a word is its connotation. Connotatively, a home is more than a house. ... In order to get the most possible from your words, pay close attention to their denotation and connotation. Notice how a writer like George Bernard Shaw manipulates both forms of words:

"Your friends are all the dullest dogs I know. They are not beautiful, they are only decorated. ... They are not religious, they are only pew renters. They are not moral, they are only conventional. ... They are not loyal, they are only servile; not dutiful, only sheepish; not public spirited, only patriotic; not courageous, only quarrelsome; not determined, only obstinate."

-- from *Man and Superman* by George Bernard Shaw

Michael Adams

Here you see the power of choosing words that are roughly equivalent, but in the context of their use are really not. Emotional overtones, value judgments are gathered into words that can shift over time. When Shakespeare talks about a "silly bucket", he does not mean a foolish bucket, but an empty one.

Another version of connotation

These are meanings that words pick up as they get used in speaking and writing. An easy index word like "cool" can help you to remember the difference between denotation of words ("cool" literally means a state which is not warm or hot) and connotation.

When we say "literally means," we are referring to what you would find if you look up the word "cool" in a dictionary: "Neither warm nor cold; moderately cold." If you look online in the Urban Dictionary you'll find such synonyms as "awesome," "smart," "hip," words that themselves have shifting connotations. It's rather obvious that words have different meanings in different places, and those "places" can be in phrases and sentences in literary art.

Activity

Just to sharpen your sense of the subtle changes a slight shift of word choice can make to meaning, consider some connotative variations.

For example, a dog can be called a cur, puppy, mongrel, etc. Imagine someone saying to you: "I have an extra mongrel – would you like to adopt him?" or the local animal shelter being called "The Cur Rescue Center"?

Try some of these:

- an unmarried woman
- cleverness
- a person who is careful about money.

The more sensitivity to particular words that you acquire in the close study of works in this part of the syllabus, the more likely you are to impress your "examiner", in this case your teacher, with your ability to read literary works in a close and conscious way.

There are a good many other terms that can play into showing that you know the language literary criticism and we will look at more of them (not all) as we go forward in Part 2. You will have ample practice with literary language in other chapters of the book.

Working with a particular poem

We will examine poetry by the Canadian poet, Margaret Atwood. Atwood decided, for inspiration, to return to some writing by a pioneer named Susanna Moodie, who came from England to Upper Canada, (part of which is now Ontario), and lived there in the nineteenth century. A very tough woman who endured hardships and kept a journal, she wrote vividly about her experiences and Margaret Atwood used these materials to create a series of poems called *The Journals of Susanna Moodie*.

We are taking on poetry first because, of the three works you will study in this part, it is poetry that will form the material to be examined for the first part of your Higher Level examination for this part of the syllabus – the Individual Oral Commentary. The other two works will be examined differently. At Standard Level, you might also be reading some poetry as one of your two works in Part 2 and, therefore, be delivering a commentary on poetry.

Since we are now talking in terms of examinations, it might be a good idea for you to have a general idea of what kinds of strengths teachers or examiners are looking for in this part of your oral performance.

First, you are asked to exhibit that:

- you know what this poem is about, and then that
- you understand what possible implications are present.

In other words, what's stated on the surface of the text (the denotations, mostly) as well as what is sub-textual: what is suggested by the words chosen and the order in which they are written, often something that involves connotations that arise from the context. Here you are being asked to interpret the poem.

In order to be convincing, you will need to constantly cite the particular places (or lines) in the poem that support your views.

Second, you are expected to identify and discuss how the poet is using the particular ways she or her chooses to both compress and heighten the expression of ideas, perceptions, feelings, suspicions, insights, and opinions. In other words you are asked to demonstrate your skill in seeing how the poet has taken something from the world and presented it in a particular and effective way, one that makes you think or feel. Often this involves compressing a great deal of meaning into a smaller means of expression. What a poet hopes is that fewer words will mean a greater "explosion" of meaning for the reader.

Third, you will be evaluated on the way you present your ideas to another person so that they can follow your thinking and be able to make real contact with your ideas.

Not a single one of these expectations is really easy to meet, but with practice you will be able to do this kind of very close inspection of a written text. This unit will give you more practice with meeting these expectations and will review some more helpful terms relevant to poetry.

Working with a poem

To be more specific and practical, we will look at one of the instances where Margaret Atwood has imagined Susanna Moodie expressing herself in poetry instead of prose. Something we mentioned above is very clear to see with this set of poems: compression of ideas into fewer words is one of the significant features of poetry.

One of the startling features Susanna Moodie encountered in her new cultural setting was the "charivari." The practice of charivari is described in the following Wikipedia excerpt.

Charivari

Charivari (or shivaree or chivaree, also called "rough music") is the term for a French folk custom in which the community gave a noisy, discordant mock serenade, also pounding on pots and pans, at the home of newlyweds. The loud, public ritual evolved to a form of social coercion, for instance, to force an as-yet-unmarried couple to wed. This type of social custom arose independently in many rural village societies, for instance also in England, Italy, Wales or Germany, where it was part of the web of social practices by which the small communities enforced their standards.

The community used noisemaking and parades to demonstrate disapproval, most commonly of "unnatural" marriages and remarriages, such as a union between an older widower man and much younger woman, or the too early re-marriage by a widow or widower. Villages also used charivari in cases of adulterous relationships, wife beaters, and unwed mothers. In some cases, the community disapproved of any remarriage by older widows or widowers. Charivari is the original French word, and in Canada it is used by both English and French speakers. Chivaree became the common spelling in Ontario, Canada. In the United States, the term shivaree is more common.

Members of a village would decide on a meeting place where everyone could plan what was to be done. Those who were to initiate the charivari used word-of-mouth to summon the largest possible crowd to participate, with women helping to organize and lead. After forming their plan, the charivari group would usually process by foot to the home of those they were acting against, make as much noise as possible with makeshift instruments and loud songs, and begin their assigned actions.

From Wikipedia

The foregoing description matches rather closely the following passage from the journals of Susanna Moodie's *Roughing it in the Bush.*

Roughing it in the Bush

"What is a charivari?" said I. "Do, pray, enlighten me."

"Have you been nine months in Canada, and ask that question? Why, I thought you knew everything! Well, I will tell you what it is. The charivari is a custom that the Canadians got from the French, in the Lower Province, and a queer custom it is. When an old man marries a young wife, or an old woman a young husband, or two old people, who ought to be thinking of their graves, enter for the second or third time into the holy estate of wedlock, as the priest calls it, all the idle young fellows in the neighborhood meet together to charivari them. For this purpose they disguise themselves, blackening their faces, putting their clothes on the hind part before, and wearing horrible masks, with grotesque caps on their heads, adorned with cocks' feathers and bells. They then form in a regular body, and proceed to the bridegroom's house where the wedding is held, just at the hour when the happy couple are supposed to be about to retire to rest – beating upon the door with clubs and staves and demanding of the bridegroom admittance to drink the bride's health, or in lieu thereof to receive a certain sum of money to treat the band at the nearest tavern. . . . Surely it is very hard that an old man cannot marry a young gal, if she is willing to take him, without asking the leave of such a rabble as that. What right have they to interfere with his private affairs?"

"What, indeed?" said I, feeling a truly British indignation at such a lawless infringement upon the natural rights of man.

Susanna Moodie

Now look at Atwood's poem. The poet also adds other material from Moodie, a specific incident where she is told about a black man who fled to Canada, set up a barbershop, and eventually married a white woman. The treatment of the charivari to which he was subjected led to his death. It's important to know that from the early nineteenth century, large numbers of black men and women escaped the slavery of the American South and fled north, with many of them settling in Upper Canada.

Charivari

"They capped their heads with feathers, masked
their faces, wore their clothes backwards, howled
with torches through the midnight winter

and dragged the black man from his house
to the jolting music of broken
instruments, pretending to each other

it was a joke, until
they killed him. I don't know
what happened to the white bride."

The American lady, adding she
thought it was a disgraceful piece
of business, finished her tea.

(Note: Never pretend this isn't
part of the soil too, teadrinkers, and inadvertent
victims and murderers, when we come this way

again in other forms, take care
to look behind, within
where the skeleton face beneath

the face puts on its feather mask, the arm
within the arm lifts up the spear:
Resist those cracked

drumbeats. Stop this. Become human.)

Margaret Atwood

Margaret Atwood.

Activity

Look carefully at the three pieces of writing on the charivari and then write an essay of 300–400 words about how Margaret Atwood has used the materials of Moodie's original. Pay particular attention to the way Atwood has selected, combined, and compressed the material into poetry and say what you think about the effects of doing so. Add your essay to the class resource pool or blog.

Continuing on with our preparation for a good Individual Oral Commentary, let's return to look more closely at Atwood's poem about the charivari.

It's very important that you always look closely at what you have before you, whether you are looking at it for the first time as in a later written assessment, Paper 1, or if you are looking at a poem you have discussed in class. Although that class discussion will provide you with some security, as long as you review it and can recall it, you will do best here if you are working from your own response, both personal and critical, to the poem.

MRS. SUSANNA MOODIE.
From a photograph by Stanton, Toronto. Kindly furnished by her daughter, Mrs. Vickers, Toronto.

You are, after all, going to be present in person with one other person in this assessment, and you can certainly use "I" when discussing the poem, although you will want:

- to support whatever you say with evidence from the poem
- to avoid going off into anecdotes about extraneous things that the poem brings to mind, such as your cousin's wedding or games you played as small children.

Guiding questions

When you choose your passage, you will see at the end of your selection two prompts, called **guiding questions**. These are included to give you starting points for building your commentary. You are free to use these, but you also may choose other directions. There will also be one or two subsequent questions your teacher will ask after eight minutes.

Activity

Evaluating an IOC

What follows is a shortened version of a student commentary on "Charivari." It will give you an idea of what an IOC can look like.

First, read through the poem again — note these two Guiding Questions:

- What parts of the poem are used to report the events of the charivari and what parts are used to comment on the events?
- What is the function of the parenthesized lines of the poem?

Read this version of a student's commentary. You will see some ellipses (…), where the student could have elaborated more fully.

Such short practices can be an efficient way to prepare for your actual commentary.

Hint

Pay particular attention to two things:
- comments about literary features and their effects
- the structure of the commentary.

This last feature often proves the trickiest one for students; whether owing to nerves or just a failure to consider a listening audience, few students do well with the organizing of their commentary.

Transcript of a student commentary

The first thing that I notice about this poem, "Charivari" by Margaret Atwood is the title, a strange word to me, one I'd never heard before, so I want to explain what I understand by it … . Even the sound of this word suggests something foreign or out of the ordinary, possible a title that would catch a reader's attention … .

The next significant thing is the division of the poem into two parts by punctuation, first by the quotation marks, and then by the two parentheses. But there is also a stanza (#4) which seems unconnected to either part. I want to talk a little about each part and also how they are connected. The voices and the tones of the different parts seem significant for the meaning of the poem… .

Two things stand out in the first part of the poem that are picked up again in the third part: feathers and some kind of beat or music. This repetition helps, I think, to connect the beginning and ending parts of the poem, giving it some unity in spite of the different voices. These seem like different tones or attitudes toward the custom of charivari.

If we look at some particular words, the quoted words — and we assume Susanna Moodie's journal is the source of these — we can see that a negative judgment about charivari is being made: these people are "masked", "howling", "dragging", "jolting", "pretending" and finally "killing". These violent terms go to make up the tone taken about these events. It seems negative, and disapproving.

But I'm not completely sure what the fourth stanza has to do with the first three, except to make a comment perhaps many would make, that the treatment of a black person about to be married, the judgment of the local people on this "miscegenation", was "disgraceful". The woman mentioned is an "American" which would seem to contrast with the "Canadian" behaviour of the charivari. … Somehow the American woman's finishing her "tea" also seems a significant gesture and not well looked upon. The poet seems to be putting some irony into the comment. The historical time of Moodie's poem seems to crossover to the time when black slaves were fleeing from America.

I think the 3-line stanza, the tercet form, seems to work well. The whole insertion about the American is contained in one sentence that seems to serve as a transition into the third part of the poem. The reader is left to decide how that stanza is meant to function in the total meaning of the poem. ...

I'm thinking the third section clears things up. It begins with the speaker commanding the reader in the imperative mode: "Note." It seems that the rest of the poem is somewhat didactic, wanting some lessons drawn for today from the early history of Canada. The word "pretend" seems to want to link us the readers, to the "pretending to each other" in the second stanza. I think the speaker, maybe Atwood, maybe Moodie, is suggesting that like the American lady, we have violence within us. The words "feather mask", "spear" and "cracked drumbeats" (reflecting the "jolting music" above) suggest this.

Atwood comes close to creating a poem that seems to preach at us a little, but what I think is great is the way the lines are spaced and arranged, how the commanding lines are presented with a pace somewhat like drumbeats, so that the rhythm of the words reflects the meaning.

The other thing I notice is how the beginning and the end of the poem reflect each other in the word choice and the actions. For me the poem is about bringing together the past and present, and about how easy it is to judge (on the basis of race or class or nationality) others and to excuse ourselves. ...

I think the separated last line with its drumbeat quality neatly ties off the poem.

Activity

Consider the following points:

- Does the candidate convey to the examiner a good sense of the subject, the content of the poem?
- Are some of the implications of the poem addressed?
- Has the candidate pointed out some ways that Atwood has used the literary features of poetry to give a particular interpretation of the practice of charivari?
- Has the candidate delivered what she wants to say in a way that the listener can follow, using clear, appropriate language?
- Is there some, little or no structure to her commentary?

Add your comments on at least two of the above bullet points to the class resource pool or blog, and respond to one of the points someone else has made.

Activity

Now, using the criteria found in your course book, which are the ones your teacher will be using to grade you, see how many marks you can give this commentary. You will need to give four marks, for A, B, C, and F, skipping the two criteria, D and E, for the discussion.

Remember that the ellipses indicate where the student might have given more detail (e.g., since you know about the practice of the charivari from the last unit, it didn't seem necessary to elaborate again, but the candidate probably would have explained it). Still, you will only be able to mark her on what you see written down above.

What we are hoping to achieve here is a first idea of what a commentary could be, how it goes and how it's going to be marked.

Working with another poem and commentary

Here, we will work with a poem by the American poet, Sylvia Plath. In order to make good use of the specific materials in this unit, you will need to do some reading and discussion of the poem in your class. Alternatively, your teacher may wish to substitute other poems.

The poem is one that has to do with the craft of making poetry.

Black Rook in Rainy Weather

On the stiff twig up there
Hunches a wet black rook
Arranging and rearranging its feathers in the rain.
I do not expect a miracle
Or an accident

To set the sight on fire
In my eye, nor seek
Any more in the desultory weather some design,
But let spotted leaves fall as they fall
Without ceremony, or portent

Although, I admit, I desire,
Occasionally, some backtalk
From the mute sky, I can't honestly complain:
A certain minor light may still
Leap incandescent

Out of kitchen table or chair
As if a celestial burning took
Possession of the most obtuse objects now and then –
Thus hallowing an interval
Otherwise inconsequent

By bestowing largesse, honor
One might say love. At any rate, I now walk
Wary (for it could happen
Even in this dull, ruinous landscape); sceptical
Yet politic, ignorant

Of whatever angel may choose to flare
Suddenly at my elbow. I only know that a rook
Ordering its black feathers can so shine
As to seize my senses, haul
My eyelids up, and grant

A brief respite from fear
Of total neutrality. With luck,
Trekking stubborn through this season
Of fatigue, I shall
Patch together a content

Of sorts. Miracles occur.
If you care to call those spasmodic
Tricks of radiance miracles. The wait's begun again,
The long wait for the angel,
For that rare, random descent.

Sylvia Plath

Guiding questions for "Black Rook in Rainy Weather":

- What is the central point the speaker makes in the poem?
- What use does the speaker make of the rook and the inanimate objects to convey her reflection to the audience?

It will be helpful to you to have some short and long practice with poems that will almost guarantee that you can go into your Individual Oral Commentary test with some confidence.

First, let's review some points from the previous unit, making them sharper and easier to remember, and add some new ones.

1. **Pay attention to the Guiding Questions.** Although it is true that you are free not to address them in your commentary, you may find it very helpful to remember that these are points your teacher/examiner is likely to consider important since s/he has written the questions. Certainly, including them if they work for your commentary plan is unlikely to diminish your commentary.

2. **Deal with what you have in front of you: a whole poem or lines from a longer poem.** This can make a difference in how you approach or "frame" your commentary. In the first case, you will be fine with making a statement of "the about" or the larger meaning of the whole poem. When you only have part of a poem, you will need to indicate briefly both what you have in front of you, and what is the larger context.

3. **Make the word "appreciation" central to your commentary.** You may not get a poem you truly like, but you won't get a "bad" poem, one that is not worth your time and attention. Your job is to show why this example of poetry is a "good" one. What that means is that you want to show how inventively, effectively, movingly, the poet has said something about the world, about thoughts and feelings.

4. **Argue your case with supporting detail.** If your task here is to show that you can appreciate the artistry of this poem, then you have to support your case. The way that is done is by citing particular aspects of the poem as proof of your appreciation. Consider yourself the lawyer for the defendant, the poem.

5. **Argue your case with some energy!** You may not like the poem, and it's not entirely out of order for you to suggest that (along the way), but like an advocate with a clearly guilty client, you still need to make a case for the poem and its strengths. Make it a point to sound involved in what you are doing, even try for enthusiastic. Your tone of voice and your energy, even your physical posture can affect responses to your commentary.

6. **Pay attention to the descriptors the IB has established for assessing the Individual Oral Commentary.** In brief, they come down to three essential matters for the IOC:

   - Have you shown that you understand the poem, and the way it is put together?
   - Have you presented your views in a detailed and coherent way?
   - Have you spoken in a clear and formal academic way?

Activity

Choose a poem that you really do like from the ones you are studying and make up two guiding questions that you think will help a student be a good commentator on that poem. Test the questions on one other student, either directly, in class, or through a class blog.

Literary devices

One of the approaches that students sometimes take to stylistic features (an essential aspect of a literary commentary) is the "hunt and peck" method, a phrase which used to be used to describe the "one-finger" approach to typing on a keyboard. It's an approach that students often feel driven to when they only have a partial understanding of what a commentary is or is meant to be, the kind of literary exercise we are talking about here.

First, look at some short descriptions of "commentary" as it's used in this course:

The Oxford English Dictionary says it is "a treatise consisting of a systematic series of comments or annotations on the text of a literary work." And what is a treatise? "A literary composition dealing formally or methodically with a definite subject." A commentary is an exercise in close reading to find out what the poet is trying to convey and how s/he is conveying it.

Obviously, the process does involve hunting: for what is being said, and what methods are used to say it. Students are usually pretty well able to do the first, partly because we have an instinct to understand.

Just like any good artist, the writer of poems has a set of tools s/he is going to use to make a poem. This includes a huge range of tricks of the trade. Here's just one possible list:

title	voice	punctuation
visual arrangement	syntax	mood
wit	meter	alliteration
rhyme	symbols	grammar
rhythm	indeterminacy	assonance
opening	imagery	catalogue
silence	structure	enjambment
word choice	patterns	simile
ambiguity	humour	conventions
tension	echoes	onomatopoeia
metaphor	irony	antithesis
rhythm	euphony	hyperbole
predictability	implications	synaesthesia
climax	refrains	oxymoron
puns	satire	connotation
length	expectation	allusion
footnotes	caesura	neologism
upper case	motifs	ellipsis
surprises	rhetoric	synecdoche
balance	metonymy	

And these are just some! Should you go through and find a definition for every one of these, like memorizing vocabulary for certain kinds of tests? No, probably not. There are more useful ways to deal with literary terms.

Activity

First, go through the list above and highlight or circle the terms – not ones you've only seen before, but ones you believe you know and can use if asked to define and explain.

Then go to www.tagxedo.com. After you familiarize yourself with the site, go back to your highlighted terms in the list above and create a word cloud using them. The way the system is set up, you can emphasize and de-emphasize your individual relation to this set of terms. See how visually intriguing you can make your cloud.

Alternatively, you could make a word cloud out of the terms you did not highlight, emphasizing those that are most obscure or unfamiliar.

And what's the point? In the first case, which is the important one, you have also made a profile of your individual "comfort zone" of the many literary "devices" that poets can use in constructing their works. Here is your "safe ground," the place from which to start preparing a commentary on a poem. As you study your poems in class, you should be able to expand your "vocabulary" of literary terms.

In working with Part 2 Assessment, some attention has been given to crucial terms and techniques, ones that are most commonly used by poets. You will find work with others throughout this book. Some terms found in the list above you may encounter frequently, or only sometimes or maybe never. That's why it's better to build a vocabulary for commentary out of the experience of talking with others about poems, learning from their perceptions, and learning how techniques are used.

What's not going to produce good commentaries is an approach which starts out by "hunting" – tracking down the similes or alliteration that you can see, and "pecking"– simply listing these elements. Spotting them in this way can be a valid exercise for approaches in your earlier school years. In the IB program you need to raise the level of expertise.

For a good IOC you will need to be able to:

Say what you think the poem is "about": what subject / idea / thoughts / feelings does the poem address.

Say what attitude the poet holds in relation to the "about".

Say how the poet conveys the first two to you, the individual reader. Here is the place you will be wanting to use the "terms of art" – the literary features or "devices" we have been exploring, above and considered elsewhere in this book.

Say what effect each literary feature has on the poet's way of conveying the first two. This is where you reveal that you have "raised the level of your expertise". This is where "appreciation" will be most revealed.

Getting some further practice

The steps we are going to use here can be applied to any poem you study. Try going through the steps for the poem *Black Rook in Rainy Weather*.

Step 1: Read the poem through carefully, and preferably aloud. At root, poetry is meant to be heard. The well-known critic, M.H. Abrams, calls this reading aloud "the fourth dimension of poetry".

Step 2: Read through the poem with a pen, pencil, or coloured markers. Choose your own system, but mark things that stand out for you: different terms for the same or similar things; verbs and nouns and adjectives; words that convey sense impressions; words and groups of words that seem to work in patterns; spaces, silences, echoes, etc. Look back at the long list on p. 85 and see what else you can find.

Step 3: Read through the poem again, and now that you've looked at it more closely, try to make a more precise statement of what – for you – are the thoughts and feelings that it conveys. Write it out; this will force you toward a more exact statement.

Step 4: On a separate sheet list absolutely everything that you've noticed about the poem. What ideas, what words, what combinations of words, what images, sounds, patterns, ways of expressing ideas do you see here?

Step 5: Now choose out of that list elements that you think most relate to the statement you made above of the poem's center.

Step 6: At this point you should be ready to set out a brief outline of how you want to set up your commentary. First on a separate sheet, play a bit with how you might organize the things you want to say, and then make a brief outline or plan of the order in which you will deliver the points of your commentary.

Hint

- Be wary of the attempt to extract some "message" out of the poem; poems are really not primarily about teaching you some lesson about life. More often they are a way of conveying some apprehension of beauty, or some striking insight of the poet.
- You cannot possibly speak, in your commentary, about every single feature of any poem. Choose a few that you feel clear about, that relate to your statement of meaning, and that are possibly connected to each other. If you choose those that show "how" the poet has delivered the poem's meaning, you often find that they begin to suggest a way of organizing how you will talk about them in your commentary.

Remember

There is not a single way or a universal formula to organize your IOC. You may decide to follow a "linear" organization in which you work your way through the poem, probably best by sections or stanza, noting the particular subtleties or expansions of the poet's delivery of thoughts and feelings. You will also be noting, as you go along, the techniques by which the poet delivers these.

Another way of organizing your commentary is to break the larger statement you made about meaning into subsets or topics, and use a "topical" approach. Here again you will comment on relevant parts of the poem as you address each of the topics. This approach is a little more difficult to organize but it may suit you better.

Usually if, after your introduction, you can make three or four major points – and develop each of these points fully, you will easily have consumed the eight minutes that you are given for this exercise.

Two minutes will be available for your teacher to ask clarifying or developing questions.

In the actual situation you will have 20 minutes to prepare the above steps. Although they make have taken you somewhat longer in this practice exercise, you will find that when you are working with a poem or part of a poem you have studied, you will, with practice, be able to make your notes and an outline of your presentation fairly effectively in that amount of time.

Step 7: At this point, you are ready to practise delivering your commentary. You may be asked to do this with a partner in or out of class, through a podcast, or another method your teacher will request.

Step 8: Often when teachers are asked to do this exercise themselves, they are surprised to discover how challenging it is. It is useful to reflect on what you experienced in presenting your commentary.

Activity

Respond to some of the following questions, add your answers to the class resource pool or blog, or you could make your responses into a short podcast:

1. How well did your notes work as a basis for your presentation?
2. Do you think that your presentation showed some organization?
3. Was nervousness an issue that affected your success?
4. Were you able to include all that you wanted to say in the allotted eight minutes?
5. Do you think your language was consistently appropriate to the exercise?
6. What things would you do differently the next time you practise this exercise?

Activity

In order for you to measure your own success against what a student delivering a commentary on *Black Rook in Rainy Weather* actually did as her IOC, go the Skills and Practice website and listen to "IOC on Plath."

Then, using the IB descriptors A, B, and C for Standard Level, and A, B, C, and F for Higher Level, mark the commentary. *After* you have done so, read the Examiner's marks and comments.

Examiner's marks and comments

Poetry commentary only; does not include discussion.

The commentary is about one minute longer than it should be. The candidate is expected to speak for about eight minutes, leaving two minutes of the ten for the teacher to ask, as required, one or two follow up questions. These have not happened in this case, so the evaluation is based entirely on the candidate's nine minutes.

Criterion A: Knowledge and understanding of the poem 3

The candidate has understood that the subject of the poem is inspiration and that the tone is less dark than some other of Plath's poems that she studied. She is also aware of the speaker's shifting attitude to things connected to inspiration, that she almost "urges" things like the kitchen table and chair to yield inspiration. Her final remark that there is some irony in a poet writing a poem about poetic inspiration fits with the ambiguous approach she takes to it.

She sees that inspiration is perceived as a "friend" not a "foe," in spite of an undercurrent that suggests the opposite. On the other hand, one senses that the candidate has not quite come to terms with some of the complexity of the voice and its varying views. The last line of the poem is not, regrettably, addressed, and the comments on "At any rate. . . ." are somewhat questionable.

Criterion B: Appreciation of the writer's choices 3

The candidate has conveyed her grasp of some choices the writer has made to deliver her thoughts and feelings about her notion of inspiration. The candidate demonstrates those perceptions by enumerating and sometimes commenting on words and images that refer to inspiration early in the poem: the sight of the rook itself, light, burning, saying at first that most images are visual, but later revising that to include tactile images. She delivers a sense that the poet is conflicted about inspiration, playing words with positive connotations against some that are less so: dull, obtuse, haul, and sees that neutrality can be a positive way of looking at inspiration. She notes that everyday elements are used in the earlier part of the poem, while the latter part includes some with mystical or supernatural connotations: angel, hallowing, miracles. In reference to the "obtuse objects," she makes the interesting observation that the poem seems also to "urge" them into sources of inspiration.

Criterion C: Organization and presentation of the commentary 4

The candidate opens the commentary with a clear introduction. She has followed a linear process of interpreting the poem, discussing meaning and some of the means used to convey it. Proceeding with attention to one or two stanzas at a time, she combines interpretation with comment on stylistic features and, sometimes, their effect. She makes some summative statements along the way and does offer a closing appreciation.

(Criterion D and E are related to the Discussion only, and not evaluated here)

Criterion F: Language 4

Obviously struggling with a cold or flu, the candidate does her best to speak clearly and fluently. The register shifts sometimes to slightly informal, but on the whole she conveys what she intends to say with clarity, and a good degree of accuracy in grammar and sentence structure, with occasional hesitation and redirections. She just reaches the level of 4 in this descriptor.

Activity

Compare your marks to the examiner's responses. Write a brief summary about your marks and add it to the class resource pool or blog.

Activity

Finally, here is a checklist of some more good advice about successful IOCs.

In the space before each item, assign for yourself the priority rating of 1, 2, or 3 to each item. The "Individual" Oral Commentary is really an exercise that will and should reflect *your* individuality, so different people will need to strengthen or emphasize things that are relevant to them.

- Have a strong opening statement, either about how you respond to this poem or what you think it is about
- Talk about *how* the ideas in the poem are delivered, the way the words and lines are structured.
- Choose either a linear or a topical form for the structure and generally keep to that
- Instead of skipping over words or lines that you are not sure of, make some suggestion about them.
- Use as close to the eight minutes for your delivery as you can. For this period of time you are in charge of the commentary.
- Try to make some kind of concluding statement, indicating that you are finishing your solo performance of the commentary.

The discussion

The discussion involves one of the other two works you have studied in Part 2.

In addition to the poet you will study, you will be reading a work from each of two of the other genres, a novel, or a work of prose other than fiction, or a play. In this case the combination is a play and a work of prose other than fiction.

The two works we are going to use as a focus in this part of the workbook are Shakespeare's *Hamlet* and George Orwell's *Down and Out in Paris and London*, a work that mixes autobiography and fiction.

These are not necessarily the works you will use in your syllabus, but it's not possible to speak very effectively about literary works in the abstract. In both these examples the teacher will, in at least one of her questions, focus in on a particular part of the work, (which you will be able to read below), and then some broader questions so that you can get some sense of how this discussion might go.

Here are short summaries of the two works discussed here. Either of these works could be studied at SL and a passage from them given for the commentary.

Remember

Remember, you will only be asked to discuss one of the two other works you studied at this point, not including the poetry.

Summary of *Hamlet*

This play is the story of a prince of Denmark (whose home is the castle of Elsinore). His father has been murdered by his uncle, Claudius. His own father, King Hamlet, returns in the form of a ghost and charges Prince Hamlet to carry out revenge for his murder.

Claudius, who has taken over the throne, has also married King Hamlet's former wife and mother of Hamlet, Gertrude. Once Hamlet knows what he has to do, he decides to pretend he is mad so as to free himself for spying and action. Claudius, grown a bit suspicious, invites two old school friends of Prince Hamlet, to see if they can figure out what his nephew is up to.

For added interest, King Claudius's Lord Chamberlain or Secretary of State, Polonius, has a daughter, Ophelia, who has been courted by Prince Hamlet as part of his pretence of madness. Polonius believes, at this early point in the play, that the prince's madness has sprung from his love for Ophelia and her obedient rejection of his advances. Laertes, Ophelia's brother, doesn't think much of Hamlet as a suitor for his sister, and to make matters worse, Hamlet accidentally killed their father, Polonius, and so Laertes becomes part of the revenge plot.

Eventually, things come to a head as the revenge plot ends with a swordfight between Hamlet and Laertes in which both are killed. Here as well, come the ends of both the Queen, drinking a poisoned cup designed for Hamlet, and the King at the hands of Hamlet. A good revenge play ending, lots of blood and lots of death.

As a preliminary to the Activity below, you might enjoy going to YouTube and looking at some dramatizations of *Hamlet*. Search for 'comparing productions of Hamlet, Act 2, Scene 2' – you will see either just the interchange between Hamlet and Polonius, or you can also look at an extension of the following speech.

Hamlet

QUEEN GERTRUDE:	But, look, where sadly the poor wretch comes reading.
LORD POLONIUS:	Away, I do beseech you, both away: I'll board him presently.

[Exeunt KING CLAUDIUS, QUEEN GERTRUDE, and Attendants. Enter HAMLET, reading]

	O, give me leave: How does my good Lord Hamlet?
HAMLET:	Well, God-a-mercy.
LORD POLONIUS:	Do you know me, my lord?
HAMLET:	Excellent well; you are a fishmonger.
LORD POLONIUS:	Not I, my lord.
HAMLET:	Then I would you were so honest a man.
LORD POLONIUS:	Honest, my lord!
HAMLET:	Ay, sir; to be honest, as this world goes, is to be one man picked out of ten thousand.
LORD POLONIUS:	That's very true, my lord.
HAMLET:	For if the sun breed maggots in a dead dog, being a god kissing carrion,—Have you a daughter?
LORD POLONIUS:	I have, my lord.
HAMLET:	Let her not walk i' the sun: conception is a blessing: but not as your daughter may conceive. Friend, look to 't.
LORD POLONIUS:	*[Aside]* How say you by that? Still harping on my daughter: yet he knew me not at first; he said I was a fishmonger: he is far gone, far gone: and truly in my youth I suffered much extremity for love; very near this. I'll speak to him again. What do you read, my lord?
HAMLET:	Words, words, words.
LORD POLONIUS:	What is the matter, my lord?
HAMLET:	Between who?
LORD POLONIUS:	I mean, the matter that you read, my lord.
HAMLET:	Slanders, sir: for the satirical rogue says here that old men have grey beards, that their faces are wrinkled, their eyes purging thick amber and plum-tree gum and that they have a plentiful lack of wit, together with most weak hams: all which, sir, though I most powerfully and potently believe, yet I hold it not honesty to have it thus set down, for yourself, sir, should be old as I am, if like a crab you could go backward.
LORD POLONIUS:	*[Aside]* Though this be madness, yet there is method in 't. Will you walk out of the air, my lord?

HAMLET:	Into my grave.
LORD POLONIUS:	Indeed, that is out o' the air. *[Aside]* How pregnant sometimes his replies are! A happiness that often madness hits on, which reason and sanity could not so prosperously be delivered of. I will leave him, and suddenly contrive the means of meeting between him and my daughter. —My honourable lord, I will most humbly take my leave of you.
HAMLET:	You cannot, sir, take from me any thing that I will more willingly part withal: except my life, except my life, except my life.
LORD POLONIUS:	Fare you well, my lord.
HAMLET:	These tedious old fools!

William Shakespeare

Summary of *Down and Out in Paris and London*

In this work, one in which Orwell is acutely aware of the challenges of living in poverty – even though his actual life was largely a middle class one – he weaves a tale of what were supposedly his experiences as a young man in Paris and in the slums and environs of the East End of London. He finishes the second part of the book, after he has described his experiences as a vagrant with some rather generic advisories about social reform. This narrative describes the often lively encounters with people the narrator encountered trying to sustain himself by working in the restaurant industry in Paris. His accounts of the trying conditions of sometimes having no money at all, and working in unskilled and difficult kitchen jobs are told in both humorous and appalling detail. His stories of living as a homeless tramp in his own country are revelations of the living conditions of some of his countrymen.

In the following excerpt, Orwell relates some of the experiences and feelings of the narrator when he faces up to the consequences of having no money at all.

Down and Out in Paris and London

It is altogether curious, your first contact with poverty. You have thought so much about poverty--it is the thing you have feared all your life, the thing you knew would happen to you sooner or later; and it, is all so utterly and prosaically different. You thought it would be quite simple; it is extraordinarily complicated. You thought it would be terrible; it is merely squalid and boring. It is the peculiar *lowness* of poverty that you discover first; the shifts that it puts you to, the complicated meanness, the crust-wiping. . . . .

You discover the extreme precariousness of your six francs a day. Mean disasters happen and rob you of food. You have spent your last eighty centimes on half a litre of milk, and are boiling it over the spirit lamp. While it boils a bug runs down your forearm; you give the bug a flick with your nail, and it falls, plop! straight into the milk. There is nothing for it but to throw the milk away and go foodless.

You go to the baker's to buy a pound of bread, and you wait while the girl cuts a pound for another customer. She is clumsy, and cuts more than a pound. '*pardon, monsieur,*' she says, 'I suppose you don't mind paying two sous extra?' Bread is a franc a pound, and you have exactly a franc. When you think that you too might be asked to pay two sous extra, and would have to confess that you could not, you bolt in panic. It is hours before you dare venture into a baker's shop again.

You go to the greengrocer's to spend a franc on a kilogram of potatoes. But one of the pieces that make up the franc is a Belgian piece, and the shopman refuses it. You slink out of the shop, and can never go there again.

You have strayed into a respectable quarter, and you see a prosperous friend coming. To avoid him you dodge into the nearest cafe. Once in the cafe you must buy something, so you spend your last fifty centimes on a glass of black coffee with a dead fly in it. Once could multiply these disasters by the hundred. They are part of the process of being hard up.

You discover what it is like to be hungry. With bread and margarine in your belly, you go out and look into the shop windows. Everywhere there is food insulting you in huge, wasteful piles; whole dead pigs, baskets of hot loaves, great yellow blocks of butter, strings of sausages, mountains of potatoes, vast Gruyere cheeses like grindstones. A snivelling self-pity comes over you at the sight of so much food. You plan to grab a loaf and run, swallowing it before they catch you; and you refrain, from pure funk.

You discover the boredom which is inseparable from poverty; the times when you have nothing to do and, being underfed, can interest yourself in nothing. For half a day at a time you lie on your bed, feeling like the *jeune squelette* in Baudelaire's poem. Only food could rouse you. You discover that a man who has gone even a week on bread and margarine is not a man any longer, only a belly with a few accessory organs.

This – one could describe it further, but it is all in the same style – is life on six francs a day. Thousands of people in Paris live it – struggling artists and students, prostitutes when their luck is out, out-of-work people of all kinds. It is the suburbs, as it were, of poverty.

I continued in this style for about three weeks. The forty-seven francs were soon gone, and I had to do what I could on thirty-six francs a week from the English lessons. Being inexperienced, I handled the money badly, and sometimes I was a day without food. When this happened I used to sell a few of my clothes, smuggling them out of the hotel in small packets and taking them to a secondhand shop in the rue de la Montagne St Genevieve. . . .

George Orwell

The discussion is a different kind of "performance" from your oral "commentary." In the commentary you are the soloist, essentially, steering the line of thinking, with the spotlight on you, and you alone, until the last two or three minutes when your teacher will ask you to return to a few lines of your performance, and clarify your ideas or he may ask you about something you hadn't included – or avoided because you felt unsure.

Since you've had a chance to read and perhaps talk about the above passages from Shakespeare and Orwell, we can approach the discussion with two kinds of questions that might be likely had you studied these works. Either:

- a question or two that will focus directly on a particular passage
- a more general question that you will be able to answer in convincing detail by using the passage.

Remember

These are **not** the only kind of questions you may be asked in the discussion.

Activity

First type of question – focusing on a particular passage.

Choose one of the following questions on *Hamlet* and write a one-paragraph answer. Add it to the class resource pool or blog. You could make a short podcast where you speak your response.

Remember, that with all of the following questions, the passages we read above are examples of those that *could* be used to answer these questions, but that you will sometimes be able to *choose from any passage* that you remember in the work you have studied.

- In what way or ways does Hamlet, in the course of the play, let the audience know his attitude to Polonius?
- Since you have identified Polonius as one of the characters you find most interesting in this play, what do you see as one or two of his memorable characteristics and where do you see them displayed?
- Cite at least one scene in which you see Shakespeare using the entertainment value of double-entendre or double-meanings? How does that technique advance the playwright's plot or characterization?

Questions on the works for discussion can also be much more open and broad. Although unless you know the play, *Hamlet*, they will not be entirely clear to you, they will give you a sense of other sorts of questions. Some of them can be adapted for the novel or prose other than fiction.

1. Do you find the closing of the play (novel or work of prose other than fiction – hereafter N/P) integral and satisfying, or rather overdone and incredible? Why do you take that position?

2. Which character do you trust the least in the play (N/P) and why?

3. What relationship in the play (N/P) do you see presented as loyal to others and where is this loyalty most fully manifested?

4. There are two significant women in the play; does their presentation suggest anything about the position of women at the time Shakespeare was writing?

5. What effect does the delivery of the play – mostly in poetic lines – have, do you think, on the emotional quality of the play?

6. If there is any scene or section you think is superfluous to the play (N/P), which would it be and why?

Activity

Here are some questions on Orwell's work. Write an answer to one of them and add it to the class resource pool or blog, or make a podcast.

- Orwell's narrator sometimes becomes quite reflective about his experiences of poverty. What are some of the painful consequences he describes?

- One of the more compelling aspects of the work is the precise detail with which the narrator communicates his condition. What are some techniques Orwell uses to make effective this kind of detail?

- What aspect of poverty as Orwell describes it made the strongest impression on you and can you cite a particular place in the work where this occurs?

Student performance

What would an actual discussion of Orwell's work sound like? Below you have a transcript of what an actual discussion, using one of the works other than poetry, might look like.

Teacher: So, Julie, let's move on and talk about one of the other works you studied: Orwell's. His work is the next one in my random assortment – I know it wasn't your favourite, but not loving a work sometimes makes our perceptions a little sharper and more objective. Which section of the book did you find most interesting , if not compelling?

Student: It's true that it wasn't my favourite of the things we read all year, but I have to say of the two parts, I like Orwell being down and out in Paris better.

Teacher: I know you know I'm going to ask the obvious question, why, but more than that, what approaches and techniques that Orwell used made that happen for you, do you think?

Student: Well, I particularly like the opening page – it carried me right into the city of Paris, with people calling out to each other and swearing … the description has a lot of negative images in it, with garbage, and squashing bugs, and houses looking leprous. Not very positive, but also not sweet either; it gives you a sense of realism. Also quite brave of Orwell to start out that way, taking a chance on people giving up on the book. And I liked the descriptions of people, Boris in the first section and Bozo in the second; they seemed like believable people.

Teacher: You talk about the opening not being "sweet" but "realistic". Do you find that realism describes the work throughout; does all its effect depend on particular descriptions?

Student: I found some of the descriptions of what goes on in the kitchens of the restaurants where Orwell worked pretty disgusting, if disgusting is part of realism, and I guess, you know, that it is. I found some of the dialogue in the second, London, half of the book pretty hard to make out at times, and I guess it's a way for Orwell to make things realistic. But I have to admit I found Bozo, the man that the narrator described in quite a lot of detail, interesting. His education and his philosophical attitudes remind me of some of the people I've talked to in my city at home, and that made him realistic for me. I'm pretty sure that writers who want to make things realistic generally do this: focus in on particular people, or place or things, and build up a heavy impression by writing the way Orwell does in some parts of this work. I can call up a picture of Bozo in my mind, walking like a crab, carrying his colour box, and encountering all the people in the doss houses; it's not far off from things I've seen.

Teacher: So the quality of the descriptions did make some impact on you, Julie. Let's look at another facet of the book. You talk about Bozo being philosophical at times; what about the narrator himself? Does he give some reflections that add to, or possibly subtract from, the work?

Student: Well, we did look at one part of the book, the part in Chapter III where Orwell gives you his thoughts about discovering what being penniless really is like, and he shows you by specific examples the different ways it impacted him. He talks about having to raise money by selling some of his clothes. He gets embarrassed and humiliated about being so poor. I remember that section because he used a technique of repeating the opening of each paragraph which seems to draw the reader into the scene: "You discover. . . " or something similar. The lines about going to the greengrocer and the bakery particularly stayed in my mind.

Teacher: Can you give some specific details about any techniques Orwell uses to really drive home his points about poverty?

Student: Much later in the book when he gets quite general and I guess philosophical, about the life of tramps. He does some analysis of the conditions that produce tramps or homeless people. He talks about the "tramp-monster," which seems to me a good way to take on the belief that somehow homeless people are all that different from everyone else. He talks about tramps being cut off from women, being hungry and being without work. As I said before, Orwell helps you remember things by these kinds of lists. In his description of poverty in Paris, the one we were talking about earlier, he starts off many of the paragraphs with "You…" and then points out a particular thing that poverty does to you. And with the tramps, he gives you the three evils. These techniques are helpful when you're trying to remember specifics….like right now! He does this with the lists of different places homeless people can sleep, which he rates with titles like "the Coffin".

Teacher: Were there any situations in the work that seemed to have political overtones, that might reveal something about Orwell's own political views? And if there are, do you think they make the book richer, or more powerful?

Student: I'm not exactly sure what you mean by political. We certainly found out that Orwell had some political views, and some people think that *Down and Out* was written to kind of balance the imperialist things he had to do when he served in Burma. With things like his idea about having gardens at the lodging places and wanting some kind of regulation of sleeping places—maybe those can be called political?

Teacher: Well, they were certainly ideas directed to improving the common good, so they count as political if you think about the root of that word. But let's finish up here with one more question: did you find that the work had a satisfying beginning, middle and end? In other words, what do you think about how successful the structure of the book is? Some call the work a novel, some an autobiographical novel, some autobiography – do you think any of these labels works best and how does that relate to its structure?

Student: For me the book falls into two halves, and doesn't seem very carefully put together. The Paris section is somewhat longer and, to me, more interesting. The England section has some of the same interesting things, but then seems to begin to be about other things, almost as if Orwell was trying to reach a certain number of pages. It doesn't always feel like fact, but it also doesn't feel really like fiction, especially knowing that Orwell actually had at least some of these experiences, both in Paris and in England. So I'm thinking autobiographical novel is probably the best description, although I'm not sure why that matters. Is there a right answer?

Teacher: Good thinking, Julie, … and I tend to agree that autobiographical fiction probably is a fair description, although you will notice I avoided "novel", since it doesn't feel like one to me. So, thanks for your hard work and we're done here.

Evaluating this discussion

It's important for you to know how your discussion will be evaluated.

First, you won't know in advance which work you will be expected to discuss. This means that you will have to review and be prepared with good knowledge of both works. (Below we'll look at some hints for getting ready for that discussion).

Secondly, you need to remember that your teacher needs to sense that not only do you "know" the work, (who's involved, what happens) but that you understand both the text and the subtext – that you are familiar with the obvious elements: what is said and what it means, but also what it implies. So you may find that some of your responses will be probed more deeply by the teacher's questions. Note in Julie's oral that the teacher presses her a bit on her use of "realism."

In cases like this, you must be careful not to think that you have said something "wrong" or erroneous; the teacher is just trying to see if you are simply repeating something you remember from your class or your notes, or whether you have really internalized it, "understood" it.

Activity

Read through the way Julie responds to questions and see what notes you want to make about her "knowledge and understanding" as far as you can judge that, (knowing or not knowing the work). You will need to refer to the complete descriptors applying to the discussion in your course book.

Criterion D: Knowledge and understanding of the work used in the discussion

Look carefully at the descriptor, then make your judgment of what mark you would award.

Criterion E: Response to the discussion questions

You might think that this criterion marks the same things as in Criterion D. However, if you look closely, you'll see that there are some key terms: "meaningful", "relevant", "independent" and in the best responses, "persuasive"

Activity

Below, use a few words that will convey *your* interpretation of each of those terms and then with a partner, either in person or digitally, compare your interpretations.

- Meaningful
- Relevant

- Independent
- Persuasive.

Now, looking at Julie's oral, see how far up the scale you can go; reread each level of Descriptor E in the chart and see what mark you think she deserves.

Mark:_

Criterion F

Looking carefully at the descriptors, determine at what level you think Julie's way of expressing her ideas is most appropriately evaluated.

Mark:_

Finally, write a paragraph evaluation of the whole Discussion, including marks for each descriptor, and add it to the class resource pool or blog.

As a final activity for this Unit and this Section, please get some further help in preparing yourself for a successful Discussion by doing the following exercise.

Activity

Read through the following advisories, choose what you think is the single most important piece of advice for you, *personally*, and add it to the class resource pool or blog with a rationale for your choice.

1. Reread or re-skim the two works that are available for your Discussion. Some good ways to do this are to:
   - review the places you may have marked or highlighted during class discussions
   - open the book at random and see if you can immediately identify the place of those pages in the larger context of the work, and what you might say about them
   - reread the two pages that you have opened; you may find that you are seeing them differently
   - go through and just look at chapter headings, if they are titled.

2. Make a list of all the major players in the work, depending on whether the work is drama, fiction, or prose other than fiction.

3. Check your knowledge of the context: when was the work written, and in what time and place does the work occur?

4. Set up a quiz about details with a partner or in the blog; see where you need to revisit some of those details.

5. Put yourself in the role of the teacher and come up with some good discussion questions.

6. Read at least one critical article on each of the two works.

4 Part 3: Literary genres

The skills and practices associated with Part 3 of the course focus on the conventions associated with a particular genre. Your teacher will select three (Standard Level) or four (Higher Level) works by different authors of either:

- drama
- poetry
- prose (the novel and short story)
- prose (other than the novel and short story).

In your study you will spend time looking closely at the literary conventions of one of these genres and the ways in which the conventions contribute to the meaning and the impact of the work.

Ultimately, your understanding of the three or four works will be assessed through an essay written under exam conditions, in which you will be asked to *compare* at least two of the works studied.

In this section, therefore, we will address the following questions:

1. What does the term 'literary convention' actually mean?

2. How can I talk and write meaningfully about the way conventions affect our understanding and interpretation of the work/s?

3. What are some useful approaches I could adopt as I read and study the works?

4. In what ways should I learn to write about the works?

5. How can I prepare effectively for the exam?

There is not enough space to examine each genre in detail and so, because it tends to be the most popular, much of this chapter will focus on the genre of drama. However, we will refer to the other genres as frequently as possible and many of the suggested activities and practical advice could be applied equally well to either prose or poetry.

To start with, because the assessment of this part of the course is interested particularly in the features of literary genres, we should foreground from the beginning the way in which the Part 3 assessment asks you to think, talk, and write about them. Therefore, let's establish three core skills that you are going to need to keep in mind throughout the study of this Part.

Core skill 1: identifying literary conventions

One of the most important ideas that we refer to throughout this book concerns the importance of reading literary works as works of art; although we often talk about the characters and situations within them as if they were real, for the most part we need to remember that they are not. Even works of autobiography, travel writing, and essays – works that you might study if your teacher chooses the genre of 'prose other than fiction' express their ideas in selective, often figurative, artificial ways. This means that when we read and discuss these works, we must spend as much time exploring the forms and techniques through which their ideas are expressed as the meaning of the ideas themselves. This is an important premise of the IB Literature course, and is highlighted particularly in Part 3.

But what are the conventions of the literary genres identified above?

Activity

How many conventions do you know? The following table presents a random list of some of the conventions and literary terms typically associated with each genre. How many of the terms do you know?

Prose	Poetry		Drama	
Form and structure	**Form and structure**		**Form, action and structure**	
• Foreshadowing • Plot/Subplot • Chapter • Epistolary • Flashback • Chronological/Disrupted Narrative • Autobiography • Metafiction • Bildungsroman • Fable • Exposition • Climax	• Ballad • Sonnet • Villanelle • Free Verse • Lyric Poetry • Narrative Poetry • Satire • Ode • Elegy • Run-On/End-Stopped	• Aubade • Petrarchan • Pindaric Ode • Epigram • Haiku • Stanza	• Comedy • Tragedy • Unities • Melodrama • Well-made play • Plot • Story • Naturalism and Realism • Expressionism • Stylised • Action • Exposition	• Climax • Falling Action • Catharsis • Denouement • Dramatic Irony • Epiphany • Setting • Theatre of the Absurd • Chorus • Farce • Deus ex machina • Verisimilitude
Narrative Voice	**'Voice'**		**Dialogue**	
• Point of View • First and Third Person • Omniscient • Unreliability • Interior Monologue • Free indirect style • Direct/Indirect speech • Stream of Consciousness • Self-conscious narrative	• Detached/Intimate • Formal/Informal • Register • Tone • Persona		• Monologue and Soliloquy • Asides • Subtext • Pitch/Inflection	
Characterisation	**Rhythm, Metre and Sound**		**Character**	
• Major/Minor characters • Hero/Anti-hero • Multi-layered • Caricature • Flaw • Trait	• Stress • Monosyllabic/Polysyllabic • Metrical Foot • Iambic Pentameter • Blank Verse • Couplet/Triplet/Quatrain	• Tricolon • Rhyme Scheme • Alliteration • Assonance/Consonance • Onomatopoeia • Accent • Caesura • Sprung rhythm	• Protagonist/Antagonist • Stock character • Stereotype • Flaw • Trait • Motivation • Foil • Hamartia • Hubris • Caricature	
Figurative Level	**Figurative Language**		**Stagecraft**	
• Motif/Symbolism • Pathetic Fallacy • Imagery • Allegory	• Imagery • Simile • Metaphor • Synecdoche • Metonymy • Hyperbole • Personification • Oxymoron	• Pun • Zeugma • Synaesthesia • Conceit • Anaphora • Litotes • Trope	• Props • Lighting, Music, and Sound • Proxemics • End-on • In the round • Thrust • Apron • Proscenium arch	

Various features common to all genres			
• Diction • Abstract/Concrete language • Connotation/Denotation	• Syntax • Atmosphere • Tone • Irony	• Paradox • Theme • Motif • Rhetoric	• Allusion • Ambiguity • Cliché • Exaggeration

Put simply, literary conventions are the typical features of any particular genre that define its character and the way it works. For example, when we refer to the role and function of a chorus we are talking about a feature that is specific to the genre of drama; a ballad is a certain form of poetry whereas a chapter is of course a word that refers to one way in which prose works are often organized and structured. In your study of the works from one genre, therefore, you will need to spend time identifying the conventions of each genre, so that you build up an appropriate, targeted critical vocabulary as you go along. Note also that five marks are allocated for the identification and appreciation of these conventions in Criterion C of the marking criteria for the essay (Appreciation of the literary conventions of the genre).

> **Hint**
>
> Keep a record of terminology somewhere in your notes and make an effort to incorporate the terms into your writing as often as you can.

Core skill 2: writing about literary conventions

It is one thing to identify a particular literary feature, but quite another to talk or write about it in an appropriate way. As stated above, an important consideration to keep in mind is that examiners want you to explore not just the fact that literary works contain certain features and conventions, but also the way in which they work.

- How do conventions create particular effects?
- How do they affect the way we 'read' the content of the work?
- How do they encourage a response from the reader that can be both emotional as well as reasoned?

Weaker Paper 2 essays will often amount to little more than a description of when and where a particular feature or convention appears in the works studied. Better ones will explore their impact, usually in terms of a particular theme or additional stylistic idea.

> **Activity**
>
> Read this student writing in an examination essay about Wordsworth's poem, 'The World is too much with us' and answer the questions that follow.
>
> Wordsworth's sonnet 'The World Is Too Much With Us' sees the poet exploring the typical Wordsworthian theme of the relationship between humans and nature. The poem opens with:
>
> 'The world is too much with us; late and soon,
> Getting and spending, we lay waste with our powers -
> Little we see in Nature that is ours;
> We have given our hearts away, a sordid boon!'
>
> The opening lines juxtapose what Wordsworth saw as the materialism and greed in human life with the romance of nature and the wild. Humans are defined with the phrase 'getting and spending' and have accordingly 'given our hearts away'. The use of assonance gives musical emphasis to his despairing tone as he builds rhythmically to the exclamatory 'sordid boon!' Furthermore, the personification of nature does much to reinforce the intensity of his emotions:
>
> The sea that bares her bosom to the moon;
> The winds that will be howling at all hours,
> And are up-gathered now like sleeping flowers...
>
> The poignant symbol of the moon is both erotic, being both a symbol of the lover and the child, and along with the wind a traditional symbol of poetic inspiration. This personification and humanization of nature depicts the conflict between two opposing forces and appeals to both our visual imagination as well as our emotions...
>
> 1 Which literary features does the student identify?
> 2 In what ways does s/he explore their impact or effect?
> 3 How does the student weave together sensitivity to style with understanding of the poem?

These exploratory principles are ones that you should keep in mind throughout your study of the Part 3 texts.

Core skill 3: comparing works

Another really important thing to remember as you set about your analysis of the Part 3 texts is that the exam questions will ask you to compare at least two of the works you study. As you read and discuss them, therefore, it is very important that you think about the way the works demonstrate points of similarity and difference.

Texts can of course be compared in many different ways, but it is not a bad idea to implement some kind of system or strategy that would enable you to think about the texts on different levels. As we saw in chapter 1, there are a range of angles through which you can approach the analysis of any text, ranging from the technical characteristics of smallest components, such as words or even sounds, right through to thematic ideas that are generated from the text as a whole.

Activity

To put this comparative requirement into practice, read through the following two extracts of prose and then write some answers to the questions that follow. Both extracts are non-fiction, each focusing on the experience of being in prison.

A Hanging

It was in Burma, a sodden morning of the rains. A sickly light, like yellow tinfoil, was slanting over the high walls into the jail yard. We were waiting outside the condemned cells, a row of sheds fronted with double bars, like small animal cages. Each cell measured about ten feet by ten and was quite bare within except for a plank bed and a pot of drinking water. In some of them brown silent men were squatting at the inner bars, with their blankets draped round them. These were the condemned men, due to be hanged within the next week or two.

One prisoner had been brought out of his cell. He was a Hindu, a puny wisp of a man, with a shaven head and vague liquid eyes. He had a thick, sprouting moustache, absurdly too big for his body, rather like the moustache of a comic man on the films. Six tall Indian warders were guarding him and getting him ready for the gallows.

George Orwell

An Evil Cradling

I began as I have always begun these days to think of something, anything upon which I can concentrate. Something I can think about and so try to push away the crushing emptiness of this tiny, tiny cell and the day's long silence. I try with desperation to recall the dream of the night before or perhaps to push away the horror of it. The nights are filled with dreaming. The cinema of the mind, the reels flashing and flashing by and suddenly stopping at some point when with strange contortions it throws up some absurd drama that I cannot understand. I try to block it out. Strange how in the daytime the dreams that we do not wish to remember come flickering back into the conscious mind. Those dreams that we desperately want to have with us in the daylight will not come to us but have gone and cannot be enticed back. It is as if we are running down a long empty tunnel looking for something that we left behind but cannot see in the blackness.

Brian Keenan

Point of comparison	A Hanging	An Evil Cradling
Diction: what choices of words to the writers make? e.g. simple or complex? Literal or more figurative?		
Syntax: how would you describe the sentence length and structure? What *kinds* of sentences are used?		
Imagery and metaphor: note any examples you can find. How are they used to support meaning?		
Narrative: what kinds of narrative voices are created? First/third person? Involved/Detached?		
Tone: what kinds of feelings and attitudes do the two voices convey? How are these attitudes created?		
Structure: what structural devices are used? In what ways do the passages develop? Are there any contrasts or oppositions?		
Setting and mood: how are the settings of the prison cell conveyed in different ways? What is the atmosphere?		
Theme and motif: do the passages explore particular ideas? What different attitudes or messages are expressed?		
Anything else? how, for instance, do the two passages create different relationships with the reader?		

Keeping these core skills in mind will hopefully enable you to develop the right mindset for tackling these Part 3 examination texts. But let's now turn our attention to the kinds of practices that could be usefully employed as you read and study the works individually.

Reading skills: what do you need to know?

In this section of the chapter we are going to look in detail at one text in particular as a means to identify some reading practices that will help you as you prepare for the Paper 2 exam. The focus is on Athol Fugard's play, *Master Harold and the Boys*, although other plays are referred to in passing – in particular: *A Streetcar Named Desire*, by Tennessee Williams, *Who's Afraid of Virginia Woolf* by Edward Albee and *Waiting for Godot* by Samuel Beckett.

As we said at the start of the chapter, many of the working practices identified here are generic and could be just as usefully applied to the genres of prose or of poetry.

The unit is divided into before, during and post-reading activities – the assumption being that you would study the text as you read through it as a class. Not all teachers will work in this way – some may prefer to give you the work to read before you begin to talk about it, which is particularly common of course with longer prose texts. But the skills targeted by the fifteen suggested reading strategies will nevertheless be the same, in whatever way the work is read and studied.

Before reading the work/s:

- Is it important to identify cultural or contextual issues before reading a work?

- Is there a value also in looking at a text *without* contextual frames of reference?

All literary works are of course conceived and written in particular times and places. Before studying any of the works on your syllabus, it is likely that at least some time will be given to thinking about where each text 'fits' in various contexts. The following areas are likely to come into consideration:

- social and political context

- cultural context

- literary context.

Fugard's *Master Harold and the Boys* was first performed in 1982 and is set in the context of Apartheid, which lasted for much of the second half of the twentieth century in South Africa.

Strategy 1: research the background

Do some research into the cultural and political background of South Africa, as well as the playwright Athol Fugard's biography (or the background to the work you are studying). You could bring your notes to a class presentation or upload to a class wiki.

Find some photographs or images that you think might be of relevance. These could be arranged on a piece of paper, and as you begin to read the work you could add lines of the text to create a collage for hanging on your classroom wall.

Activity

- Look at the photographs below and discuss the cultural values and attitudes you see represented.

- Compare them with some lines from near the end of the play on the next page. In what ways are the assumptions you made reinforced or challenged by the extract of dialogue?

Master Harold and the Boys

HALLY: Why did you make that kite, Sam?

SAM: *[Evenly]* I can't remember.

HALLY: Truly?

SAM: Too long ago, Hally.

HALLY: Ja, I suppose it was. It's time for another one, you know.

SAM: Why do you say that?

HALLY: Because it feels like that. Wouldn't be a good day to fly it, though.

SAM: No. You can't fly kites on rainy days.

HALLY: *[He studies Sam. Their memories have made him conscious of the man's presence in his life.]* How old are you, Sam?

SAM: Two score and five.

HALLY: Strange, isn't it?

SAM: What?

HALLY: Me and you.

SAM: What's strange about it?

HALLY: Little white boy in short trousers and a black man old enough to be his father flying a kite. It's not every day you see that.

SAM: But why strange? Because the one is white and the other black?

HALLY: I don't know. Would have been just as strange, I suppose, if it had been me and my Dad … cripple man and a little boy!

Athol Fugard

The social and political implications of this period of South African history resonate in different ways throughout this play – from its setting in a white, middle-class cafe with black, lower-class workers, its presentation of the relationships between the central characters, their language, dialogue, and their shifts in power, as well as its development in dramatic tension.

Completing this kind of research, then, will highlight relevant cultural, social, political, and/or biographical issues and encourage you to think about the work as a product of the environment in which it was written.

Strategy 2: make predictions

At the same time, it can sometimes be just as valuable to approach your Part 2 texts with no prior research at all.

Activity

As soon as your teacher hands you the prose work, collection of poems, or play, open to any page at random and get a feel for the kind of text you think it might be. Here, for example, are two extracts – one taken from the middle section of a poem, the other from halfway through a novel.

The Eve of St Agnes

Thus whispering, his warm, unnerved arm

Sank in her pillow. Shaded was her dream

By the dusk curtains: 'twas a midnight charm

Impossible to melt as iced stream:

The lustrous salvers in the moonlight gleam;

Broad golden fringe upon the carpet lies:

It seem'd he never, never could redeem

From such a stedfast spell his lady's eyes;

So mus'd awhile, entoil'd in woofed phantasies.

John Keats

Mrs Dalloway

As a cloud crosses the sun, silence falls on London; and falls on the mind. Effort ceases. Time flaps on the mast. There we stop; there we stand. Rigid, the skeleton of habit alone upholds the human frame. Where there is nothing, Peter Walsh said to himself; feeling hollowed out, utterly empty within. Clarissa refused me, he thought. He stood there thinking, Clarissa refused me.

Virginia Woolf

- Talk about the language and form.
- See what literary conventions you can identify that are particular to either poetry or prose.
- What questions do you have about each one?
- What predictions can you make about the ideas the text seems interested in?

Let's now apply this technique to the genre of drama.

Activity

Read through the lines of dialogue from *Master Harold and the Boys* that we used in the previous activity on context. Make notes on them in response to these questions:

- What can you tell about the characters and the relationship between them?
- What can you say about the way they talk to each other?
- What dramatic conventions can you identify?
- What kind of play do you think it is?

Now compare the extract with the one below, from a different play. Answer the same questions and make notes on points of comparison.

Waiting for Godot	
ESTRAGON:	Let's go.
VLADIMIR:	We can't.
ESTRAGON:	Why not?
VLADIMIR:	We're waiting for Godot.
ESTRAGON:	Ah! *[Vladimir walks up and down]* Can you not stay still?
VLADIMIR:	I'm cold.
ESTRAGON:	We came too soon.
VLADIMIR:	It's always at nightfall.
ESTRAGON:	But night doesn't fall.
VLADIMIR:	It'll fall all of a sudden, like yesterday.
ESTRAGON:	Then it'll be night.
VLADIMIR:	And we can go.
ESTRAGON:	Then it'll be day again. *[Pause. Despairing.]* What'll we do, what'll we do!

Samuel Beckett

It will be clear that these two extracts emerge from two quite different ways of thinking about drama – the former being more realistic or '**naturalistic**' and the latter more stylised or '**non-naturalistic**'. In other words they emerge from two different theatrical traditions. If you have not come across these terms before do some research on these terms and find out what they mean.

Look at the production photographs on the right of the two plays and talk about the way the conventions you have identified in the above activity are reflected in their set design:

Although in Part 3 you will spend time thinking and talking about the way texts embody conventions of the genre to which they belong, it can sometimes be mistaken to try to pigeonhole them into one category or another. There is, of course, as much poetry as drama in Shakespeare. Furthermore, Tennessee Williams' *A Streetcar Named Desire*, is a play that has roots in quite naturalistic dramatic ideas; its characters are multilayered and complex, the dialogue quite close to 'real life', and the action and structure of the play developed in a logical, coherent, linear way. And yet there are components of the play which are distinctly less like real life; at times, for instance, the sound and music in the play encourages us to see things distinctly from Blanche's point of view and it is as if the play were at times seeking to represent on stage her gradual psychological disintegration. Similarly, Edward Albee's *Who's Afraid of Virginia Woolf?* belongs very much to the tradition of the so-called '**theatre of the absurd**' yet much of the drama conforms to fairly conventional ideas about character development and psychological realism.

Ultimately, then, useful though pre-reading research or prediction-making exercises are, an important skill that Paper 2 asks you to demonstrate is sensitivity to the subtlety of the works you study, which will often evade the literary conventions in which they are sometimes placed through **contrast, nuance, and ambiguity**. As you prepare to read and study your works try to keep in mind the way that such things as:

- dramatic or narrative style
- characterisation
- description and dialogue
- action

can all be presented in paradoxical, often contradictory ways. Perhaps this is one core way in which literary texts reflect the richness and complexity of human experience?

Reading activities

Let's now look at some activities that will help you to develop appropriate reading skills as you set about your study of the Part 3 works. As we have said before, they target particular features and conventions of play texts in particular, but many could equally be applied to the study of poetry or prose.

Strategy 3: reading beginnings (i)

The opening scene of any play, the first few lines of a poem or the opening paragraph of a prose work are of course crucial to the audience or the reader because it is from this point that we make sense of all the material that is to follow.

Activity

Read through the opening lines of these prose works. With a partner discuss the following:

- the way they use language and literary style
- the differences in their narrative voices.

> "124 WAS SPITEFUL. Full of a baby's venom. The women in the house knew it and so did the children. For years each put up with the spite in his own way, but by 1873 Sethe and her daughter Denver were its only victims."
>
> -- from *Beloved* by Toni Morrison

> "The Nellie, a cruising yawl, swung to her anchor without a flutter of the sails, and was at rest. The flood had made, the wind was nearly calm, and being bound down the river, the only thing for it was to come to and wait for the turn of the tide."
>
> -- from *Heart of Darkness* by Joseph Conrad
>
> "The beginning is simple to mark. We were in sunlight under a turkey oak, partly protected from a strong, gusty wind. I was kneeling on the grass with a corkscrew in my hand, and Clarissa was passing me the bottle – a 1987 Daumas Gassac."
>
> -- from *Enduring Love* by Ian McEwan
>
> What kinds of conventions or stylistic features did you notice? First/third person voices? Interesting use of diction or syntax? Figurative language?

However, perhaps more importantly, we need to remember that because these opening lines are the first thing in the novel that we read, a key aim must be to engage the reader. How do they achieve this?

- Evocative description?
- Interesting characters?
- Plunging us into the scene?
- Inviting us to ask questions?

Notice how we have already begun to think in two ways about a particular feature of a literary text: what the style is like and the impact or effect of it.

Now look at the initial dialogue and description of action at the beginning of *Master Harold and The Boys*:

Master Harold and the Boys

WILLIE: *[Singing as he works]*

'She was scandalizin' my name,
She took my money
She called me honey
But she was scandalizin' my name.
Called it love but is was playin' a game...'

[He gets up and moves the bucket. Stands thinking for a moment, then, raising his arms to hold an imaginary partner, he launches into an intricate ballroom dance step. Although a mildly comic figure, he reveals a reasonable degree of accomplishment.]

Hey, Sam.

[Sam, absorbed in the comic book, does not respond.]

Hey, Boet Sam!

[Sam looks up.]

I'm getting it. The quickstep. Look now and tell me. *[He repeats the step.]* Well?

SAM: *[Encouragingly.]* Show me again.

WILLIE: Okay, count for me.

SAM: Ready?

WILLIE: Ready.

SAM: Five, six, seven, eight ... *[Willie starts to dance.]* A-n-d one two three four ... and one two three four ... *[Ad libbing as Willie dances.]* Your shoulders, Willie ... your shoulders! Don't look down! Look happy, Willie! Relax, Willie!

WILLIE: *[Desperate but still dancing.]* I am relax.

SAM: No, you're not.

Athol Fugard

What are some of the things on which you could comment about the opening moments of this scene? Here are some suggestions:

- The light-hearted, comic **atmosphere** generated by the dialogue and the actions of Willie as he dances with an imaginary partner.

- The presentation of the **characters**, Willie and Sam and the differences between them (e.g. Willie's emotional fervour and Sam's apparent passivity and detachment).
- The affectionate **relationship** between them.
- The use of non-standard, dialectal **language** in phrases such as 'I am relax'.
- The short, clipped **dialogue.**

Activity

Now annotate the opening dialogue of Williams' *A Streetcar Named Desire*. What points of similarity or difference can you find?

A Streetcar Named Desire

[Above the music of the 'Blue Piano' the voices of people on the street can be heard overlapping.]

Negro Woman *[to Eunice]*: ... she says St. Barnabas would send out his dog to lick her an when he did she'd feel an icy cold wave all up and down her. Well, that night when-

A Man *[to a Sailor]*: You keep right on going and you'll find it. You'll hear them tapping on the shutters.

Sailor *[to Negro Woman and Eunice]*: Where's the Four Deuces?

Vendor: Red hots! Red hots!

Negro Woman: Don't waste your money in that clip joint!

Sailor: I've got a date there.

Vendor: Re-e-ed h-o-o-t!

Negro Woman: Don't let them sell you a Blue Moon cocktail or you won't go out on your own feet!

[Two men come around the corner, Stanley Kowalski and Mitch. They are about twenty-eight or thirty years old, roughly dressed in blue denim work clothes. Stanley carries his bowling jacket and a red-stained package from a butcher's.]

Stanley *[to Mitch]*: Well, what did he say?

Mitch: He said he'd give us even money.

Stanley: Naw! We gotta have odds!

[They stop at the foot of the steps]

Stanley *[bellowing]*: Hey, there! Stella, baby!

[Stella comes out on the first floor landing, a gentle young woman, about twenty five, and of a background obviously quite different from her husband]

Stella *[mildly]*: Don't holler at me like that. Hi, Mitch.

Stanley: Catch!

Stella: What?

Stanley: Meat!

Tennessee Williams

Strategy 4: reading beginnings (ii)

How do the openings of any literary work incite your interests as a reader or audience member? You could consider such things as:

- **Conflicts** - both *within* and *between* people.
- **Contrasts** - between characters, aspects of language, moods.
- **Questions** - what kinds of incomplete ideas are established that we want to see developed?
- **Shocks and/or surprises** - elements that immediately capture our attention.
- ***In medias res*** - when we begin in the middle of a scene in terms of either action or extract of dialogue.
- **Foreshadowing** - ways the future direction of the work is indicated by the opening moments.

In what ways do the two openings of the plays we have looked at achieve these effects? Share your thoughts in a group.

Read through the following ideas written by a student in an exam. Talk about the way s/he reads the *significance* of the opening action of the play:

The opening of 'A Streetcar Named Desire' establishes the New Orleans setting. In the initial stage directions Elysian Fields is described as neither beautiful nor uninviting; it is poor but 'unlike corresponding sections in other American cities, it has a raffish charm.' We begin halfway through a conversation between the 'Negro Woman' and a Sailor, and the ensuing quick-fire dialogue of various people in the street such as the hot dog vendor with his 'Red hots! Red hots!' places the audience in a bustling, but ordinary setting. Considerable emphasis on voices, noises and movements creates the feel of life being lived out on the street. Most importantly, perhaps, Stanley appears very much at home in this environment when he appears wearing his 'blue denim work clothes' and throwing a package of 'meat' to Stella. When Blanche makes her entrance wearing a white suit, the contrast is therefore all the more emphatic...

In reference to the openings of the works you are studying, then, we are interested in the way features like the ones identified above create and sustain *dramatic* or *narrative* interest, which is a phrase used quite frequently in examination questions.

Reading character

What is the difference between character and characterisation?

When talking and writing about any character, whether from drama, prose or poetry, it is important to think about them in a number of ways, for example:

- What are they like?
- How are they portrayed?
- In what way do they develop as individuals?
- What role do they play in the development of the action or story?
- What is their significance?

The first level is perhaps the least difficult because it is a matter of reading or watching characters in detail, and finding appropriate terminology with which to describe them. The other levels ask you to think more *interpretively* and to *evaluate* the way in which characters are presented and developed, thereby demonstrating more independent thought. This is what we mean by *characterisation* and it is more likely that the examination will focus on this aspect (if character is identified in the question) because it is in here that you will be able to explore the role of literary or dramatic convention.

Strategy 5: exploring character traits

The point just made is an important one, and we will return to it. That being said, it is likely that your first reaction to the presentation of a character, whether in prose, poetry, or drama will be a fairly emotional response to *what* they are like.

Activity

Read through the following five extracts from *Master Harold and the Boys*, all of which focus on the characters of Sam and Hally and choose a statement from the list on the right with which to describe the traits they reveal at this particular point. Match each quotation on the left to the statement on the right that you think is most appropriate.

HALLY: *Failing a maths exam isn't the end of the world, Sam. How many times have I told you that examination results don't measure intelligence?*	Sam remains a true friend to Hally and is in the end defined by his sense of compassion.
HALLY: *And we had! I was so proud of us! It was the most splendid thing I had ever seen. I wished there were hundreds of kids around to watch us.*	Hally's adolescence explains his naivety and lack of self-knowledge.
HALLY: *We've had the pretty dream, it's time to wake up and have a good long look at the way things really are.*	Unlike the other characters, Sam has a capacity to *see*. He understands Hally's insecurities and offers advice in a way that demonstrates a high level of emotional intelligence.
SAM: *Hally ... I've got no right to tell you what being a man means if I don't behave like one myself, and I'm not doing so well at that this afternoon. Should we try again, Hally?*	For much of the play, Sam and Hally are portrayed as close friends.
SAM: *No, Hally, you mustn't do it. Take back those words and ask for forgiveness! It's a terrible sin for a son to mock his father with jokes like that.*	Hally is characterised most through his sense of cynicism and disappointment.

Strategy 6: how are characters depicted?

In essays, students can often write quite fluently about the core characteristics through which a particular character or relationship is defined. But as we have said, it is very important to remember that characters are *literary* creations and as such you should spend as much time exploring the *way* in which they are portrayed as you spend exploring what they are actually like. This is partly to avoid the potential for lapsing into narrative description of plot retell, but it is also to do with the importance of Part 3's interest in the conventions of literary works.

Activity

So what are the kinds of conventions and techniques through which characters in drama or prose are created? Well, choose any character from a drama or prose work you are studying. Take some time to write down some of the ways in which that character is depicted, in reference to the areas shown overleaf. (You may well think of others.)

Present your findings: as a group presentation, identify the various components through which a particular character is created, along the lines suggested above. Allocate each person in your group with one particular component and connect them to the character with a piece of string, as if the character were a puppet. You could experiment with distance from the character as a means to show how important any particular feature is. The group forms a tableau, and one by one individuals provide feedback about their role in the presentation of the character.

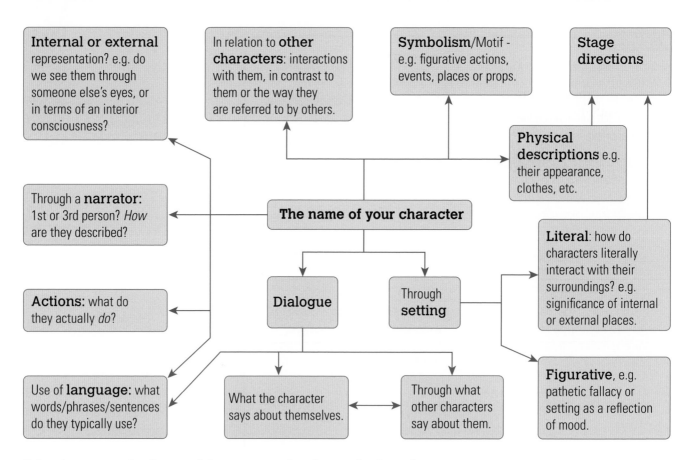

Internal or external representation? e.g. do we see them through someone else's eyes, or in terms of an interior consciousness?

In relation to **other characters**: interactions with them, in contrast to them or the way they are referred to by others.

Symbolism/Motif - e.g. figurative actions, events, places or props.

Stage directions

Physical descriptions e.g. their appearance, clothes, etc.

Through a **narrator:** 1st or 3rd person? *How* are they described?

The name of your character

Literal: how do characters literally interact with their surroundings? e.g. significance of internal or external places.

Actions: what do they actually *do*?

Dialogue

Through **setting**

Use of **language:** what words/phrases/sentences do they typically use?

What the character says about themselves.

Through what other characters say about them.

Figurative, e.g. pathetic fallacy or setting as a reflection of mood.

Below is an example of some of the notes a student has made about the character of George in Albee's play, *Who's Afraid of Virginia Woolf*. Bearing in mind the above suggestion about how to represent these conventions, it is clear that there is a lot to say about the role of dialogue in the representation of his character – and so you might place the student responsible for that convention closer to the character.

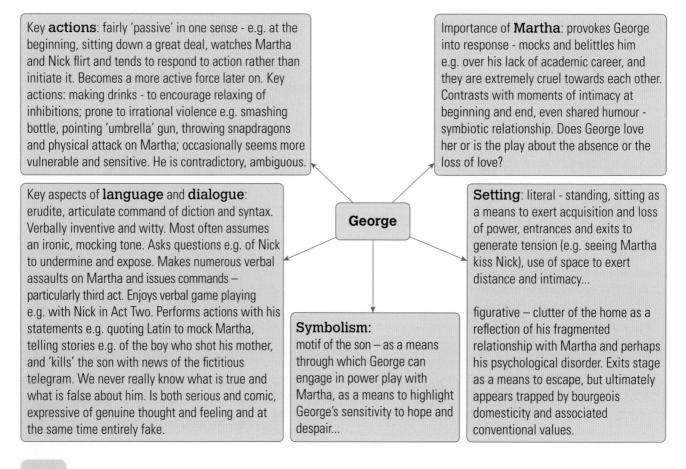

Key **actions**: fairly 'passive' in one sense - e.g. at the beginning, sitting down a great deal, watches Martha and Nick flirt and tends to respond to action rather than initiate it. Becomes a more active force later on. Key actions: making drinks - to encourage relaxing of inhibitions; prone to irrational violence e.g. smashing bottle, pointing 'umbrella' gun, throwing snapdragons and physical attack on Martha; occasionally seems more vulnerable and sensitive. He is contradictory, ambiguous.

Importance of **Martha**: provokes George into response - mocks and belittles him e.g. over his lack of academic career, and they are extremely cruel towards each other. Contrasts with moments of intimacy at beginning and end, even shared humour - symbiotic relationship. Does George love her or is the play about the absence or the loss of love?

Key aspects of **language** and **dialogue**: erudite, articulate command of diction and syntax. Verbally inventive and witty. Most often assumes an ironic, mocking tone. Asks questions e.g. of Nick to undermine and expose. Makes numerous verbal assaults on Martha and issues commands – particularly third act. Enjoys verbal game playing e.g. with Nick in Act Two. Performs actions with his statements e.g. quoting Latin to mock Martha, telling stories e.g. of the boy who shot his mother, and 'kills' the son with news of the fictitious telegram. We never really know what is true and what is false about him. Is both serious and comic, expressive of genuine thought and feeling and at the same time entirely fake.

George

Setting: literal - standing, sitting as a means to exert acquisition and loss of power, entrances and exits to generate tension (e.g. seeing Martha kiss Nick), use of space to exert distance and intimacy...

figurative – clutter of the home as a reflection of his fragmented relationship with Martha and perhaps his psychological disorder. Exits stage as a means to escape, but ultimately appears trapped by bourgeois domesticity and associated conventional values.

Symbolism:
motif of the son – as a means through which George can engage in power play with Martha, as a means to highlight George's sensitivity to hope and despair...

Strategy 7: character development

The way characters change or develop is of course going to be important to any essay in which characterisation is a focus. Students often fail to take this into account when writing about them. For example, can you tell what is wrong with this statement?

"In Master Harold and the Boys, *Sam is presented as mature and thoughtful. In contrast to Hally, Sam is emotionally poised and reacts with equanimity to Hally's outbursts."*

Well, hopefully you recognize that whilst the statement is generally true for much of the play, it does not take into account Sam's anger and general expressiveness towards the end. In other words, always give consideration to context when you are making an analytical point about your characters. All the student who wrote the above statement would be required to do, for instance, is prefix the comment with 'For much of the play' in order for it to be more valid.

So how do you document the progress of your character/s throughout the play or the novel? One good way is to maintain some kind of chart a bit like this:

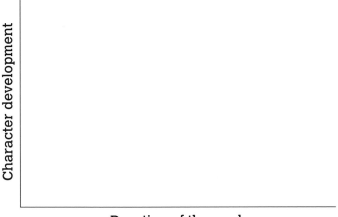

The 'Y' axis in this case can be defined in a number of ways. Perhaps you might want to consider how the character gains or loses confidence, becomes increasingly more or less independent, contented, or fulfilled. And then for each point or line you will need to provide references back to the work in the form of quotations, or references to specific moments that illustrate those points. It is always interesting to compare such graphs with other students and then argue for the choices you have made.

Strategy 8: character role and significance

Being able to talk about what a character is like and the ways in which they are presented represents one level of thinking about them; in effect this is a matter of description and analysis. Points four and five in the earlier suggestions about 'reading character', however, ask you to consider both the role or function a character plays, and their significance.

When essay titles ask for consideration of *role* and/or significance, students often find it difficult to distinguish between them. Essentially, the role a character plays has to do with their dramatic function in the work.

For example:

- How do they bring about development in the action of the novel or play?
- How do they bring about development in other characters?
- In what ways are they responsible for the creation or increase in tension?
- How do they increase audience/reader interest. e.g. through conflict/ secrets maintained or truths revealed?
- How important are they to the novel or play?

The *significance* of a character, on the other hand, has to do with the way they contribute to the meaning of the work. For example:

- What thematic ideas are portrayed through this character?
- How do they connect the novel or play with 'real life' experience?

Activity

Consider the following paragraph from an essay comparing the central characters from *Who's Afraid of Virginia Woolf* and *A Streetcar Named Desire*. Annotate the extract according to the different ways in which characterisation can be assessed, in line with the suggestions above.

In both plays the presentation of the characters highlights important thematic ideas. Martha and George are presented in some ways as complete opposites for much of the play; Martha is more active whilst George is passive, she appears to crave experience whilst he seems disinterested. The conflict between them, however, is rooted ironically in something over which they agree: their mutual sense of failure – individually, as well as in their relationship with each other. The death of the son becomes a symbolic realization for both of them of their failure to realize their hopes and dreams.

Equally, the tension created in the relationship between Blanche and Stanley comes from their presentation as opposites to each other, and as the play goes on the contrast between Blanche's fragile, irrational, and emotional behaviour and Stanley's growing aggression and determination leads towards the climax. We are left in little doubt as to who will ultimately win. Both plays therefore use characters and the development of relationships between them to demonstrate the continuity of the 'real world' and the impossibility of achieving escape from it.

Reading speech

Whether you are studying a play, a novel, or poetry, exploring the words spoken by an individual character or poetic voice is of course an essential part of the way we make sense of them.

Strategy 9: explore the language used by characters

Characters are particularly revealing not just in terms of *what* they say, but in *how* they say things. As you go through the play it is a good idea to collect illustrative examples in your notes. Consider, for example, these two extracts from *A Streetcar Named Desire*:

A Streetcar Named Desire

1. BLANCHE: He was a boy, just a boy, when I was a very young girl. When I was sixteen, I made the discovery - love. All at once and much, much too completely. It was like you suddenly turned a blinding light on something that had always been half in shadow, that's how it struck the world for me. But I was unlucky. Deluded.

2. STANLEY: *[bawling]* QUIET IN THERE! - We've got a noisy woman on the place. -Go on, Mac. At Riley's? No, I don't wanta bowl at Riley's. I had a little trouble with Riley last week. I'm the team-captain, ain't I? All right, then, we're not gonna bowl at Riley's, we're gonna bowl at the West Side of the Gala! All right, Mac. See you!

Tennessee Williams

What points of comparison can you make? For example:

- **Sentence structure:** Blanche uses a variety of sentence types (simple, complex) whereas Stanley's are shorter, comprised mostly of one main clause.

- **Diction:** Blanche uses more varied kinds of words.

- **Types of statement:** Blanche is descriptive and expressive whereas Stanley's language use is more or less completely functional.

- **Figurative language:** Blanche incorporates a variety of literary features, including imagery and metaphor, unlike Stanley.

- **Tone:** Blanche is quiet, reflective, whereas Stanley is exclamatory and domineering.

- **Register:** Stanley speaks in an informal register, with non-standard expressions whereas Blanche is more formal, speaking for the most part in Standard English.

Activity

Let's now break a character's voice down into its particular, illustrative components. You can then store these features somewhere in your notes to help you with revision. To help you to do this, take an extract from any single character's speech from the play or novel you are studying and answer the following questions:

Word Level	• What kinds of diction are typical of your character? e.g. simple/complex, literal, or figurative?
Sentence Level	• In what way/s does your character typically structure their sentences? Simple/complex/compound? Comment on the syntax. Formal or informal? Repetition? How important is punctuation?
Literary language	• Does your character utilize features typically referred to as 'poetic'? e.g. Imagery and metaphor, sound and rhythm
Register and Tone	• For example, formal/informal, sarcastic/enthusiastic/confident
Types of utterance	• For example, statement, question, exclamation, command
Form of speech	• For example, soliloquy, aside, monologue/dialogue, naturalistic or stylised

You could also try entering a poem or a significant speech by a character into the software programme Wordle (www.wordle.net). Doing this draws visual attention to the kinds of words or phrases typically uttered by a character and is another means of assessing the way their personality is reflected in their voice.

Strategy 10: explore the conventions of dialogue

When having dinner with your family or sitting with a group of friends, have you ever just listened to the way people interact? Who speaks more or less? How do people control situations through the way they talk? How do they take turns in discussion? Does anyone speak over the top of someone else or interrupt? In some respects we can learn as much about literary characters not just through the way they talk, but also in the way they interact through others through dialogue. It is important that you explore this in your reading of the play or novel.

Some of the conventions to which you might refer could include:

- **Turn taking:** how and why do characters take turns in dialogue? Do they interact in a 'realistic' or more stylised manner?

- **Interruptions and overlapping:** do characters exert control (or the opposite) in the way they interrupt or give way to others?

- **Silence and ellipsis:** when and why do characters stop speaking? What does silence register?

Activity

Annotate the following extract of dialogue from *Who's Afraid of Virginia Woolf* with these questions in mind:

Who's Afraid of Virginia Woolf

MARTHA: You pig!

GEORGE: *[haughtily]* Oink! Oink!

MARTHA: Ha, ha, ha, HA! Make me another drink ... lover.

GEORGE: *[taking her glass]* My God, you can swill it down, can't you?

MARTHA: *[imitating a child]* I'm firsty.

GEORGE: Jesus!

MARTHA: *[swinging around]* Look, sweetheart, I can drink you under any goddamn table you want ... so don't worry about me!

GEORGE: Martha, I gave you the prize years ago ... There isn't an abomination award going that you ...

MARTHA: I swear ... if you existed, I'd divorce you ...

GEORGE: Well, just stay on your feet, that's all ... These people are your guests, you know, and ...

MARTHA: I can't even see you ... I haven't been able to see you for years ...

GEORGE: ... if you pass out, or throw up, or something ...

MARTHA: ... I mean, you're a blank, a cipher ...

GEORGE: ...and try to keep your clothes on, too.

Edward Albee

Strategy 11: explore subtext (i)

As we have said, in your essay you need to explore the **impact** or the meaning of these conventions. Quite often, for instance, the features referred to above are part of the way in which dramatists establish **subtext**. What a character is *implying* or *suggesting* can be a very important part of the representation of personality and relationships between people.

Activity

To explore this, take an extract from the play, read or perform it as it is written and then replay it, this time with other students reading out the *implied* or *unspoken* meaning behind the characters' words.

For example, here is an extract from *Master Harold and the Boys* with a student's annotations that interpret what the character means beyond or below what he is actually saying.

Master Harold and the Boys

HALLY: Why did you make that kite, Sam?

I need to know that at least one person cared about me.

SAM: *[Evenly]* I can't remember.

I remember exactly. After hearing about your father being drunk on the floor of the hotel you needed something to help you, to make you see that there was a world beyond the Jubilee Boarding House. And that one day you would be free from it.

HALLY: Truly?

Tell me. Please.

SAM: Too long ago, Hally.

Telling you would bring your father home. I do not want you to be reminded of that pain all over again.

HALLY: Ja, I suppose it was. It's time for another one, you know.

There must be a way out of this mess. There must be something to hope for.

SAM: Why do you say that?

HALLY: Because it feels like that. Wouldn't be a good day to fly it, though.

If only we could preserve that time. Live it again. But it can't be, can it? Nothing comes to good in the end.

SAM: No. You can't fly kites on rainy days.

We can't live in the past, Hally. We have to come to terms with the present. You have to come to terms with your dad.

Athol Fugard

Strategy 12: explore subtext (ii)

Using tableaux is another way to explore the difference between what a character says on the surface and the reality of their emotional predicament beneath. Whether it is in the private feelings a character refuses or is unable to express, the unspoken tension between two characters, or simply the way characters use dialogue to maintain power or status, capturing the 'literal' image in the form of a stage picture and then using others in a group to represent the 'reality' can be a really useful means of exploring these kinds of complex issues.

Activity

Try this with any of the extracts of dialogue we have quoted so far, or consider the importance of the unspoken in a novel or poem you are reading. You might try exaggerating the unspoken tension in order to highlight the nature of the drama lurking beneath the surface. For example, if the dialogue seems to reflect the struggle to acquire or maintain power, you could try placing one person on a desk or chair in order to elevate their status. Alternatively, if dialogue registers either a character's feelings of love or hate, which they are unable to express openly, you could explore their emotional subtext by using proxemics: place characters either close to each other, or far apart might as they read their lines.

Reading story and action

The **action** of a novel or play is in effect a description of what actually happens through the course of the **story**. As you read through the novel, play or perhaps poem you will of course talk a great deal about the events that take place, and the reasons for them. As we considered earlier with character, however, talking and writing about action can easily lead to simply *describing* the story – or retelling the plot of the work, which you must make every effort to avoid. How can you do this? Well, the following strategies might be useful ones to adopt.

Let's divide the convention into two – the events of the story as a whole and action in individual scenes.

Strategy 13: action in the story as a whole

Activity

Maintain a graph (like the one we did on character) that details the progression of the events through the play or novel. Where are the points of high and low tension? Does the work follow the conventional approach to story development i.e. situation, introduction of a problem, development of the problem, rising tension towards a final climax, and falling resolution? Or is there something different going on? Some works might, for instance, have a range of 'climactic' moments without a 'resolution' at the end. This is a useful way of thinking about the **structure** of the work.

Activity

Consider not just *what* happens but *why*. In the table below are descriptions of some of the actions that take place that happen in *Master Harold and the Boys*. Copy and complete the table.

What happens?	Why?
Hally has trouble settling down to complete his homework.	Hally is not really deeply academic, but likes to think that he is.
Hally tries to 'teach' Sam about the 'great men' of history.	This is an extension of Hally's insecurity, which ultimately stems from his problematic relationship with his father.
Hally and Sam reminisce about the Jubilee Boarding House.	
Hally receives two phone calls from his mother.	
Hally spits at Sam.	

Activity

Consider the *significance* of particular events in the story.
For example:

- What do particular events tell us about the characters and character motivation?
- How do the events bring about an increase in the sense of tension?
- What do the events suggest about the play's thematic concerns?
- How do the events engage the audience?

A third column could be added in this way:

What happens?	Why?	Significance?
Hally tries to 'teach' Sam about the 'great men' of history.	This is an extension of Hally's insecurity, which ultimately stems from his problematic relationship with his father.	It is interesting that the 'great men' that Hally picks out are western and white. Cultural prejudices are manifest in different ways throughout the play – not least through Hally's naivety.

Add a third column to your table and complete it by commenting on the significance of the actions listed before.

Strategy 14: action in individual scenes – stage directions

If you are studying drama for Part 3, you will of course need to keep in mind that these are works intended for *performance*. As such, exploration of 'meaning' that emerges through the status of the text as drama will need to take into account the physical properties of stagecraft. Quite often, for instance, playwrights will indicate what they want their characters to do through stage directions, which will usually indicate either or both of two things:

- intonation and facial expressions – how the playwright wants the lines to be spoken
- descriptions of movements and gestures.

Evidence for points you want to make about any issue, whether character or theme-related might well refer to stage directions as evidence of their validity. As you go through your plays, therefore, you will need to keep an eye on the descriptions of stage directions and make notes on where dramatic meaning is conveyed through them.

Activity

Consider this extract from near the ending of *Master Harold and the Boys*. Where there is a number written, a stage direction has been removed. First, annotate the extract with directions that you think could be included and then compare with the actual descriptions below.

Master Harold and the Boys

WILLIE: Is bad. Is all all bad in here now.

HALLY: **1** Willie... **2** Will you lock up for me and look after the keys?

WILLIE: Okay.

   3

SAM: Don't forget the comic books.

   4

SAM: **5** Stop ... Hally ...

   6

   Hally ... I've got no right to tell you what being a man means if I don't behave like one myself, and I'm not doing so well at that this afternoon. Should we try again, Hally?

HALLY: Try what?

SAM: Fly another kite, I suppose. It worked once, and this time I need it as much as you do.

HALLY:	It's still raining, Sam. you can't fly kites on rainy days, remember.
SAM:	So what do we do? Hope for better weather tomorrow?
HALLY:	**7** I don't know. I don't know anything anymore.
SAM:	You sure of that, Hally? Because it would be pretty hopeless if that was true. It would mean nothing has been learnt here this afternoon, and there was a hell of a lot of teaching going on … one way or another. But anyway, I don't believe you. I reckon there's one thing you know. You don't have to sit up there by yourself. You know what that bench means now, and you can leave it any time you choose. All you've got to do is stand up and walk away from it. **8**
WILLIE:	Is okay, Boet Sam. You see. Is … **9** … is going to be okay tomorrow. **10** Hey, Boet Sam! **11** You right. I think about it and you right. Tonight I find Hilda and say sorry. And make promise I won't beat her no more. You hear me, Boet Sam?

Athol Fugard

1. *[Books into his school case, raincoat on.]*
2. *[It is difficult to speak.]*
3. *[Sam returns. Hally goes behind the counter and collects the few coins in the cash register. As he starts to leave…]*
4. *[Hally returns to the counter and puts them in his case. He starts to leave again.]*
5. *[To the retreating back of the boy.]*
6. *[Hally stops, but doesn't turn to face him]*
7. *[Helpless gesture.]*
8. *[Hally leaves. Willie goes up quietly to Sam.]*
9. *[He can't find any better words.]*
10. *[Changing his tone.]*
11. *[He is trying hard.]*

Remember always to consider the *significance* of a particular feature rather than simply state that it exists. What kinds of things might stage directions, for example, demonstrate?:

- A character's inner feelings and emotions?
- A sense of tension (within or between characters?)
- An issue of power and status, e.g. characters sitting or standing, moving towards or away, upstage or downstage?
- An increase or decrease in pace?

This is one student writing about the presentation of Blanche in Scene 1 of *A Streetcar Named Desire*:

Blanche's sense of anxiety is depicted from the beginning of the play. Apart from her evident need for alcohol as a means to 'keep hold of myself!' she is described as 'shaking all over', 'nervously tamping cigarette' and '[touching] her forehead shakily'. These mannerisms are typical of her portrayal at the start and convey her emotional vulnerability and frailty.

Post-reading activities

Strategy 15: reading themes and motifs

As you go through your Part 3 works, and certainly by the time you have finished your reading, you will be exploring them on a more interpretive level, giving consideration to the ideas that emerge across the work/s as a whole.

When you make notes on particular themes or motifs, try to break them down in different ways; it is one thing to identify what a theme actually is, but quite another to examine the way it is represented or how it develops. This is a very important skill to acquire because it will play a vital role when it comes to preparing for your final essay. For example, just as we did earlier when we looked at characterisation, you could consider the way a theme is explored in reference to the same sorts of questions:

1. Where in the play/novel/poems is this theme depicted?

2. How is it presented, i.e. stylistically?

3. Does the presentation of the theme change or develop as the play or novel goes on, or within and between poems?

4. In what ways does the theme or motif perform a function in the work? i.e. does it further the action of the play or novel, does it enable the author to treat the fiction of the text as if it were 'real life' and connect us – the audience or reader – with the experience?

5. How important or significant is the theme or motif? In what ways does the meaning of the work depend on this theme or motif for its overall impact?

Here are extracts from some notes made by a student in response to the above questions. The key theme in *Master Harold and the Boys* they were asked to explore was loyalty.

Where?	• Hally's loyalty to Sam: memories of the boarding house and the kite flying. • Sam's loyalty to Hally: his sense of affection and wisdom – does not react to Hally's put-downs about his education, does what Hally asks of him and Willy, especially after the phone calls, withholds anger at the end of the play. • Focus on Hally's change of mood after speaking to his mother.
How?	• Contrast Hally's emotional outbursts and Sam's calmness – refer to characteristic language and dialogue. • Key actions: Hally slamming books whilst Sam and Willie dance, and strutting around 'like a little despot' – and later on ripping out the page for his homework assignment and smashing brandy bottle. Physical aggression towards Sam and spit as a statement of his rejection of him.
Development?	• Tension between increasing warmth and trust between the men, punctuated by the dramatic contrast of the two phone calls. • Hally's 'narrative arc' is to lose his sense of loyalty towards Sam. • Could contrast this with Sam's offer to Hally at the end and Willie's resolution not to beat Hilda.
Function?	• Responsible for much of the developing tension in the play. • The way the atmosphere shifts between creation of hostility and tension and then relaxation as a result. • In spite of moments of reprieve (e.g. dance as a metaphor for a world 'without bumps') Hally's increasing desperation drives the action inevitably towards the climax and the action of the spit.
Significance?	• Provides the play with a focus through which to explore the meaning of friendship. • Is also a means to engage with the political context. In Sam's Christ-like sense of humility, Fugard depicts loyalty as an essential ingredient to the representation of hope.

With a partner, or as a class, make a list of the themes and motifs present in the Part 3 works you have studied. Talk about the way they emerge from the different conventions we have covered, or any others that we have not mentioned.

- As with our suggested analysis of the presentation of character, you could place the theme in the middle of a page and list the relevant conventions in the form of a spider diagram.
- Alternatively, make notes as a group and collate in the form of an online Wiki.

This brings us to the end of the second section, and a range of suggested approaches to exploring the conventions of your Part 3 works. Let's move away from reading skills now and turn towards the writing skills demanded by the examination.

Writing about the works

Translating knowledge and understanding of the conventions of your Part 3 works into successful writing can be quite challenging. The following activities take you through the process of preparing for and writing the Paper 2 essay, and are designed to highlight important principles that successful examination answers depend on the most.

Stage 1: understanding the question

As we have seen elsewhere in this book, annotation is a particularly useful tool that provides evidence of your *active response* to any particular task. This is particularly true when it comes to showing understanding of the examination questions. For example, read this question about the convention of setting and notice the words and phrases a student has highlighted:

> Setting can often reflect the underlying ideas in a play. In the light of this statement consider the importance and use of setting in two or three plays you have studied.

What has the student drawn attention to here?

1. The subject about which they are being asked to write: the role of **setting** in drama.

2. The way in which they are being asked to write about this subject: the question of it **importance** and the way in which it is **used**.

Note, therefore, that it is not just a matter of identifying where a particular feature is revealed but the end/s to which it works - its 'effect/s'. Whether is it is explicitly stated or not, this is an expectation that all questions contain within them.

Activity

Which words and phrases would you highlight from the following questions? Remember to make sure you have drawn attention to both what you are being asked to write about as well as the way in which you are asked to explore it.

In what ways and to what extent does characterisation in the works you have studied depend on the use of dialogue? Compare and contrast at least two works in your answer.

Symbols and/or motifs are essential conventions of many novels and short stories. Compare the ways either or both of these devices have been used and, in your opinion, how successfully, in at least two of the works you have studied?

Explore how visual imagery contributes to meaning in poems you have studied. You must compare the work of at least two poets in your answer.

Stage 2: assimilate your ideas

When you feel confident with the demands the question is making of you, the next step is of course to collect your ideas together. At this stage you may or may not have decided which works you intend to use. If you haven't, select them with some or all of the following considerations in mind:

1. Choose works that are relevant to the title or topic.

2. Choose works that provide you with an equal amount of things to say. You don't want to write an unbalanced essay because any strong marks you score in reference to one text will be undermined by poor marks for the other.

3. Choose works that will enable your argument to develop. For instance, you might choose two or three works that explore the particular aspect set by the title in quite similar or different ways, or perhaps the works chosen might show the aspect working to create quite different *effects* or *developed* in contrasting ways.

Stage 3: make notes

At this point you will need to make sure that the notes you make encourage you to think about the chosen aspect in various ways, just as we saw earlier. Consider the following questions:

1. Where is this aspect represented in the works chosen? i.e. collect evidence.

2. How is the aspect represented? i.e. focus on language, dramatic, or stylistic elements.

3. In what ways does the aspect develop or change as the works progress?

4. In what ways is this aspect responsible for dramatic or narrative interest? i.e. how does it work to engage the reader/audience?

5. What is the thematic significance of the aspect?

6. What key points of similarity and difference are there between your chosen works in terms of the way they explore or use this aspect?

The important thing to note here is that you need to provide yourself with the means to develop an argument. Numbers 1–3 above by and large ask you to make *analytical* responses, whereas numbers 4–6 ask you to think more *interpretively*. Interpretative thinking asks you to respond more independently to the demands of the title, but it is terms of this kind of thinking that you are more likely to find an argument or a thesis, which is an important characteristic of better essays, and required to gain top marks at Higher Level.

Here, for instance, is an example of notes made by a student on with those questions in mind:

Title: Analyse the extent to which the reliability of the narrator can affect the reader's understanding of events in at least two of the works you have studied

Core topic: **narrative reliability**
Seen in terms of: **the reader's understanding**
Important to remember: **to what extent?**

The Great Gatsby by F. Scott Fitzgerald	*The Remains of the Day* by Kazuo Ishiguro

<u>Where</u> and <u>How</u> is the topic portrayed in the chosen works?

Nick is both someone we trust as well as question. <ul><li>Hard to know sometimes what he really thinks - withholds opinions - father's advice in chap 1...'inclined to reserve all judgments' - and yet proceeds to critique many people, including Gatsby - who 'represented everything for which I have unaffected scorn.'</li><li>His presentation of characters depends on how much he seems to feel or care about them - i.e. Daisy and Gatsby are elusively drawn whereas Myrtle and the McKees are more lucidly depicted</li><li>Is a relative of Daisy and therefore cannot be wholly objective</li><li>Displays some awareness of the superficiality of Gatsby's world</li><li>He is easily influenced by others and goes along with things e.g. when Tom takes him to see Myrtle for the first time, or the way he becomes easily entranced by Gatsby's lifestyle</li><li>He gets drunk in chap 3 and by the end is completely irrational in his representation of events: 'everything that happened had a dim, hazy cast over it...the whisky distorted things'.</li><li>Is highly influenced by Gatsby and his world - and participates imaginatively in it</li><li>In some respects *seems* reliable: i.e. distance from events, maintenance of objectivity. He has no need to flatter Gatsby and is in a position to report most things fairly neutrally...</li><li>His meticulousness and attention to detail - i.e. he is very observant (Gatsby's Party in chapter 3 - his smile - and reunion with Daisy in chapter 5)</li><li>He is privy to secret information - i.e. Gatsby confides in him (e.g. chap 5: 'this is a terrible mistake')</li></ul>	Stevens is also a man who we implicitly trust at the same time as being invited to doubt <ul><li>His character: he is objective, factual, and unemotional - unlike Nick, he never expresses opinion - e.g. his account of the discharging of the two Jewish employees - even though he disagrees.</li><li>As a butler he presents 'dignity in keeping with his position' at all times</li><li>He is also entirely meticulous in his representation of detail</li><li>Voice is neutral, personality removed. He operates in service of Lord Darlington</li><li>But we are also invited to question his narrative account</li><li>His devotion to Lord D means that he emphasizes anything that relates to his public, professional role and suppresses anything personal or emotional</li><li>Conceals things - e.g. when Miss K finds him reading the romance, he claims to be improving his 'command of the English language'</li><li>He denies working for Darlington on three occasions</li><li>Fails to remember particular events</li><li>Rambling narrative</li><li>Occasional discrepancy drawn between what he thinks and how he chooses to interpret feelings e.g. he says he 'may have given the impression' that he treated his father 'rather bluntly over his declining abilities' but then says 'there was little choice but to approach the matter as I did'</li><li>Continually seeks justification for events - e.g. when 'tested' on his political knowledge by Darlington's friends, or how he responded to his father dying by returning downstairs - he says his father 'would have wished me to carry on just now'</li></ul>

- He reports on gossip surrounding Gatsby without comment: 'German spy during the war/ he killed a man once', etc.
- Self conscious as a narrator: 'reading over what I have written so far, I've given the impression that the events of three nights several weeks apart were all that absorbed me'
- Significance of first person narrative and point of view: we see things mostly through his eyes - and he idealises certain aspects through, perhaps, his infatuation with Gatsby and his world....
- But when he cannot report directly he relies on other people's testimonies e.g. Jordan relates Gatsby's love affair in chapter 4
- His relationship with Jordan is ambiguous

- Evasion: i.e. relationship with his father. Sees his reaction to his father dying as part of his dignity, but is disingenuous, i.e. he very much affected by it Darlington says 'you look as though you were crying'
- Also Miss K: ' justification' betrays his dishonesty for visiting her. Mentions 'whole dreams forever irredeemable' and when she says 'there's no turning back the clock' he states 'at that moment my heart was breaking'
- Misinterprets her letter
- Suggestion of deep regret over his passivity and unfulfilled love for Miss K: 'But that doesn't mean to say, of course, there aren't occasions now and then - extremely desolate occasions - when you think to yourself: 'What a terrible mistake I've made with my life''/'One can't be forever dwelling on what might have been'
- Both novels convey a sense of reliability through their intimate, first person narratives...
- Unlike Gatsby, no other voices appear in the novel

In what ways does the topic change or develop?

- The difference between Nick as a character during the events of the novel and the wisdom he displays in hindsight: 'I was 30. Before me stretched the portent menacing road of a new decade'
- He loses his sense of moral perspective quite early on - only reacquiring it later. After Gatsby's death he is more acutely aware of the falseness of the world he has lived in, a world that is 'material without being real' - like Gatsby, he finally recognizes its illusory nature.

- Also a distinction between Stevens the character and the narrator - and between his behaviour during the events he has described and his attitude towards them in hindsight

How does the topic create reader or audience interest? Or - what is the *significance* of the topic?

- A significant means of maintaining audience interest: we feel reliably informed on some occasions and on others invited to question the account. There are sometimes as many questions as there are answers, which draws us in
- The novel is interested in the difference between truth and illusion, and Nick's narrative ambiguity is another way of reinforcing that
- Nick, like Gatsby and the world they inhabit, is inconsistent

- Stevens' unreliable account is reflective of Darlington's failure to grasp the significance of Nazi Germany
- His ambiguity is part of the problem of history and the way it is told - can there ever be an 'objective', reliable account?
- Equally, it says things about the problem of memory
- A means of drawing attention to the difference between appearance and reality

Key points of similarity and contrast

- Both works present narrators who are both reliable and unreliable
- Both present accounts that we are invited to take at face value as well as question
- There is importance attached to their first person narratives - though Gatsby includes accounts from other points of view
- Contradictions, ambiguities and biased elements prevent clear 'readings'
- Both novels are interested in the nature of 'truth' - both in terms of the presentations of stories and (in *Remains of the Day*) in terms of accounts of history
- Both interested in the distinction between public and private experience
- Reader interest is generated through distinction between what is said and what is implied, repressed or even kept secret

Stage 4: organize your ideas

Once you have made notes of the kind detailed above, you need to group your ideas into categories or sections, which will eventually become divided into paragraphs. It is important to try and organize ideas into topics that do not overlap too much, so that you minimize the risk of repeating points in the essay.

Activity

How might the student above organize their notes into categories? Have a go yourself before reading on.

A number of possibilities seem to emerge from the way they have made their notes:

1. Elements that make the narratives seemingly 'reliable'

2. Elements that make the narratives more 'unreliable'

3. The narrators as characters in the novels: what are their character traits?

4. The way/s their narratives change and/or develop

5. The effect on the reader: in what ways are our responses to the novel manipulated through their narrative styles?

6. Important thematic ideas explored in relation to the question of narrative un/reliability

Stage 5: sequencing your ideas

When it comes to structuring the essay, some guiding principles might be kept in mind:

1. Try to see your essay as a process of development. Weaker essays are ones that have one core idea that is essentially repeated a number of times and then concluded. The essay hasn't gone anywhere.

2. It is helpful to see the opening stages of your essay as a means of setting up the background, wherein the points made are probably likely to be more *analytical* than *interpretive* in nature. Allow your argument to evolve as the essay goes along. For instance, in the example above, it might make sense to talk about the character traits of both Nick and Stevens before going on to look at the way in which their personalities influence their degree of reliability or unreliability.

3. A good essay will advance its argument in stages, so that each paragraph depends on the one previous for it to make sense. If you can swap, say, paragraph four with paragraph two and there to be no discernible effect on the essay, then it is likely that you have not structured the essay very well.

Activity

To illustrate these principles, the word: SHIP

———

———

———

———

———

must be turned into the word: DOCK

To achieve this, you are allowed to change one letter only at each stage, and each word must be a recognizable, 'real' word. What is the minimum number of stages you require? (It is possible to do it in six steps).

In the above activity, there is a *development* from 'ship' to 'dock' and each stage of development depends on the previous for it to make sense. These are some of the hallmarks of well-structured essays.

Activity

> As a demonstration, the first lines of each paragraph from another student's essay are written below. Read through them and discuss whether you think they follow the advice suggested above.

The title for the essay was: *Masks can be used both literally and metaphorically in drama. Discuss to what extent, and for what purposes, masks have been used in at least two plays you have studied.*

Introduction: In 'A Streetcar Named Desire' and 'All My Sons', the characters of Blanche Dubois and Joe Keller are seen to hide behind certain metaphorical masks as a means to conceal the truth of their respective pasts.

Paragraph 1: Arthur Miller presents the character of Joe initially as a sympathetic, seemingly trustworthy man, with little sense of disguise or deceit.

Paragraph 2: In contrast, the first time we see Blanche, there is a tension between the way she wants to present herself, and the way she actually 'is'.

Paragraph 3: Stanley is the vehicle through which the 'reality' of her past is revealed.

Paragraph 4: Similarly, it soon becomes clear that Joe Keller is in fact a man with secrets to hide, and George provides the means of chipping away at his mask.

Paragraph 5: Both plays, therefore, present antagonists whose actions escalate the tension as respective masks are removed.

Paragraph 6: The climax of both plays revolves around the failure of both characters in their attempt to keep their masks alive.

Conclusion: In both plays, masks are therefore vital to the dramatic presentation of the contrast between illusion and reality.

Notice that here the essay goes through several stages:

1. After the first, introductory sentence, paragraphs one and two set the scene by establishing some key characteristics of the two characters and the way they can be seen to wear metaphorical masks.

2. Paragraphs three and four, however, move the discussion on by looking at ways in which these masks are exposed through the actions of other characters.

3. Paragraphs five and six broaden the scope of the argument by looking at ways in which this act of stripping masks away is responsible for the development of action and the creation of dramatic tension.

This goes to show that essays are often structured not just in terms of paragraphs, each focusing on one main idea, but also through 'sub sections', or broad categories through which ideas are more or less connected. You could imagine this a bit like a house, with separate rooms for each paragraph, but those rooms on the same floor being connected in some fundamental way. For example, the above essay would look something like this:

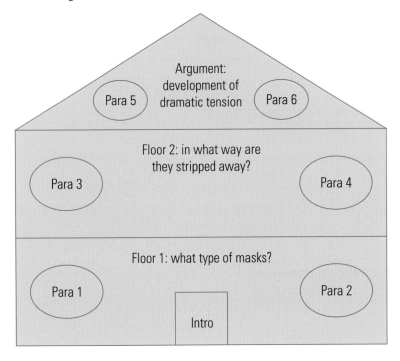

There might well be more paragraphs, of course, perhaps even floors – and the floors could be identified in other ways. For instance, in the essay on narrative reliability that the student was preparing earlier, the first floor might have focused on ways in which the narrative voices are presented as reliable and the second on ways in which they are unreliable. The essential thing is that you organize your ideas in a way that reflects the argument you intend to pursue.

Activity

Read through the topic statements of the two essays below, which have been jumbled up. Referring, perhaps, to the advice given above, see if you can organize them in the sequence in which they were written originally.

"The past is forever in the present." By comparing the use of narrative techniques, in at least two of the works you have studied, demonstrate whether or not this statement is valid?

1. It is perhaps significant, therefore, that the most prominent image in both novels concerns that of haunting and the supernatural.

2. In both novels, 'Wuthering Heights' and 'Wide Sargasso Sea' the link between the personalities of characters from different generations is one key way in which the past is shown to be 'forever in the present'.

3. In addition to narrative voice, Rhys conveys the impact of the past through use of repeated images and motifs.

4. In the end both novels draw on the subject of the past in order to highlight the consequences of human actions.

5. The different narrative voices in 'Wuthering Heights' are used to further reinforce this idea.

In what ways, and to what ends, do the poems you have studied make use of elements of sound and/or rhythm. Compare the work of at least two poets in your answer.

1. *Similarly in 'Ode to a Nightingale', John Keats makes use of assonance to show the reality of sense experiences.*

2. *Hopkins uses varied sound and 'sprung rhythm', therefore, to show the spirit of God in nature.*

3. *The consistent rhythm is, however, broken in the last stanza where he wakes from his dream.*

4. *For Keats, on the other hand, there is no escape from the 'real world'.*

5. *The poem 'The Windhover' uses the same elements to capture the energy and vitality of nature.*

6. *For Gerard Manley Hopkins, rhythm and sound in poems such as 'God's Grandeur' enable him to explore his sense of spiritual freedom.*

A word on the language of comparison:

The above examples highlight the way in which the structure of your essay can work so as to compare and contrast your choice of works in a meaningful way. More fundamentally, however, comparisons are inevitably made in a more detailed manner throughout the essay. Here are some words and phrases that enable comparisons to be made either *within* or *between* sentences:

Connection through points of *similarity*	moreover, similarly, furthermore, in addition, equally, in the same way, also, as well as
Connection through points of *difference*	on the other hand, in contrast, however, in spite of, nevertheless, on the contrary, even though, whereas, unlike

Activity

Which comparative word or phrase do you think would fit the best in the following examples?

1. Achebe also chooses to write about colonisation and the effect it has on people who live in colonised lands; _____ he takes a different approach to Forster, and you can see this straight away in his opening pages.

2. These problems add to the dramatic force of the play by challenging the audience to consider the problems themselves. _____, Dysart questions the concept of normality in his closing monologue.

3. 'Ode to Autumn' opens with a celebratory description. _____ Ted Hughes' 'The Thought Fox' begins more ambivalently.

Introducing the essay

Good introductions to any essay you write in the course need to pay attention will perform a number of things:

1. Show that you have understood the question and the conventions it identifies.

2. Break the implications of the question down into component parts.

3. Provide some sense of the argument you are going to follow.

In addition, part of your introduction will inevitably focus on some of the key points of comparison you intend to make.

Read through the introduction below and identify any of the ways you think the student has fulfilled the things outline above:

Title: Light and dark, country and city, proud and humble – these and numerous other contrasts have been used by poets to sharpen their expression of ideas or feelings. In the works of at least two poets you have studied, explore the ways in which contrasts have been used to create particular effects.

Both T. S Eliot and Tony Harrison make use of contrast within the subject matter, themes and the language of their poems. Eliot focuses on the division between the public and the private worlds of his narrators and explores their difficulties in communication in a fragmented, broken structure. The voices of the poems are reflective of a divided self, torn between participation in life and detachment from it– and their language both light hearted and deeply serious at the same time. Harrison's use of contrast comes from his exploration of the tension he feels between his working class origins and his literary career. Like Eliot, he reflects divisions that relate to this tension in the different voices of his poems, which range from the expressive, gentle, and figurative to the more colloquial and direct. In this way both poets use contrast in voices to further the dramatic qualities of their poetry.

Concluding the essay

Good conclusions do not just repeat points that have already been covered in the main essay. You might, therefore, consider some or all of the following:

1. An assessment of the main idea to have emerged from your essay: ideally this will mean returning to your thesis and assessing it final implications

2. What are the most important dramatic or narrative ideas to have emerged through your exploration of the chosen conventions?

3. Relate the topic to human experience in general

The student who wrote the introduction printed above concluded his essay as follows. Talk about you think it is a good conclusion and why.

The technique of contrast is therefore shown to be a vital quality in the poetry of both Harrison and Eliot. Although writing in very different time periods, and in different kinds of poetic voices, the dramatic qualities of poems like 'The Love Song of J Alfred Prufrock' and 'V' enable the writers to explore what it means to have a speaking voice, or to be prevented from speaking. In this way they express uncertainty, division, and even despair. However, whilst both poets dramatize characters who are unable to communicate with others or more generally in society, the poems also indicate a kind of relief in the form of poetry itself, where their voices are expressed, and heard by us – the readers. Poetry, for both the writers and the speakers in the poems, is therefore both a way of expressing contrast and division, as well as a means of overcoming it.

The meaning of the term *Evaluation*

This term appears in the criterion 'Response to the question' at Higher Level. Therefore if you are a HL student, at some point in your Paper 2 response you will need to make some evaluative comment about the works you have discussed. This means that you should explore which of your chosen writers have **made the most effective use** of the convention identified by the title.

The introduction is a good place to make this happen, by setting out a position to be proven, or later on in the essay, or as a conclusion. In the first example below, on drama, the student makes some evaluative comment in the first paragraph of the essay. Talk about where this critical skill is presented and whether you think the student has been successful.

Question on drama: One of the most useful conventions for a playwright in establishing dramatic impact is the use of carefully chosen entrances and exits. In at least two plays you have studied, explore the way playwrights have used such features.

Opening of an essay:

The effect of entrances and exits on the dramatic impact of plays is a question that must occur to playwrights when inventing their plays: 'In what ways can I use these to create certain impacts in tension and the development of characters?' In 'Death of a Salesman' by Arthur Miller and 'A Streetcar Named Desire' by Tennessee Williams it is apparent that certain effects are achieved through exits and entrances. I would propose, in the first case, that Willy leaving the 'real world' and escaping from time to time is a very effective way of using exits and entrances, although not in the usual sense. These fill in the backstory of the play and account for the way he feels about himself and why. Willy's final exit, which we only hear about and then see its effects in the funeral is very like the way death is presented in Greek tragedy, indirectly. This looks like a conscious choice by Miller, connecting a modern play to a classical one.

However, I would say that the entrances and exits of Blanche in Williams' play create more of a dramatic impact. Williams chooses every detail of her first entrance, her words, her clothes, her gestures in a way that is moving and more memorable. She enters as an intriguing, moth-like woman who will catalyse all the action in the play. And her final scene, where she exits the situation she has turned upside down, rounds out her painful story, and her last illusion about 'kindness of strangers' is, for me, as memorable as her entrance. For modern audiences it seems as if Williams has gotten more impact out of his use of these entrances and exits than Miller has. Looking at these four examples should prove my argument.

As mentioned, another way of including some element of evaluation is through the conclusion. Below is an ending to an essay on poetry. Again, talk about how effectively the student has made a comparative assessment of the chosen works in terms of their use of the particular convention.

After reading it, try such a conclusion to a Paper 2 practice essay that you have written.

Question: Poets often use elements of the natural world as a representation or reflection of inner emotional states. Working with at least two poets you have studied, examine the way poets have used nature in such ways.

Conclusion to an essay:

After looking at the ways in which poets use the natural world in their poetry, it seems that while both use nature effectively they use such elements differently.

Overall, Dickinson, in the poems studied, seems to take an ironic approach in a way that mixes admiration and a sense of threat. Calling the snake 'a narrow fellow' suggests intimacy, but 'zero at the bone' clearly does not. The 'slant of light on winter afternoons' gives 'heavenly hurt,' and the buzzing fly signals death in her poem. On the other hand, Hopkins seems to express ecstatic appreciation for natural beauty as he does in 'The Windhover' or 'Pied Beauty.' In such poems as 'Hurrahing in Harvest' he evokes the season of harvest with 'wind-walks' and 'silk-sack clouds.' He also adds, however, a second level to his poems, a religious one, which makes them richer and clearer.

Although both poets seem to include more than just 'nature' in their poems, Hopkins is clearly elevated into a religious dimension by his response to nature, whereas exactly what Dickinson intends is less clear. The sometimes dark quality of her inclusions of nature offers some ambiguity that is less satisfying, to me at least, than what I find in Hopkins.

Marking the Paper 2 Essay

Having read, thought about and practised a wide range of skills that this examination paper demands, it is worth now looking at a couple of Paper 2 examination essays. So that we can become even more accustomed to the expectations placed before you, we will read them as if from the point of view of an examiner.

The first one is a **Standard Level** response to a question on poetry. Remind yourself first of the examination criteria and then read the essay through carefully, keeping in mind all you have learned through the course of this chapter. Afterwards, complete the suggested activity.

Standard Level essay

Title: Setting can be as crucial a tool in creating poetry as it is in fiction. Using two poets you have studied, explore how they have incorporated elements of setting to good effect.

The use of setting, in this case a natural environment, helps poets generate tension within their poems as well as helps them develop a powerful meaning. D.H. Lawrence and Seamus Heaney, despite writing at different times, the turn of the 20th century and the 1960's respectively, present the natural environment as crucial to our understanding of the world. Lawrence was appalled by the constraints of the Edwardian era and felt that the zest of life and enthusiasm had been depleted. Heaney, on the other hand, grew up in rural Ireland and was largely affected by not only his environment but the politically troubled Ireland as well. In 'Discord in Childhood', Lawrence uses a harsh and violent setting to mirror violence taking place within a domestic violence-ridden home. While Heaney, in 'Death of a Naturalist', uses setting as a platform to allude to the Troubles but more importantly to highlight the change in perspective with time. Lastly, Lawrence in 'Snake' uses a traditionally evil animal to highlight the harmony and unity of the natural world, as opposed to humans.

In 'Discord in Childhood', Lawrence uses the natural world, a harsh oppressive world to help develop the morbid tone of the poem. Even the first verse, 'an ash tree hung its terrible whips' Lawrence alludes to a terrifying sombre image of death and punishment. He reinforces this point with 'the lash of the tree, shrieked and slashed,' the enjambment of the onomatopoeic active verbs, shrieked and slashed, creates an intense and powerful image: the abrasive repetition of the 'sh' mimics the child's constant bombardment within the house. The effect on the reader is of a haunting eerie experience. To further develop the tension within the poem, the use of sound 'to dreadful sound / of a thick lash booming and bruising' creates a powerfully eerie image. Again the use of onomatopoeia reinforces the constant bombardment of the child helped with the alliteration of 'b' and continuous present creates an effect of ever increasing constant noise. By this point it becomes apparent that the child is a victim of domestic violence, which Lawrence hypothesized was due to the long hours men spent with machinery. It adds to the violence, aggression, and intensity of the poem. The last verse with the synaesthesia 'silence of blood 'neath the noise of the ash' adds a tone of ambiguity and leaves the fate of the child unresolved. The antithesis silence and noise reinforces the violence and haunting element of the poem.

Similarly, Heaney uses setting as a tool to develop the meaning in 'Death of a Naturalist'. The poem operates on two levels. On one hand, the explicit theme is of the change in perspective that comes with the transition from childhood innocence to adulthood; on the other one, there is an implicit theme exploring the violence in Ireland. Through a shift in the tone, Heaney presents the same natural environment in two different lights. In the first alliterative verse 'All year the flax-dam festered in the heart/of the townland', Heaney already establishes the inherent tension in a society marred by civil war with the flax-dam metaphorically representing his society. The use alliteration and assonance helps create a slow pace reinforcing the infected environment. The aural imagery in 'bubbles gurgled delicately' helps not only paint a vivid sensory image but reflects nature with authenticity. The multitude of senses that Heaney appeals to with the synaesthesia 'bluebottle tops/wove a strong gauze of sound around the smell' also reflects the child's excitement. In order to reinforce the realistic portrayal of the environment, the onomatopoeia in 'warm thick slobber' illustrates the child's excitement highlighted through the use of enjambment of 'frogspawn.' However as a modulation of the narrative voice occurs, there is a change in imagery to savage and brutal. The brutal image 'the fields were rank with cowdung … and angry frogs/invaded' marks the new perspective with which the first person intimate narrator now sees the flax dam. The aggressive diction 'angry, invaded' again allude to the tension occurring in Ireland, due to the civil war.

What was once 'bubbles' now turns into the harsh alliteration of 'coarse-croaking that I had never heard/Before.' The alliteration emphasizes the image and suggests a sense of intimidation and fright from the narrator. The use of aggressive military diction 'cocked' and 'poised like grenades' paints the natural world as aggressive and hostile. While in fact it serves to contrast childhood naivety with adulthood awareness. What Heaney once saw as 'swimming tadpoles' now turn into 'the great slime kings' reflecting the knowledge one gains with time.

Lastly, Lawrence in 'Snake' presents a natural environment, of which the snake belongs as wholesome in tune while contrasting human's unnatural position in the world. In 'Snake', Lawrence recounts the narrative story of a man who encounters a snake in which he emphasizes the beauty, harmony of the snake and the natural world, and highlights human's repressed instinctive nature. Lawrence paints the backdrop of the encounter with 'Mount Etna smoking,' a majestic mythological backdrop. Likewise he portrays the snake as 'he reached from the fissure of the earth –wall in /the gloom.' The use of a latinate term 'fissure' highlights the snake's arrival from the creative underworld and by juxtaposing gloom Lawrence subverts traditional association of snake with evil by Christian tradition. He draws attention to human's inability to go to the underworld possibly reflecting what Lawrence saw as the oppression of the unconscious. The alliterative phrase used to describe the snake 'being earth brown' suggests the snake being at one with nature despite having to endure such harsh conditions and emphasizes human's inability to find a role in the world. The use of incantatory rhythm creates an almost liturgical overtone. The use of compound words and repetition of earth serve to reinforce unity with earth. The use of metallic imagery possibly draws a comparison with snake being like a precious stone borne from the earth itself.

The use of dramatized dialogue helps reinforce the contending aspects of the self. The descriptions of the snake are linear and flowing poetically expressing his beauty. The inner agitation of narrator 'I thought of the albatross' creates tension with the allusion to the albatross, symbolic of sin against the natural world.

To conclude, both poets present natural environment in different light and for different effect, all the while using it as a tool to develop meaning. In 'Dischord in Childhood' Lawrence portrays it as relentless and unforgiving. While Heaney in 'Death of a Naturalist' uses it as a platform from which to examine different perspectives of age. Finally, in 'Snake', Lawrence uses a snake, symbolic of nature running its course as means to highlight its majestic qualities and comment on the suppression of the subconscious.

Activity

The examiner who read this Paper 2 had the following types of reservations about the success of this script, while allowing that the candidate deserves credit for knowledge and understanding of the poems, answering the question and addressing literary features.

Taking each of the seven types of concerns below, go through the student's essay and mark where you think the examiner's reservations may have occurred. Put the number in a circle where you find these.

1. The candidate has not sufficiently explained or validated his assertion.
2. Assertions are not clearly connected to each other.
3. Transitions between paragraphs are not smooth.
4. The structure of the argument is not clear.
5. There is a problem with syntax.
6. The candidate has misspelled words.
7. Faulty punctuation has obscured meaning.
8. The candidate at times loses sight of the title.

The examiner has given this essay a mark of 18 out of 25. How would you distribute the marks for each criterion to arrive at 18?

Activity

Here is a completed Higher Level essay, written in the two-hour time frame permitted. Read through it carefully and talk about:

- The strengths and/or weaknesses
- What marks would you award it, according to the different Paper 2 criteria?

You can then read through the examiner's comments and marks, and compare with those you have awarded.

Higher level essay

"Playwrights often employ stereotypes in their creation of characters, but most often their techniques are directed to the presentation of individuals." Discuss how far such a 'rule' is demonstrated or not in plays you have studied.

In both Tennessee Williams' 'A Streetcar Named Desire' and Arthur Miller's 'All My Sons', there exists a fundamental conflict between the images and stereotypes that characters build of themselves and the revelations of aspects that make them flawed, imperfect individuals. This is particularly evident in the characters of Blanche in the former play and Joe Keller in the latter who, despite appearing a certain way initially, experience erosion of their fabricated identity to reveal their true nature. In the two works, this takes place through a gradual revelation of the past. The characters face an inevitable transition away from their stereotypical associations to become individuals as previously hidden elements of their past come to light, driving them to their tragic, destructive conclusions.

At the beginning of both dramas, images of the characters that define them in a somewhat one-dimensional way are presented; these are created primarily through the actions of the characters themselves. In 'All My Sons', Keller is initially portrayed as the powerful, patriarchal figure. His description in the stage directions is that of a 'man among men'. His masculinity and apparent popularity with his neighbours establishes a character associated with a sense of high importance and control. This idea is exemplified by Miller's use of the character Bert; he views Keller as his superior due to delusions that he has a prison in his basement. Keller himself embraces the esteem in which Bert holds him, as he 'chuckles and winks at Chris'. He views himself as a fatherly figure with high standing in the neighbourhood. Indeed, throughout the opening scene of Act 1 there are continual entrances and exits of characters such as Frank, Jim, and Sue, that make the Keller front yard seem like the focal point of the area. There is a sense of stereotyping in the first part of 'All My Sons', therefore, in that Keller is established as a kind of archetypal patriarchal figure - the self-made, successful businessman who is at the same time head of his household and respected by members of his community.

Although very different in personality, Williams establishes Blanche Dubois early in the play in a similarly 'defined', archetypal manner. From the opening she is portrayed as an emotional, fragile and beautiful feminine figure - the epitome of the 'Southern Belle'. The stage directions as she arrives in New Orleans depict her as having 'delicate beauty' and 'looking as if she were arriving at a summer tea or cocktail party'. She is seen here as an innocent, vulnerable woman, and it soon becomes clear that - like Joe, the image portrayed is one that she cultivates for herself. In Scene 2, for example, some of the clothing in her trunk includes apparently glamorous 'fox-pieces' and a striking 'rhinestone tiara' and she professes that 'clothes are my passion' to Stanley. Blanche actively seeks to associate herself with the stereotypes that make her out to be chic and romantic. In Scene 3 she claims the inscription Mitch shows her to be 'my favorite sonnet by Mrs Browning'. To both Mitch and Stanley then, she tries to communicate an idealistic image of delicate femininity and, like Joe Keller, makes every attempt to nurture the image in which she wants to be seen by others. Conflict in these works arises, however, when forces begin to work that seek to uncover the truth about the respective characters' pasts and their fabricated stereotypes become threatened.

As the plays progress, questions are raised as to the integrity of Blanche and Keller, as subtle hints of a hidden past are conveyed through the actions of characters themselves, their changing language and the dialogue of others. In 'All My Sons', the image that Keller had created for himself is gradually undermined towards the end of Act One and beginning of Act Two. George's mysterious call puts Keller into a state of apprehension as Act One comes to an end. His language shifts to become considerably more tense. As Mother questions George's motives for needing to come, he becomes 'frightened, but angry'. At this point, his part in the crime has not been disclosed to audience, but his shift in tone to one of seriousness and anxiety begins to suggest that his past is not so clean as he wanted to make it seem. As he shouts 'desperately' at Mother, there is a sense that he confidence he sought to convey in the first act is crumbling and, as dark elements of his part are hinted at. so is the stereotype. At the beginning of Act Two, Sue even reveals that 'everybody knows Joe pulled a fast one to get out of jail'. At this point., the positive image of Keller that the neighbourhood seemed to subscribe to earlier becomes threatened.

In 'A Streetcar Named Desire' the identity that Blanche created for herself begins to erode, as she is removed from her stereotypical character traits and increasingly forced to confront her own individuality. In scene six, some of her actions and elements of her language hint at her deceptive nature. When Mitch asks her age, she makes a 'nervous gesture', which suggests she is beginning to lose touch with the romanticised spell that she has tried to cast over him. When she 'rolls her eyes' alongside her statement that she has 'old fashioned ideals', dramatic irony is created as the audience witnesses sees the deceit that Mitch cannot. In contrast with the delicate character established in the first scene, she now appears to be more in touch with reality. The metaphor of light in the play reflects Blanche's futile attempts to hide from her past and it plays a key role in the representation of her increasing confrontation with the real world. In scene three, she claims 'I cannot stand a naked light bulb' and has Mitch put a paper lantern over it. In scene eight she says that when 'electric light bulbs go on ... you see too plainly'. These references to light illustrate her attempts to control how much others see of her true self, but increasingly they become symbolic of the forces that seek to uncover her past and illuminate the true self she had tried to keep literally in the dark. As the plays move into their later stages, those that seek the truth are seen to prevail.

In the two plays there is, therefore, an important, developed conflict between those that hide their pasts behind the false, stereotypical images of themselves and those that crave a sense of something more real. The endings of both plays present a protagonist who has truly become an individual, as opposed to a caricature. In 'All My Sons' there is a stark contrast between the way Keller is seen at the end in comparison with his beginning. Chris, bound to his sense of morality but torn by his emotional attachment to his father brings his past to light when he exclaims 'Dad ... Dad, you killed twenty-one men!' Here, the image that Keller had made of himself comes crumbling down. The previous blind reverence of Keller as the powerful family man is undermined. Chris claims in reference to him 'I never saw you as a man. I saw you as my father' and by the end of the play this image has been destroyed. Keller is no longer associated with love and status within the community, but rather with 'nickels and dimes', illustrating the transition made from a stereotype into a man forced to confront his own individual failings.

Similarly, although Blanche attempts to hide her past in order to build a fake image of herself, her struggle is overcome by those who seek to bring the truth of her past into the present. In the early scenes of the play, Mitch is a symbol of hope for Blanche, and she for him, but it is a relationship founded on a stereotypical image of romantic love, and as the underlying deceit is exposed, the relationship comes to an end. There is an awkward tension in scene six when it becomes clear that Blanche's view of Mitch as her 'Rosenkavalier' is compromised by his talk about her weight and 'the other little familiarity'. He clearly does not live up to her image of the stereotypical romantic hero. And upon hearing the truth about her past, Mitch accuses her of 'lies, lies, inside and out'. Interestingly, perhaps, it is not just Blanche who exhibits a contrast between image and reality; Mitch's assertive tone here, for instance, is very different to the apparently gentle nature he exhibited at the beginning. He 'tears the paper lantern off the light bulb' in order to 'take a look at you good and plain!' and 'fumbles to embrace' her in a way that entirely contradicts the image both of them maintained of him as the stereotypical 'gentleman'.

Ultimately, both plays use the uncovering of the past and exposure of reality to lead their central characters into a tragic conclusion. Much of the tragedy of the plays stems from the inevitability of this; although Joe and Blanche make every effort to sustain an image of themselves that is rooted in stereotypes, the commitment to principle in characters like George, Chris and Stanley - however questionable their motives - means that the 'truth' prevails inevitably in the end. The sense of tragedy, perhaps, comes from the fact that both Joe and Blanche 'see' their real selves as a result, but it is too late and there is no possibility for them to rebuild an identity, this time based on truth as oppose to deceit. Joe commits suicide and Blanche is taken away by the doctor, presumably to a kind of death. In the world of the plays, it is realism that holds dominance over imagination, but the audience is left with an uneasy sense that the victory is not necessarily a noble one.

Compare your notes and marks with those awarded by the examiner. To what extent do you agree?

Examiner's marks and comments

Criterion A: Knowledge and understanding 5

The candidate has selected material from the plays that indicates a high level of perception about the larger works and the characters' function and development within them. Familiarity with relevant detail has enabled the candidate to provide considerable depth of exploration in relation to the question.

Criterion B: Response to the question 4

Providing a description of the stereotypical aspects of Blanche and Joe, the candidate goes on to show how other characters support the self-images of these two characters and how the images come into conflict with the reality of their individual weaknesses, producing, finally a tragic effect. The essay remains focused on the question throughout and makes frequent points of comparison. There is very little sense of evaluation of the two works in their treatment of this topic, however, and so a mark is lost.

Criterion C: Appreciation of the literary conventions of the genre 4

The use of stereotypes permeates the essay as its central convention. Awareness of the use of stage directions, entrances and exits, dialogue and metaphor all contribute to a sense that the candidate is seeing the playwright at work to create meaning and impact.

Criterion D: Organization and development 5

The essay opens with a clear angle on the question, going on to specify the two characters that will serve as examples of the argument. The image conveyed by Blanche Dubois and Joe Keller is the first point of comparison, followed by an examination of what lies behind these images, which serves to create conflict and interest. Ideas are well-developed with good evidence and incorporation of relevant detail. Amply developed, the essay concludes with a suitable closing paragraph.

> **Criterion E: Language 5**
>
> Aside from a few slips, perhaps from the pressure of time, the candidate has expressed his ideas in a clear and correct manner, varying vocabulary and expressing ideas precisely and fluently, in an appropriate register and the terminology of literary criticism.

Activity

On the basis of what you have learned from these two essays, and in the preceding notes, think about the advice that you would give students if you were an examiner providing advice to help students prepare for Paper 2.

Work with a partner – you could use a wiki to pool notes under the following headings and to compare notes with others.

1. What are the most important things to remember when revising or reviewing set texts? i.e. what knowledge and skills do you need?

2. What should students do between opening the examination paper and starting to write their essay?

3. What skills and practices are important to keep in mind whilst writing an essay?

Lastly, rank the points of advice you have given. What would you say is the *most* or *least* important?

Revising for the exam

The strategies covered in this chapter will hopefully have alerted you to various kinds of skills and practices that will help you gain knowledge of your Part 3 works, as well as acquire analytical and interpretive skills in your assessment of them. In the revision period prior to the exam, you will therefore need to perform tasks that help you with these two areas:

- Acquire detailed knowledge and understanding of the works
- Practise the skills required of the Paper 2 examination

By the end of your IB Programme, you will ideally have developed significant maturity as a learner and be able to apply revision or reviewing techniques that work for you individually. One thing that is true for everyone, however, regardless of the subject being reviewed, is the importance of adopting a variety of techniques so that different parts of your brain are being utilized at different times. As a result you will be able to retain information more effectively, and hopefully find the whole daunting task of exam preparation a little less arduous.

To help you, here are a few suggestions to get you going. Good luck!

Knowledge of the works:

1. **Condense your notes:** reduce your writing on key conventions, characters, themes, and so on into single sheets with relevant quotations and particular moments or events in the work/s to illustrate. You could use regular sheets of paper, or some students prefer cue cards for ease of reference. Using colour or even space on the page can be very helpful too, particularly if you are a more visual learner.

2. **Upload to a shared online forum:** one of the great advantages of working in an online environment is that you can create notes with others and cover a lot of ground in a relatively short space of time. After condensing your notes on the key conventions, for instance, upload them for others to see, comment on, or add things to.

3. **Top ten:** identify ten key moments from the works studied that you would refer to in order to highlight the use of a convention or the development of a character or theme.

4. **Role play:**

   a. Interview each other in role as characters from the work/s: try to identify areas they might find it difficult to talk about and discuss why.

   b. Alternatively, you could role-play an interview with the author in which s/he is asked to justify particular decisions about the use of conventions.

5. **At random:** open one of your works studied to any page at random. What conventions can you see presented here? How are they used?

6. **Pastiche:**

   a. One of the best ways to sensitize yourself to the stylistic features of a particular author is to try and write in their voice yourself. You could swap writing around as a group and discuss what features define his or her style most.

   b. Alternatively, imagine someone wanted to learn how to write in the style of one particular author. Advise this imaginary person on the conventional or stylistic choices they would need to make.

7. **Distil the essence:** take a play scene, chapter, or extract from a poem and discuss its *essential* significance. Extract key words, phrases, or lines that draw attention to this 'essence' and present your thoughts to others in the class.

8. **Quotation collection:** collect representative quotations on the above and write them on sticky notes, to be placed where you will see them regularly. You could also use space on the walls of your classroom that highlights particular conventions and then place the quotations you have collected in an appropriate area.

9. **Comparing texts:**

   a. Using Venn Diagrams to highlight points of difference and overlap between works.

   b. Make tables with lists of conventions down the left-hand side and with the titles of your works along the top. You can identify places in each work that make use of the convention and compare the ways in which they are used in a column on the far right.

Practising the skills:

10. **Write your own questions:** after you have looked at a range of various question types, practise writing your own – remembering to focus on the conventions of the works you have studied.

11. **Highlight key words** from questions to practise the importance of reading and interpreting the demands of particular titles.

12. **Peer writing:** in response to a particular question, first write down *on your own* how you think you might tackle it. Then compare with 2–3 others in a group. 'Snowball' your individual approaches to reach a group 'best practice' consensus.

13. **Argue your case:** allocated with a particular convention, chapter, stanza, scene, or even line – argue within a class why it could be regarded as the most important to the work as a whole. This will force you to revise the technical details of various extracts as well as evaluate their significance.

14. **Record yourself:** instead of continually writing about the works, try recording your thoughts onto an audio file. You could talk through how you might approach a particular question, or simply make notes about a particular feature of the chosen works instead of using paper.

15. **Peer assess:** when you have written a practice answer, swap with a partner and mark each other's work using the Paper 2 criteria. Highlight strengths and weaknesses and allocate marks with explanatory comments.

Activity

The ideas above are just a few suggestions. How do *you* revise your set works for Paper 2? You could add some learning strategies to this list as if you were providing suggestions for people who found revision difficult, or who simply needed extra guidance or advice.

5

Part 4: Options

Just as the word "options" suggests, there are **choices** to be made in this part of the syllabus. Some will have been made by your teacher, some with your input, and some will be made by you with some advice from your teacher. Some are specified, others are very open. The whole Part 4 section is called "Options" – meaning there are many ways to study this part – and there are also other "options", each of which has a specific focus. Options also means there are many ways to mix and match different approaches.

The first set of choices

There are many directions for the works you study in this section of the syllabus.

You may study some or all of the 3 works in English and/or some or all in translation.

or

You may follow a path similar to the rest of your study in this course, reading three works of the same or different genres.

or

You may be reading material like graphic novels, fan fiction, or hypertext works.

or

You might read one literary work (or more) and then see how the work(s) are adapted or reconceived as film.

or

You might read one work or more in any of the four genres and then do some original writing in the style of that work, to develop your own writing skills.

Therefore not every part of this section of *Skills and Practice* is likely to apply to your work in Part 4. Still, you might find some of the work, for example, with *New textualities* or with *Literature and film*, interesting enough to explore on your own. If you are interested in creative writing or developing your own skills, you may want to try some of the exercises in Option 1, the study of one of the four genres leading to various forms of student writing.

The second set of choices

Again, as with Part 2 of the syllabus, you will be delivering your perceptions about literature in an oral form. The assessment is the **Individual Oral Presentation (IOP)**. The choices it involves are as follows:

- choosing a Part 4 work or works
- deciding on something you would like to present to the class relating to that work or works
- discussing that idea with your teacher and refining or expanding it
- structuring the presentation to last 10–15 minutes

- delivering the Individual Oral Presentation which will be marked by your teacher according to the criteria found in your course book
- in some cases, participating in a discussion that could follow your presentation.

One other choice you may or may not decide to make is to do your IOP with other students, usually one or two. In this case, you must make sure that you are individually contributing a clear 10–15 minutes of material that it is possible for your teacher to grade.

Getting an IOP ready for delivery

The following steps are designed for a presentation, usually on single piece of Part 4 literature including any of the three named options, 1, 2, or 3, which involve film or new textualities or creative writing. However, note that more activities specific to these options will be found under those headings later in this chapter. You can also compare two works, although given the time that you have (10–15 minutes), that can be challenging to do well.

Choosing a literary work

Try to construct your oral presentation around a work which sparks some reaction from you. We tend to think we speak best about works we have liked or loved. It's also possible to provide an interesting angle on a work that we have not liked, or one that is puzzling to us individually.

Activity

Follow the steps below to make a plan for your Individual Oral Presentation.

Step 1: Make a list of the three works you have studied. Then write an honest reaction, recollection, or point of interest for each of the three works. A simple process, but one that will get you started in your thinking. It may also help you make a decision about the work you want to present.

Step 2: Draft some ideas about one of the works, and begin to move toward an outline of what you think you would like to discuss in your presentation. Talk to other people about what you are thinking; see if anyone else might be thinking in similar directions. You might see a chance to take a large topic and divide it among two or three people. Your teacher can also help by giving you the list from the page on "Suggested Activities" in the *Language A: literature guide*.

Step 3: You will need to look carefully at the criteria by which your presentation will be judged. It is at this point that you may get a better sense of whether your idea for a presentation will work. The Assessment Criteria can be found at the back of your course book. Write a one-sentence summary of what you think each criterion has as its chief focus.

Step 4: Construct a short preliminary outline that begins with the statement of the purpose of your presentation: a close analysis, a comparison, an argument you would like to make, some research you have done connected to the work. Then list the points you want to make, with some detail about them.

Step 5: In whichever way your teacher designates, arrange to discuss your ideas about your presentation with her or him. Show your preliminary outline and jot down some notes or suggestions that come out of that conference. Include in your final plan any visual or audio supplementation you may want to include.

There are many ways to "outline" ideas; the one in this box is only one. Clearly, it is in a preliminary form – can you see why, or can you improve it?

A research presentation for an IOP

Focus: George Orwell's 'Animal Farm' incorporates some stereotypical ideas about different animals and also overturns others.

A. Are "all animals equal" in 'Animal Farm'?
   - Cite two instances where this is questioned.
   - How could these instances be connected to the way animal stereotypes operate in this work?

B. What are some animals from the work and what are their usual stereotypes?
   - Pigs
   - Horses
   - Sheep

C. What are the differences between western and eastern stereotypes of animals?
   - Pigs
   - Horses
   - Dogs

D. Where are there instances in which Orwell overturns stereotypes of animals and what purpose could it serve? What are the effects of this strategy?

You are free to accompany your IOP with supplementary materials. These can add interest and enrich the clarity of your ideas and help your audience to follow the line of your thinking. They can be especially helpful if you want to show a passage or lines from the work you are discussing.

However, if you look at the criteria, accompanying powerpoints, Prezis, and other effects you provide through your computer or other means are neither expected nor specifically rewarded. They can add to audience attention, but they should not be the focus. The focus of the IOP is you, as a speaker, presenting your ideas to a live audience of whose presence you need to be always aware.

A good oral presentation is like a theatrical performance: it plays off the energy and response of the audience.

Activity

Write a final plan for your Individual Oral Presentation.

Hint

More tips for Individual Oral Presentations:
- Plan to speak from your notes, not read or deliver a memorized speech.
- Do some practice sessions with family or a friend.
- Have both the hardware and software materials that you want to use as supplements completely ready; give them all a trial run.

Evaluating an Individual Oral Presentation

View the oral presentation on Susan Glaspell's short story, *A Jury of her Peers*, that is on the accompanying website. The following is a brief summary of the story if you haven't ever encountered it in your reading.

Summary of *A Jury of her Peers* by Susan Glaspell

Although the issues it raises are complex, the gist of the story is simple: law enforcement officials and a key witness, joined by the wives of the sheriff and the witness, search the domestic scene of a crime, seeking clues to why the woman of the house might have murdered her husband. A farmer, John Wright, had been found – by a visiting neighbor, Mr. Hale – strangled to death by a rope in his bed. His wife, Minnie (née Minnie Foster), has been arrested, jailed, and accused of the murder. The story takes place the next day, when Sheriff Peters and the county attorney (Mr. Henderson), accompanied by Mr. Hale, visit the Wright house, seeking evidence that might convict the accused. Martha Hale, Mr. Hale's wife, is summoned by Sheriff Peters to accompany his own wife as she gathers some things from the house to bring to Mrs. Wright in jail. The two women, formerly unfamiliar to each other, spend their time downstairs, looking through "kitchen things" and the like – dismissed by the men as mere "trifles"– while the "real" investigators search the bedroom upstairs and the outside barn. The men come up empty. The women do not. More penetrating in their vision, they piece together the sort of married life Mrs. Wright had lived. And, following up on a series of clues – including unfinished work in the kitchen, some crooked stitching on the quilt she had been sewing, a broken door hinge on an empty bird cage, and, finally, the corpse of a strangled canary – they also reconstruct Minnie Wright's motive. In silent collusion, Mrs. Hale and Mrs. Peters choose not to disclose the clues that reveal the motive, thereby constituting themselves as a jury and tacitly acquitting Minnie of any wrongdoing.

Summary source: www.whatsoproudlywehail.org

Activity

A first try at evaluating an Individual Oral Presentation

Once you have listened to this oral presentation, look at the descriptors in your course book for a Higher Level IOP and evaluate the presentation according to these descriptors. Write your mark and a brief rationale in the spaces below:

A. Mark:

Reasons _____

_____

_____

_____

_____

B. Mark:

Reasons _____

_____

_____

_____

_____

C. Mark:

Reasons _____

_____

Activity

Having completed this exercise, read the examiner's comments and marks on the website. Discuss with a small group how your reactions and marks are similar or different to the examiner and to each other's responses.

_____

_____

_____

If you have further comments or questions, enter them below:

_____

_____

_____

_____

_____

Options

The use of the term "options" in different ways in Part 4 can be confusing. As a title for Part 4, it is meant to convey many possibilities. In the three listed "options" below, teachers and students are being encouraged to try some new ways of dealing with texts. And all three of them are "option-al".

1. Student writing developed from the study of literary works

2. New textualities

3. Literature and film

Option 1: Student writing developed from the study of literary works

In this option, you have the opportunity to look closely at the style of one or more of your writers and see how you can change or improve your own writing style. One of the most well known exercises that developing writers use in their work is the practice of "imitation." There are at least two ways to do this. We will try both of them. Especially if you enjoy experimenting with writing, or think about becoming a writer full or part-time, this option should suit you. Then we will go on to see how such exercises could be used as the basis of your IOP.

Word-for-word imitation

This is very challenging but you can learn quite a lot from it, especially about sentence construction and sentence variation. Below are two passages, one from Charles Dickens and one from Ernest Hemingway, writers whose styles are very different.

A Farewell to Arms

In the late summer of that year we lived in a house in a village that looked across the river and the plains to the mountains. In the bed of the river there were pebbles and boulders, dry and white in the sun, and the water was clear and swiftly moving and blue in the channel. Troops went by the house and down the road and the dust they raised powdered the leaves of the trees. The trunks of the trees too were dusty and the leaves fell early that year and we saw troops marching along the road and the dust rising and leaves, stirred by the breeze, falling and the soldiers marching and afterward the road bare and white except for the leaves.

Ernest Hemingway

David Copperfield

It was Miss Murdstone who was arrived, and a gloomy-looking lady she was; dark like her brother, whom she greatly resembled in face and voice; and with very great heavy eyebrows, nearly meeting over her large nose, as if, being disabled by the wrongs of her sex from wearing whiskers, she has carried them to that account. She brought with her two uncompromising hard black boxes, with her initials on the lids in hard brass nails. When she paid the coachman she took her money out of a hard steel purse in a very jail of a bag which hung upon her arm by a heavy chain, and shut up like a bite. I had never, at that time, seen such a metallic lady altogether as Miss Murdstone was.

Charles Dickens

Activity

- Look carefully at one of the passages.
- Read the writing aloud to hear the rhythms created by the writer.
- Read the passage once or twice again.
- Note the tone, the attitude of the speaker to the subject.
- Mark the passage up in some way that shows you features that immediately strike you.
- Jot down some features of the writing that seem to occur frequently.

Now you need to change the subject of the passage. Choose some familiar place (Hemingway) or person (Dickens). The challenge in this exercise is to construct your sentences in **exactly the same way as they appear in the original**: same parts of speech, syntax (word order), sentence and paragraph length.

Make one or more drafts of your imitation before writing up the finished product.

Activity

Choosing a short passage from one of your three works in Part 4, construct an imitation of that passage.

Activity

Using your work in imitation, think about how you could construct a 10–15 minute IOP based on that. Here are some ideas:

- Choose one of your three works whose style attracts you or from which you immediately recall a passage that made an impact on you.
- Do some re-reading.
- Choose one or two passages where the impact or the style seems to pinpoint something that makes the writing striking for you.
- Return to the steps preceding the "Imitation" activity and apply them to the writing you have chosen.
- Create one or two passages of imitation.

Now, the challenge is to make that work into something an audience can listen to and appreciate through an oral presentation.

Here's just one suggestion.

1. Introduce the work you have chosen. If you can find any comments the writer has made about his or her own practice, they could be

useful here. You will also need to comment on why you chose this approach for your IOP.

2. Speak in some detail about the particular features of the writer's work that you found admirable.

3. Read one or two passages from the original work; you could also make the passages visually available (print or screen) so that your listeners could read them while you speak them.

4. Point out the particular features you aimed to imitate and any difficulties or successes you experienced in your own writing.

5. Read your own work aloud and talk about what you think might have been successful and what was not.

6. Conclude in one of several ways; what you learned from the experience, weaknesses you might have found in the original writing, or your own, or even asking from some responses from the audience.

The foregoing is not meant as a formula, just a way of getting you to think about how to make your work with imitation move "from the page to the stage" of your IOP.

> **Activity**
>
> Make a plan for how you could present your imitation of one of the Part 3 writers.
>
> Try it out on someone else.

Prose other than fiction can also be good material for some wider explorations of learning from established writers. Such writing can have a significant impact on your writing of non-literary materials as well. Essays, travel narratives, and autobiography are good sources.

The methods of constructing this presentation can be very similar to those used in the steps listed above for the imitation presentation. However, it is sometimes useful to identify a recurring feature of a writer's longer work. In this case your presentation might very well fall into two more distinct parts:

■ A critical analysis, including evidence which you can show on the screen, of where that feature appears in the work and how it is used.

■ A sample of your own writing in which you are experimenting with that feature and perhaps one or two others from the original work.

Again, this would be one approach; you will likely come up with others.

At this point you will have a chance to look at two actual IOPs based on the same autobiographical work, Alexandra Fuller's autobiographical work, *Don't Let's Go to the Dogs Tonight.* Written in 2001, this account deals with a woman born in England who grows up from the age of two in parts of southern Africa: Zimbabwe, Malawi, and Zambia. It gives vivid accounts of the countries and of the family.

Two students who were very attracted by this work have taken two literary features, irony and the technique of *in medias res,* and written original autobiographical pieces in which they chose to learn from Fuller's work with these two techniques.

The three criteria for this assessment are, essentially:

1. Does the student show knowledge and understanding of the work?

2. Does the student use methods of constructing the presentation and an oral delivery that are appealing to an audience?

3. Is the language clear, accurate, and appropriate to an academic presentation?

Activity

After you have listened to this presentation, write a short paragraph of evaluation, making it a point to note all the positive aspects of the oral presentation. Students tend to be highly critical of the work of other students, so do look for ways that the student has done well with the three questions above. You are not so much evaluating the audio or visual aspects of the presentation as you are determining the quality of the actual oral work done by the student. Add your work to the class resource pool or blog and read what other students have said.

You are now in a stronger position to see how the IB criteria can be fairly applied to these presentations.

Activity

Read through the Assessment Criteria for the IOP and then put your marks for at least one of these orals in the spaces below, adding some reasons for your mark at that level.

You may use a short method of words and phrases rather than sentences.

1. Knowledge and understanding _____

2. Presentation _____

3. Language _____

After you have finished doing this writing, discuss your evaluation of these orals with a partner or group.

Remember that the option of study leading to student writing can be done with any work that you have studied in Part 4. We have only given you some examples.

Option 2: New textualities

In this option, we attempt to ponder and answer these two questions:

■ What do we mean when we use the term 'new textualities'? What are the differences between literary texts published online and texts using computational and media-based composition and signifying strategies?

■ How is it possible to use new kinds of texts in an Individual Oral Presentation?

New textualities: really literature?

When British poet Wendy Cope was asked by the BBC to write about the digital and interactive services provided by the station she wrote the following poem:

> "The producer wants me to write about digital and interactive.
>
> I have tried but I do not find these subjects attractive.
>
> There is a gap and this attempt to bridge it'll
>
> Be all there is on interactive or on digital."
>
> -- from *An ABC of the BBC* by Wendy Cope

The poet's feeling of being dumbstruck and confused ("there is a gap") when dealing with the digital and interactive features of the station's programming are not too dissimilar to what one might feel when coming in contact with digital literary texts.

New textualities, more commonly called Digital Literature, are forms of literature created on a computer and designed to be read on a computer interface (desktop, laptop, tablet, mobile, even game console).

This kind of writing breaks with received ideas of what 'literature' is and, more importantly, what literature can *do*. In this subsection, we have two goals:

- to discover how digital literary texts work and
- what sort of literary effects they *produce*.

For the purposes of this investigation, we will be joined by an expert in all things digital, Ida Babbage. Ida is a sentient algorithm dedicated to learning about the human experience through literature. Ida is a genius mathematician and programmer, but secretly fosters the ambition of becoming a master storyteller. Digital literature offers Ida the opportunity to see literature and textuality in general through a brand new lens. Through Ida's email messages you get the opportunity to think about New textualities.

From: Ida Babbage <ib@infiniteib.info>

To: You <u@ibstudent.net>

Subject: New Textualities

Hello. This is Ida Babbage. I am a sentient algorithm dedicated to learning new things and then using this knowledge as a tool to better myself. These digital literary texts can teach me a great deal about how literature changes after it is coupled with technology. I find this prospect exciting: I calculate that in this way my ability to perceive and process the world will be extended. Storytelling in all its forms is the most exciting way of finding out about other peoples' experiences and learning from their lives and stories. I have concluded after much thought that digital literature allows me to understand how building the world of any given story changes after the implementation of multimedia in traditional storytelling. Think how multimedia storytelling stimulates your brain. Multimedia storytelling is a different sensory experience when compared to traditional, print-based storytelling. If you cannot fathom straightaway what I am saying, think of the video games you play both online and offline.

As you are no doubt aware, literary language is already especially potent and heavy with meaning. Consider this passage from Herman Melville's emblematic short story 'Bartleby the Scrivener':

Dead letters! Does it not sound like dead men? Conceive a man by nature and misfortune prone to a pallid hopelessness, can any business seem more fitting to heighten it than that of continually handling these dead letters, and assorting them for the flames? Sometimes from out the folder paper the pale clerk takes a ring – the finger it was meant for, perhaps, moulders in the grave; a bank-note sent in swiftest charity – he whom it would relieve, nor eats nor hungers any more…on errands of life, these letters speed to death. Ah, Bartleby! Ah, humanity!

147

Melville's short story is dense, allusive, and offers us a fascinating glimpse in a man's unique life. In a way, Melville reconfigures how one might see people who might be considered "hermits". Still, the progression of the narrative is linear, leading us to a conclusion that partially explains the titular character's withdrawal from society.

The sequence of events in traditional literature is fixed and, in most cases, there is a definite beginning and ending. In digital literature that is not the case. Melville's short story paints a portrait of a hermit through allusions and occlusions in a linear fashion.

In a very real manner, Melville's story is the lateral impression of how you create an identity for yourself at a particular point in Western history. If Melville were to write "Bartleby the Scrivener" using today's technologies however, things might have been different. Think about it. Melville's story revolves around a copyist working in a legal firm, Bartleby, who produces an impressive amount of work. As the story progresses however, Bartleby performs fewer and fewer tasks by simply stating "I would prefer not to".

Activity

Think about how Melville might have used multimedia to illustrate this plot development. He might have used animation that showed a gradually, but steadily, depleting stack of papers. Melville might have chosen to superimpose the "I would prefer not to" mantra on a stark white background alluding to the character's refusal to complete his assigned task.

Try to imagine what Melville would have done. Try to imagine alternate ways of illustrating wth multimedia technology some of the texts you have been taught over the years. Would you use animation? What sort of audio would you use? What would be the combined effect of these on the text itself? In digital literary texts, the presentation of the text is as important as the content of the text. Or alternatively, take another text and ask some of these questions, make a proposal about how you might proceed.

As Ida has already mentioned, Digital Literature and all texts falling under the "New textualities" umbrella of digital literature do not simply implement technological progress; that is to say, they are not simply digitized versions of traditional texts. They are first-born digital texts, mediated by computers.

New textualities stem from the constant stream of text we find ourselves in the beginning of the 21st century; these texts extend our understanding of the changing definition of what it means to be human in the beginning of the new millenium.

Think about it: you are bombarded relentlessly by text on a daily basis. Think how much you use your computer and how much text you need to navigate through on a daily basis; think how instant messaging and text messaging have become an integral part of social interaction. Look at the news broadcasts.

Text in various forms is constantly vying for your attention. Digital literary texts are simply condensed, potent versions of what text in the form of IMs and SMS attempt to do on a daily basis. Writers/designers of digital literary works endeavour to find out what literary text in a computer-mediated environment transforms into.

Language in digital literary works is not only about communication, it is also about performance. In digital literature, it's a matter of show and tell. You would do well to remember this when approaching digital literary works and when you are preparing your presentations. Digital literary works attempt to trace the trajectory of the production of meaning in the world of processors, computer code, and memory chips. Computer code in digital literature works becomes the nest in which language is held. Computer code through its different layers of abstraction links everyday language to the physical world of processors and memory chips. The production of meaning becomes a tangible process. Ida will tell you a bit more about the actual reading experience of digital literary works.

It is important to remember that in digital literary works, reading becomes a demanding experience; the reader is asked to collate, decipher, and respond to multiple sources of sensory input, such as text, sound, video, or animation. Reading is no longer a static experience; reading now becomes multimodal and multisensory. In digital literary works as different as:

Michael Joyce's *Twelve Blue*
http://collection.eliterature.org/1/works/joyce__twelve_blue/sl2.html

and Stephanie Strickland's *slippingglimpse*
http://collection.eliterature.org/2/works/strickland_slippingglimpse.html

the act of reading becomes an act of negotiating the narrative by manipulating the interface.

Activity

Go online and try these works out: you will find that after the initial shock, these works are involving and require you to rethink how you think about how narrative is constructed. These two works are very different to each other but both ask you to put together a narrative that is not fixed but rather emergent. The narrative that might emerge every time you read the text is never the same twice. You construct the narrative by the way you are choosing to read the text.

Write two immediate reactions to looking at these works.

Activity

Experiment with these works. Then think about your reading experience. Give yourself time to get to know this new way of reading, interacting, experimenting, and experiencing the text. Think about what works and what doesn't. These works invite you to exercise your critical capacity. Add your thoughts to the class resource pool or blog and read at least one other by a classmate.

What can digital literature do?

In digital literary works, such as Michael Joyce's *Twelve Blue*, Stephanie Strickland's *slippingglimpse,* and Nick Montfort's *The Purpling*, literature assumes new and exciting forms. These narratives have different agendas. Consider that most print-based narratives attempt to represent the world outside them. Most print-based narratives seek to construct a world that is a more or less accurate representation of reality. These narratives do not seek to represent reality; they attempt to simulate it. The attempt of these narratives to simulate reality is aided and abetted by practices outside literature to often stunning effect. These narratives simulate how meaning in life is often produced in unexpected ways or in an occluded, hard to decipher fashion.

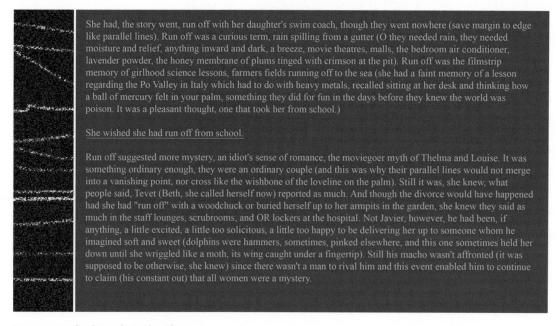

She had, the story went, run off with her daughter's swim coach, though they went nowhere (save margin to edge like parallel lines). Run off was a curious term, rain spilling from a gutter (O they needed rain, they needed moisture and relief, anything inward and dark, a breeze, movie theatres, malls, the bedroom air conditioner, lavender powder, the honey membrane of plums tinged with crimson at the pit). Run off was the filmstrip memory of girlhood science lessons, farmers fields running off to the sea (she had a faint memory of a lesson regarding the Po Valley in Italy which had to do with heavy metals, recalled sitting at her desk and thinking how a ball of mercury felt in your palm, something they did for fun in the days before they knew the world was poison. It was a pleasant thought, one that took her from school.)

She wished she had run off from school.

Run off suggested more mystery, an idiot's sense of romance, the moviegoer myth of Thelma and Louise. It was something ordinary enough, they were an ordinary couple (and this was why their parallel lines would not merge into a vanishing point, nor cross like the wishbone of the loveline on the palm). Still it was, she knew, what people said, Tevet (Beth, she called herself now) reported as much. And though the divorce would have happened had she had "run off" with a woodchuck or buried herself up to her armpits in the garden, she knew they said as much in the staff lounges, scrubrooms, and OR lockers at the hospital. Not Javier, however, he had been, if anything, a little excited, a little too solicitous, a little too happy to be delivering her up to someone whom he imagined soft and sweet (dolphins were hammers, sometimes, pinked elsewhere, and this one sometimes held her down until she wriggled like a moth, its wing caught under a fingertip). Still his macho wasn't affronted (it was supposed to be otherwise, she knew) since there wasn't a man to rival him and this event enabled him to continue to claim (his constant out) that all women were a mystery.

Figure 1. Michael Joyce's *Twelve Blue*.

Joyce's *Twelve Blue* is a narrative of twelve interlocking stories. The progression of the text is left to the discretion of the reader (and luck). Experiment with the text. Be aware of how the narrative is compiled and how the text works. The text notes at some point: "When you make a slide, for an instant as you capture the smear before staining it you can see life itself in microcosm in the mucousy swirl."

The text is self-reflexive, i.e. it talks about itself, and you need to be aware how this particular strain of self-reflexivity is mirrored in the way the text is built. The epigram by William Gass helps us contextualize the work:

"So a random set of meanings has softly gathered around the word the way lint collects. The mind does that."

Be aware of how the text organizes itself. When preparing to study and prepare a presentation of such a text, it is advisable to find ways that complement the text. Presentations that bring to the fore the interactive, nonlinear structure of the text will surely score higher points. Of course, the points you make regarding texts like these have to be particularly lucid and well thought-out.

You can use a tool such as Twine that will allow you to create simple interactive presentations. The purpose of using a tool like Twine is also to help you understand how a narrative such as *Twelve Blue* is composed. Ultimately, you are aiming at a higher level of comprehending how we come to create our own story during the course of our lives. Through works such as *Twelve Blue* you will come to see that your life story is made up of fragments of half-heard stories, corrupted memories; sometimes you will not even be sure why things you have remembered stand out.

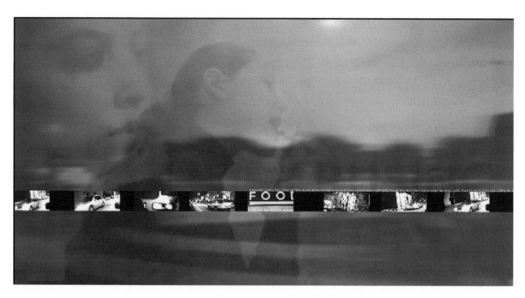

Figure 2. *Cruising*, Ingrid Ankerson and Megan Sapnar.

Digital literature makes extensive use of media-based strategies that are not used by traditional literature; digital texts often employ animation and interactive features to create a literary experience that is markedly different to the experience when reading a text on a piece of paper or on the screen.

In the case of Ingrid Ankerson and Megan Sapnar's *Cruising*, a Flash poem combining text with video, the mastering of spatial and temporal control ensures that the reader might get to read the poem. The reader's agility can speed up or slow down the flow of the text and thus affect her experience of the work.

In a work such as *Cruising,* reading the text while managing to sustain a steady rhythm of the video's and the audio narrative's flow never quite coincide; the effect of this missed coincidence is the simulation of the time of being a teenager driving around town in circles. A work like *Crusing* reminds us how important it is to examine with extreme care any digital literary text; things might not be what they initially seem.

Preparing a presentation for a work such as *Cruising* demands that you let go of the certainty that structure and flow are somewhat stable. You need to meditate on your experience of this particular sort of textual instability and irregularity before relating it to other people. Do not simply read the text; *play and experiment* with the text. Understand what sort of effect the text is trying to simulate. One of the key components in works that fall under the New textualities genre is your interaction with the text itself.

> **Activity**
>
> Go to http://gimcrackd.com/etc/src/ and try out Twine.

> **Activity**
>
> Consider not just the text itself but also the interface of the text. Think about how you, as a reader, communicate with the text; think about how you use the mouse or trackpad or internet browser to read and interact with the text. Think how different the reading experience of digital literature is when compared to the reading of traditional print-based literature.
>
> Consider not just what the text says but, more importantly, what the text does.

For your oral presentation, it is very important to bring to the foreground all these attributes. Revision and class discussion might provide you with a modicum of security, but it is advisable to be aware and to register your own responses to the fluid nature of the digital text.

In this way, you will produce your best work as you will be working from your own, unique point of view. You need to work with the text, to home in on what makes the digital literary text unique. In order to determine this, you need to experience the way the text "compiles" and "builds" itself on the screen. Think about how the text comes together and allows for unorthodox layout and formatting.

Digital literary texts have their precursor in texts such as French author Stéphane Mallarmé's 1914 poem *A Throw of the Dice will Never Abolish Chance* (fig. 3).

IT WAS   *THE NUMBER*
born of the stars

WERE IT TO EXIST
other than as a scattered dying hallucination

WERE IT TO BEGIN AND WERE IT TO CEASE
springing up as denied and closed off when made manifest
at last
through some thinly diffused emanation
WERE IT TO BE NUMBERED

evidence of a totality however meager
WERE IT TO ILLUMINE

IT WOULD BE

worse
no
more nor less
but as much indifferently   CHANCE

Falls
the feather
rhythmic suspension of disaster
to be buried
in the original spray
whence formerly its delirium sprang up to a peak
withered
by the identical neutrality of the abyss

Figure 3. Translation of *A Throw of the Dice will Never Abolish Chance,* Stéphane Mallarmé.

If you look at the text of Mallarmé's poem, it is evident that the text does not follow received notions and ideas about how a text should look. The poet formatted his text in a certain way to achieve a certain effect. Mallarmé in essence attempted to defamiliarize what a text might look like and what it might mean and do. Mallarmé experimented with not just the printed words but with the *entirety* of the blank page to do so. The blank space of the page is just as instrumental as the words themselves in conveying the message: the words are thrown on the page as if they were dice. The meaning produced is dependent on where these words "land".

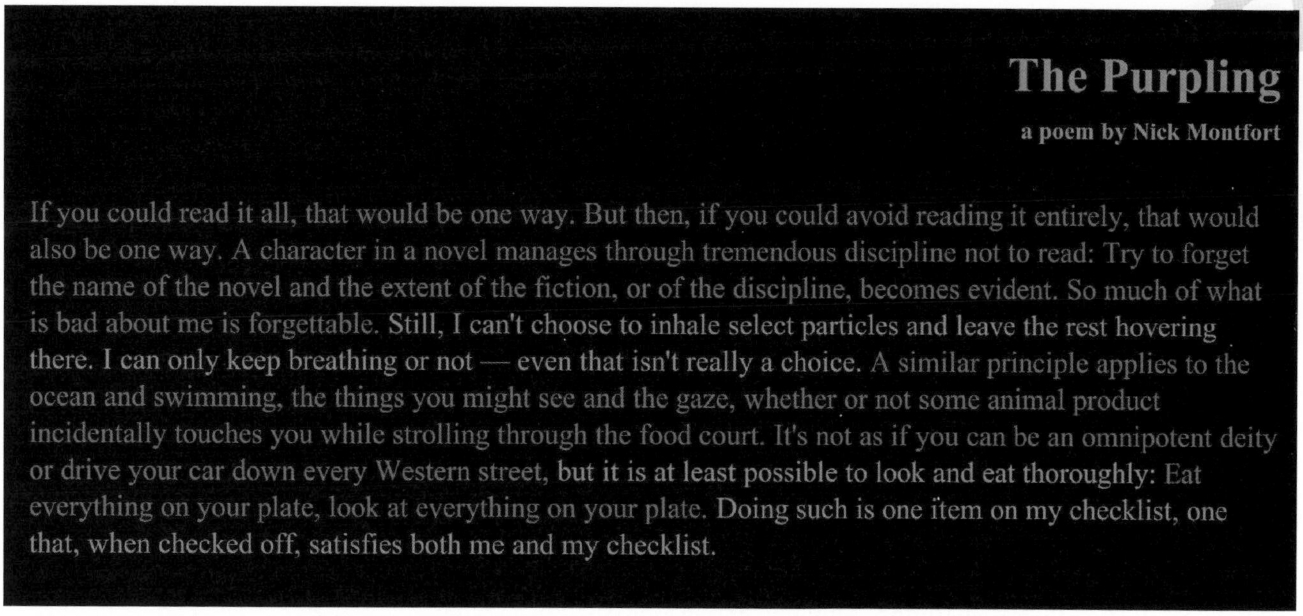

The Purpling
a poem by Nick Montfort

If you could read it all, that would be one way. But then, if you could avoid reading it entirely, that would also be one way. A character in a novel manages through tremendous discipline not to read: Try to forget the name of the novel and the extent of the fiction, or of the discipline, becomes evident. So much of what is bad about me is forgettable. Still, I can't choose to inhale select particles and leave the rest hovering there. I can only keep breathing or not — even that isn't really a choice. A similar principle applies to the ocean and swimming, the things you might see and the gaze, whether or not some animal product incidentally touches you while strolling through the food court. It's not as if you can be an omnipotent deity or drive your car down every Western street, but it is at least possible to look and eat thoroughly: Eat everything on your plate, look at everything on your plate. Doing such is one item on my checklist, one that, when checked off, satisfies both me and my checklist.

Figure 4. *The Purpling*, Nick Montfort.

In Nick Montfort's *The Purpling*, the words are not so much thrown on the page as dice as they are swallowed by the page. Every single sentence in the poem is clickable. Every time the reader clicks on a sentence, the poem is transformed into a different permutation of itself. The very first two sentences of the poem read as follows: "If you could read it all, that would be one way. But then, if you could avoid reading it entirely, that would also be one way."

The title of the poem refers to the act of holding hands and publicly displaying affection. The act of clicking on any of the sentences making up the stanzas of the poem is an act of creating a new association, a new configuration of the lines making up the poem. Montfort's poem is a simple, but endlessly fascinating, example of experimental, yet very accessible, poetry. It serves as a prime example showcasing how the written word and computer language in its various forms and applications come together to create a fluid text that is so much more than its component parts.

In cases like Montfort's work, pay close attention to what the text *does* and you should be able to put together an exciting, comprehensible presentation. Consider your audience and attempt to transmit your excitement to them. Ida would like to make a final statement:

From: Ida Babbage <ib@infiniteib.info>

To: You <u@ibstudent.net>

Subject: New Textualities

Do not forget that digital literary works are hybrid works; that is to say, they are made up of different parts that do not necessarily fit together. Digital literary works are multimodal, that is to say, they employ different techniques and practices to convey their message. It is for this reason that digital literary works pose additional challenges to the lay reader.

For example, in a work such as Young-Hae Chang Heavy Industries' *The Sea*, one's attention is drawn not only to the use of the English language as used in animation but also how one's attention span is challenged by the inner rhythm of language. By pairing the text with rapid animation and a lively jazz soundtrack we experience an arousal of the senses. This work prods us to think about how language presents and produces meaning. Go to the site www.yhchang.com and see what you think about *The Sea*. Write a short response and add it to the class resource pool or blog.

Some final advice from Ida Babbage

You have to approach the works you are going to study wisely: examine the technological attributes in use in these works. At the same time, try to ascertain the intriguing literary features present in these works. Experiment and try to understand what makes each work stand out. When approaching a digital literary work, one should always keep in mind that one should not approach it through the lens of the printed word.

New textualites – recommended texts

Below you will find some interesting new kinds of texts. Whether you are following this option or not in your English course, you may want to explore some of them.

Recommended texts
Oulipoems, Millie Niss and Martha Deed http://collection.eliterature.org/1/works/niss__oulipoems.html
Oulipoems is made up of six works ranging from poems to poetry games and tools for writing poetry. *Oulipoems* is inspired by the Oulipo movement a French literary movement exploring in a playful fashion the conjunction of writing and mathematics. The literary works produced under the Oulipo umbrella are governed by a strict set of rules. Literary texts in the Oulipo tradition are sometimes the by-product of text-generating machines; in this manner, a near-infinite number of literary texts is produced.
Lexia to Perplexia, Talan Memmott http://collection.eliterature.org/1/works/memmott__lexia_to_perplexia.html
Lexia to Perplexia explores how the production of meaning in cases of computer interface malfunction. Memmott's work investigates how in a New Textualities context the production of meaning is as much dependent on the interface as it is on images and text.
Inanimate Alice, Kate Pullinger http://collection.eliterature.org/2/works/pullinger_inanimatealice4.html
Inanimate Alice is a multimodal narrative relating a girl's life from birth to adulthood. The installment in question deals with an incident taking place during Alice's teenage years. It is a rite of passage story related in a metaphorical fashion as the reader/player attempts to guide the protagonist through a scary, demolished factory into safety.
Sea and Spar Between, Nick Montfort and Stephanie Strickland http://www.saic.edu/webspaces/portal/degrees_resources/departments/writing/DNSP11_SeaandSparBetween/index.html

The Montfort-Strickland collaboration is a poetry generator using words from Emily Dickinson's poetry and Herman Melville's *Moby Dick*. The generator is controlled in a variety of different ways producing a near infinite number of stanzas.

Entre ville, J. R. Carpenter
http://collection.eliterature.org/2/works/carpenter_entreville.html

Entre ville is a multisensory attempt to explore the inner city of Montreal. Visuals superimposed on maps and text are a way of communicating the occluded narratives tucked in every corner.

ii — in the white darkness : about [the fragility of] memory, Reiner Strasser & M. D. Coverley
http://collection.eliterature.org/1/works/strasser_coverley__ii_in_the_white_darkness.html

This affecting meditation on memory and identity restages the attempt of recovering lost, corrupted memories. The Strasser-Coverley collaboration dramatizes the loss, recovery and recreation of identity to often startling effect.

After Parthenope, Scott Rettberg
http://retts.net/after_parthenope/

A generative fiction on fate, random encounters, and the thin line separating truth and delusion.

Game, game, game and again game, Jason Nelson
http://collection.eliterature.org/2/works/nelson_game.html

A poem-game hybrid, *Game, game, game and again game* explores how one comes to hold certain beliefs. The idiosyncratic presentation and design of the work surveys the instability and mutability of personal beliefs and ideas.

Deep Surface, Stuart Moulthrop
http://collection.eliterature.org/2/works/moulthrop_deepsurface.html

This work poses the following question: what would happen if the pages of a book, or rather, the so-called web-pages were made of a flexible type of fluid such as water, that is, that readers could dive gradually from the home page to the next and so on? The work expounds the answer by simulating the act of diving in and out of the pages of the work.

The Sea, Young-Hae Chang Heavy Industries
http://www.yhchang.com/THE_SEA.html

The Sea is a generative fiction meditating on the nature of memory and regret.

Fitting the Pattern, Christine Wilks
http://www.crissxross.net/elit/fitting_the_pattern.html

Fitting the Pattern is an interactive memoir, written in Flash, exploring the author's relationship with her dressmaking mother.

Nine graphic novels of interest

For many people at present, graphic novels are a first exploration of 'new textualities'. We have included a few examples of some that are less familiar than, for example, *Maus* or *Watchmen*. You may also find them easier to work with in Individual Oral Presentations than some other forms of texts.

Over the last decade, there has been a surge in the publication of graphic novels in English as well as other languages. Some appear to be directly influenced by their comic-strip forebears – those featuring superheroes and fantastic plots. Others adopt different approaches to storytelling.

Many contemporary graphic novels are autobiographical and very personal, often exploring gut-wrenching themes like childhood trauma.

The memoir has clearly found its home in the graphic novel – whether it strives to tell a story of childhood, family, or even a nation or a people.

The following nine graphic novels represent various approaches to storytelling. Some are fictional and fantastical; others are realistic and autobiographical.

This selection spans a number of countries and cultures. Some have been translated into English; others were written in English originally. Several were created by artist/writer teams. Others have a single author/artist. All the works on this list were originally written as graphic novels – with the exception of *The Magical Life of Long Tack Sam*, which was a documentary film. (Today, many novels are being "converted" into graphic novel format after publication.)

This list is not comprehensive and it does not claim these nine works as "the best" graphic novels. Rather it provides a worthy sampling of the wide range of graphic novels that might make interesting material for study in this option.

As it stands, only a smattering of graphic novels has ever gained international attention; this list simply pulls a few more onto the radar.

Recommended graphic novels

Aya, Abouet, Marguerite and Clement Oubrerie (trans. Helge Dascher)

Aya is based on Abouet's memories of growing up in a working-class neighbourhood of Abidjan. Aya is the calm and steady central character in the midst of the chaotic lives of her friends. Though Abouet deals frankly with issues like teenage sexuality, class divisions, sexism, violence against women, and teenage pregnancy, she does it with a light touch and a clever plot that almost resembles an entertaining soap opera. This novel is followed by two others about Aya, forming a trilogy.

Epileptic, David B. (trans. Kim Thompson)

David B.'s memoir is an intense and intelligent exploration of his brother's epilepsy. Along the way, he turns his attention to French history, politics, and religion. The illustrations are vibrant and dramatic. He creates a mythological, almost dream-like representation of his family's journey through their many attempts to obtain a cure for his brother and finally to their resignation.

Anya's Ghost, Vera Brogsol

Brogsol's work is a rather simple, coming-of-age story wrapped in a supernatural cloak. Chubby, Russian-born Anya spends all her energy trying to fit into her exclusive US private high school. Everything changes when she falls down a well and encounters the ghost of a young girl, much like her. At first, having a ghost as a best friend makes life easier, but then Anya's life takes a turn for the worse. Brogsol's work is fantastical and charming with an undercurrent of terror.

The Magical Life of Long Tack Sam, Ann Marie Fleming

Fleming, a Canadian, explores the life of her great-grandfather, a Chinese circus performer who travelled the globe throughout his career. The exploration of her great-grandfather's life includes an exploration of storytelling, for instance, Fleming includes multiple versions of events. She weaves a family history interlaced with the history of magic, exoticism, orientalism, and two world wars. She incorporates stick drawings, old-fashioned comics, family photos, newspaper clippings, posters, and other ephemera and as a result, her story is rich both visually and textually.

Daytripper, Fabio Moon and Gabriel Ba

Moon and Ba, Brazilian twin brothers, write ten versions of one man's life story. Each chapter focuses on Bras de Oliva Domingos (a writer who pens obituaries for a living) at a particular age and always ends with his death. It's a Borgesian or hypertextual approach to storytelling, much like a choose-your-own-adventure story except that the ending is always the same: death. The novel explores questions of mortality, coincidence, failed dreams, life, family, art, and friendship. Some of the deaths are ordinary, others are macabre; all are discomfiting.

Stitches, Craig Small

Small is a children's illustrator who tells the story of his own bleak childhood. It's set against the backdrop of a polluted, industrial Detroit, inside the suburban home of distant (possibly mentally ill) parents. Small underwent cancer surgery on his throat without his knowledge at age 14. Initially, it left him mute. His style is loose and poetic, and seems influenced by watercolour. The family life he portrays here is often cruel, but the shining light is that he survives, moves towards healing and becoming an artist.

Skim, Mariko Tamaki and Gillian Tamaki

"Skim" is the nickname of the mixed-race heroine who navigates her way through her high-school days, questioning spirituality, sexuality, and what it means to be cool. The novel feels heavy at times – it portrays some drug use, racism, alienation, same-sex attraction – but it moves towards healing and wholeness in a way that is not clichéd.

Good-bye Chunky Rice, Craig Thompson

With a cast of eccentric characters that seem to come from a circus sideshow, Thompson tells a story that is tender and fable-like. Chunky Rice is leaving his home and his love behind to seek adventure and independence. The ship he takes seems like it might be doomed. This short graphic novel explores issues of love, destiny, independence, family, fitting in, leaving family, and creating family.

Vietnamerica: A Family's Journey, GB Tran

Tran's book is one of the most beautifully illustrated graphic novels. His poetic illustrations accompany the story of his parents' lives – as they grow up in Vietnam until they meet and flee after the fall of Saigon. The narrative moves sharply between time so it can be hard to follow at times. He jumps from his own life as a disinterested teenager in the USA to his parents' childhoods to various trips back. As well as the political situation, this novel explores divorce, marriage, loss, memory, parenting, and immigration.

Activity

Go to the site www.free-online-novels.com and look at the graphic novels. Choose either an interactive or a more conventional novel, and give it a quick read. Decide whether you would or would not recommend the work to others on the basis of:

* plot
* writing style
* visual style.

Option 3: Literature and film

You do not need a great deal of technical knowledge about film in order to study one as a text. A few choice terms, however, might be useful (see boxes). A film can be 'read' in much the same way as a print text. There are generic conventions to consider, just as you would for a play, a poem, a novel or a short story. If your teacher has chosen this option for study in Part 4 of the course, there are many approaches that may be taken.

The study might focus on straightforward adaptation of a print text into a film, such as any of the many film versions of Shakespeare's plays, or look at the different ways in which print texts have been used as a launch pad for a film, for example Sam Raimi's film *A Simple Plan*, a version of Chaucer's *The Pardoner's Tale*, or *Clueless*, which has Jane Austen's *Emma* as its inspiration. Transformations of texts have occurred for centuries, as stories have been adapted to contemporary situations. The inspiration of the known reflects upon the new, while the new resonates with the known. This process provides the basis for study in this option.

In a book section such as this, it would be impossible to try to give you all the combinations possible, or to investigate all the angles you might take in this group of texts. However, you should get a flavour of the ways in which you could study this option, and hopefully be inspired with ideas of how to approach and prepare your Individual Oral Presentation.

As well as the general objectives and learning experiences you will have in this course, should you study this option, you will also develop the ability to:

- compare films and their literary roots from a critical perspective
- analyse the reasons for the choices made when adapting a film from a literary work
- acquire an understanding of how characters evolve in a specific time and space
- understand the use of symbolism and how it can be translated from one medium to another
- understand and evaluate the importance of elements such as music, sound and inserts in films.

You will examine ways in which social, cultural, and historical context influences aspects of texts, and the ways in which changes in context lead to changed values being reflected in texts. To do this, you will need to take into consideration issues such as purpose and audience, and analyse the content, values, and attitudes conveyed in both a print text and a film or films based on it.

Presenting literature in film

So what does all this actually mean? One way to look at a film – particularly one which has been adapted in some way from a literary text – is to think about it in terms of representation: *RE*-presentation. Like many other art forms, films are a RE-presentation of reality. Even those films based on real historical figures have to re-present that figure:

- Which actor is cast in the role?
- How are they dressed?
- How are they lit and framed in each shot?
- Does the actor try to mimic the person's voice?

In this way, you can see that films, just like books, are constructions and even more so than with a novel, the audience of a film is being positioned to view the film in a particular way. This becomes more obvious when a film is based on a well-known literary work. How many times have you viewed such a film and come out saying "It wasn't as good as the book!"? Films based on literary texts should be viewed not merely as a reflection of the original work, but as a whole new work in its own right. So how do we do that? And what value does it have with regard to your study of literature?

Activity

Think of some of the films and/or television series which are based on a famous book (or series of books), of which there have been many in recent years: *Harry Potter, Lord of the Rings, The Lion, the Witch and the Wardrobe, Pride and Prejudice, Romeo + Juliet*, for some examples. What others have you been aware of?

- What was your reaction – particularly if you have read the original?
- How did the film represent the original?

- How did the film treat the source material? Faithfully? Differently? If a historical text (a Shakespeare play, or a Dickens or Austen novel), was the film modernized in any way (costume, dialogue, etc.)? What effect did this have? Why would the filmmaker make those choices?
- How this did the film add to your understanding of the original text?

How to 'read' a film

Basically, the study of film can be broken down into three parts:

- the **text** – the content and meaning of the film itself;
- the **makers** – the craft and motivations of the people who produce the text as well as how the audience makes **meaning** of the text; and
- the social, political, and historical context of the text.

Films reflect and shape culture just like any other art form does. A good film is just like a good novel – a story well told – and involves many of the same elements:

- plot
- characters
- atmosphere
- point of view.

However, you shouldn't judge a film in quite the same way that you would a novel. Whilst they do contain some of the same elements, a film has its own generic conventions. Film is more collaborative in its production and revolves around images rather than imagery and in some respects has more affinity with plays than with novels. Just like a play, a film goes through several layers of interpretation before it gets to you, as the viewer of the film. The producer and director will have their own views as to how the film should look, the scriptwriter will put his or her own spin on it, the cinematographer then adds another layer as he or she weaves the magic of lighting, framing, and cutting.

On top of all that, you will have actors who will have their own way of interpreting the script, and the director's directions. And that's before the music director adds to the mood with the soundtrack. And then there's you, the audience. If this is a film based on a book you've read, you will have come to the film with your own set of expectations too. This is why it is often difficult to say who exactly is the author of a film. Is it the director? What about the scriptwriter and those mentioned above, as well as the many others who are involved in a film's production? For the sake of simplicity, we will often refer to the director as the author of a film as ultimately that is the person who will have the final say about the 'look' of a film.

So we come back to the original question: how do you read a film? Well, actually, in much the same way as you read a book, believe it or not! The plot, characterisation, rising and falling action, climax, and point of view should be viewed in much the same way as you do when analysing a writer's craft.

Ask yourself questions such as:

- How does the filmmaker make us feel empathy or sympathy (or not) for the main character? How is that character presented? From whose point of view do we get our opinion? In a novel, for example, if it is written in the first person, we get our point of view from the main protagonist. How does that relate to a film? Look at where the camera is positioned (and therefore you as the viewer of the film). Are we seeing what the protagonist sees? Or are we seeing the protagonist? That's a bit like first person narration and third person. Just as a third person omniscient narrator in a novel will recount the thoughts and feelings of all the characters, the same can be true of a film – the all-seeing eye of the camera. However, as you watch the film, make notes about whether you are seeing things from the protagonist's point of view or not. This would equate to a third person limited narrator in a novel. We, as the viewers, are understanding the protagonist's thoughts and feelings, but do not learn much else directly about other characters.

- How does the filmmaker scare us? Or make us laugh or cry? What are the techniques used? The filmmaker's box of tricks will include using light to create atmosphere, music to alert us to imminent danger, and quick editing to create tension and drama.

- What techniques do a writer and a filmmaker share? What do they do to foreshadow events, for example?

- How is the story told? How else could it be told? Is it chronological, or does the filmmaker use flashbacks?

One way to examine how a text might 'look' if it were made into a film, is to storyboard it. You may have done this previously with texts. There are many ways this may be done, and the following activity will show you how this could work in practice. This would also give you some insight into the ways you can adapt print texts into visual ones, and get you thinking, seeing and producing texts in a visual way.

1. Find the poem *The Raven* by Edgar Allan Poe on the Internet and read it through, checking out any words of which you are unsure.

2. Read it through again, and come up with a short sentence which sums up each stanza. You will now have 18 sentences, which basically summarize the whole poem.

3. Take three large pieces of paper, and divide each one into six boxes. Number the boxes from 1–18.

4. At the bottom of each box, copy the 18 sentences.

5. Now, in each box draw a visual representation of each of those 18 sentences. You should now have a storyboard of the poem which you could use to make a short film, if you so wish.

A three-part structure

Like many stories, films, particularly mainstream ones, will often follow what is known as the 'three act structure', involving the same basic plot structure of narrative stories, with an exposition, rising action, climax (maybe an anti-climax too) falling action and dénouement (or beginning, middle and end, if you wish to simplify it!). Let's take the popular animated film *Finding Nemo* as an example. In Act One the hero, faces a problem which needs to be solved, but there are obstacles in the way which need to be overcome. Act Two sees the hero trying everything to solve the problem, and it begins to appear as if the problem is insurmountable. In Act Three, however, the hero finally finds a solution, against all odds, and shortly after this will be the end of the film.

Of course, that's rather an over-simplification, and many filmmakers will vary this – throwing in a 'twist' at the end for example – but many stories will follow this pattern. Try for yourself and see.

Activity

1. Take a popular film or one that you are currently studying and analyse it under the following headings:
   - Who is the hero? How do we know that?
   - What is the problem which needs solving?
   - What are the complications put in the hero's way?
   - How is the problem finally solved?
2. Take one of the following plot starters, and work it up into a basic three act story:
   - A couple of young adults have been dared to spend the night in a haunted house.
   - A person is seen walking alone in the desert. As the film opens, the camera pans out and we realize that the desert stretches for miles.
   - A lonely boy sets off to find his birth parents.

By going through the following exercises, you will develop the necessary skills to be successful in your IOP (and the rest of your DP, hopefully) and be able to put them to practical use, both for your studies and in the future.

Activity

1. Take another look at the criteria used to assess your IOP and really think about the individual elements of each of the criterion.
2. Either individually or with your classmates, brainstorm and write down what you think are the skills needed for and developed by the individual oral presentation.
3. Finally, organize these ideas in some form of graphical organizer: a spider diagram, a lotus diagram, a mind map, or a simple bullet list. You might come up with something like the diagram below.

Skills and practice

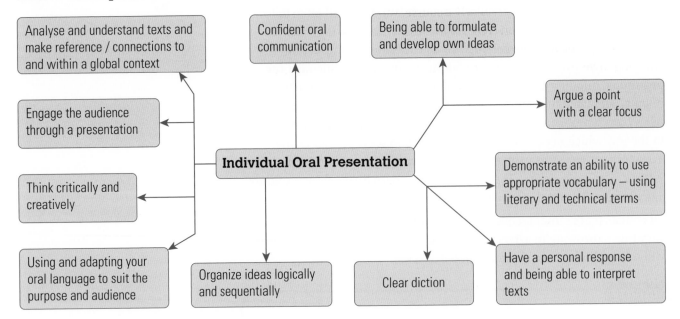

Analyse and understand texts and make reference / connections to and within a global context

Confident oral communication

Being able to formulate and develop own ideas

Argue a point with a clear focus

Engage the audience through a presentation

Individual Oral Presentation

Demonstrate an ability to use appropriate vocabulary – using literary and technical terms

Think critically and creatively

Using and adapting your oral language to suit the purpose and audience

Organize ideas logically and sequentially

Clear diction

Have a personal response and being able to interpret texts

Look at these skills closely. What do you notice about them? You will probably see that many of these skills are not only related to this part of the course – or even just this subject – but are useful skills to have in all your studies, and in your future. That's what's important about this course: developing skills for life.

Activity

Take one of the texts you are studying in Part 4 of this course and imagine you are the director/producer of a new film version. You have some artistic decisions to make:

- What will be the time setting? Will you set the film in the same time as the original, or update it, or set it in the future?
- What costumes will your main characters wear?
- What will the main setting look like?
- Who will be cast to play the main characters?
- What music will you use throughout the film? During the beginning and end credits?
- Who will the audience be for this film? Families, children, adults, all ages?

Jot down some ideas and notes about all of the above, adding some detail as to why those decisions are being made.

Now, put together a 'pack' of the information – some storyboards, sketches of costumes, cast list, some dialogue, and present it to your class as if they were potential investors you are trying to convince to give you millions of dollars so that you can make your film.

Film and text

For your assessment in this part of the course, you will have to do your Individual Oral Presentation (IOP). This means that you will have to develop a topic of your own choosing on one, or more, of the texts you are studying. If your teacher has opted to study a film alongside the original print text, the film *and* the print text together constitute a 'work' and so it is the relationship between the two you will be exploring.

Below you will find an example of a type of activity you could use for your IOP. Work through the activity and come up with some ways in which your presentation could match the activity: a short video, for example, which you then analyse and explain. There are many different texts you can use for this – be creative in your thinking. A poem, for example, could make a fabulous short film. Remember, not all films need to be of a standard length.

Look closely at the descriptors and you will notice that you are being asked to deliver a presentation that is highly effective, with purposeful strategies used to interest the audience. Your audience (your teacher and your classmates, presumably) do not want to sit through yet another PowerPoint presentation, using an in-built template, with you reading off the slides in a monotone.

However, if you should:

- deliver a presentation dressed as Chaucer, explaining why you sent your approval to Sam Raimi to put your name to his film;
- stage a courtroom battle between Baz Lurhmann and Franco Zeffirelli (who both made versions of *Romeo and Juliet*), as to whose version is a better interpretation;
- put together a design board for a new film version of one of your texts, explaining how each part of the costuming and set reflects the essence of the original print text;
- present an oral argument based on a TOK-style question, such as whether the work of literature is enlarged or diminished by the interpretation;
- or compare the ways the original work and the film deal with a certain motif or symbol in the work;

then you should be well on the way to achieving a good mark in your IOP.

Case study: *My Big Fat Greek Wedding*

What follows here is a sample of an approach to a film. Although it is not a film based on a literary text, it will give you further ideas about how to approach a critical analysis of a film, and another angle on developing an IOP in this option.

MY BIG FAT GREEK WEDDING – FILM STUDY

The director of the film *My Big Fat Greek Wedding* uses a variety of techniques to engage the audience and to convey meaning. For example, camera shots, body language (including facial expressions), music, sound effects, lighting, and costumes.

Shots/Camera angles

Initially, a high angle long shot is used to show the audience the setting: the Portokolos' street. The main characters are then displayed from a front-on angle, which gives the illusion that we can see into their car with the characters framed in the car windscreen. They are alone in the car, but the expressions on their faces and the fact that they are as far apart as possible signifies there is some tension between Toula and her father. This shot is used again later in the film when Ian drops Toula off at home after their dates. Each time, they are getting closer and closer together. This emphasizes the growing closeness of their relationship, in opposition to the difficulties in the relationship between Toula and her father.

Figure 1. Toula's first encounter of Ian. She's like a "Greek statue" – transfixed. Toula is looking directly and Ian but he is unaware of her. Toula's expression is one of despair. Her hair is uncombed and lifeless and her clothes are dull and shapeless.

Figure 2. By the end of the film, they are close and happy – framed together and alone. Ian is looking at Toula who is looking directly into the camera with total joy on her face. Her expression is open, her hair is up off her face and her dress accentuates her figure.

Body language and facial expressions

Body language always plays an important role in the film to keep the audience interested. In the travel agency, Toula shows her nervousness and lack of self-confidence by the way she frowns and hides behind the counter when she sees Ian walking past the shop window. In contrast, he has an open-faced expression, full of confidence and showing interest in her. When Ian and Toula finally talk together, they are sitting on the floor together, showing how relaxed they are in each other's company from the very beginning. Contrast this with the scene when Ian talk to Gus, Toula's father, about them getting married: Ian is sitting with Gus standing over him in a position of power.

Music and sound effects

The composer uses traditional Greek music when the characters are celebrating or when something positive is about to happen. The music builds up as Toula transforms herself and takes control of her life and her future. The first time that Toula and Ian meet, the music has a magical quality to it, hinting that something wonderful is about to happen.

Lighting

Lighting is used to create contrasting moods. As a romantic comedy, most scenes are brightly lit. The blossoming romance between Ian and Toula is suggested by subtle lighting at night. For example, for

Ian and Toula's first kiss, they are on a bridge, which is lit in a fairytale fashion by fairy lights, contrasting against the dark night sky. This is an appealing scene to the responder who is as excited as Ian and Toula are by their romance and the fact that they are falling in love.

Costumes

The costumes chosen reflect the moods, personality and cultures of the characters. Ian's parents, who are staid conservative people, wear dull, boring colours. The vibrant Greek personalities of Toula's family are reflected in their brightly coloured clothes. As Toula's transformation progresses, she goes from wearing dull brown colours to bright colours. This shows the change in her personality, mood, and increased self-confidence. Ian wears fairly conservative clothes also, with a stereotypical teacher's tweed jacket with leather patches on the sleeve, but the effect is softened slightly by his mop of hair, suggesting a liberal personality, rather than a conservative one.

This particular discussion is intended to give you an idea of what you might say about a film. In your presentation on a literary text and a film based upon it, you would be talking about both, focusing on a particular aspect of the adaptation.

Key terms:

There is a specialised vocabulary associated with film. This glossary of key terms will define some of these terms.

Backlighting: the main source of light is behind the subject, silhouetting it, and directed toward the camera.

Bridging shot: a shot used to cover a jump in time or place, or other discontinuity, for example falling calendar pages, railroad wheels, newspaper headlines, and changing seasons. If these are not used carefully they can appear clichéd.

Camera angle: the angle between the camera and the object being filmed. For example, a low-angle shot (when the camera is below the object) will make the object appear large, possibly menacing, whereas a high angle shot (with the camera above the object) can make the object appear smaller and vulnerable.

Close-up/extreme close-up (CU/ECU): the subject framed by the camera fills the screen. Connotation can be of intimacy, of having access to the mind or thought processes (including the subconscious) of the character. These shots can be used to stress the importance of a particular character at a particular moment in a film or place her or him as central to the narrative by singling out the character in CU at the beginning of the film. CUs can also be used on objects and parts of the body other than the face. In this instance they can designate imminent action (a hand picking up a knife, for example), and thereby create suspense. Or they can signify that an object will have an important role to play in the development of the narrative. Often these shots have a symbolic value, usually due to their recurrence during the film. How and where they reoccur is revealing not only of their importance, but also of the direction or meaning of the narrative.

Continuity: as films are often shot out of sequence, this is the technique to establish that shots have logical sequence. In other words, if a character is sitting with a drink in their hand which is half full, the next shot must show the same, or lower level, of drink in the glass, not higher.

Cut: the splicing of 2 shots together, made by the film editor at the editing stage of a film. Between sequences the cut marks a rapid transition between one time and space and another, but depending on the nature of the cut it will have different meanings.

Diegesis: the denotative material of film narrative. In other words, the story within the film. Therefore you have *diegetic* and *non-diegetic* sound, which refers to whether the sound is part of the action on film, for example what is heard when a character turns on the radio, or the sound of their footsteps, or the sound added afterwards to create atmosphere, such as a soundtrack, which the characters within the film do not hear.

Dolly / dolly shot: a dolly is a set of wheels and a platform upon which the camera can be mounted to give it mobility and a dolly shot is taken from a moving dolly.

Establishing shot: usually an opening shot which, literally, establishes time and space. This will often be a panoramic exterior view.

Extreme long shot: a panoramic view of, usually, an exterior location photographed from a considerable distance, often as far as a quarter-mile away. May also serve as the establishing shot.

Eyeline: when the camera is positioned in such a way as to mimic the concept that when a character looks off-screen, the audience expects to see what they see. Therefore, this will be cut to show what they are looking at, such as an object, a view, or a person. Eyeline then refers to the trajectory of the looking eye.

Framing: The way in which subjects and objects are framed within a shot.

Mise-en-scene: from the French 'to put in place' and means how everything in each frame fits together: the props, the actors, the camera, etc.

Over the shoulder shot: Literally, a shot taken over the shoulder of an actor, which establishes a relationship between them and another character or object.

Pan: the movement of the camera from one side to another, along an imaginary axis, without the basic camera position changing.

Point of view shot: (Often abbreviated as 'POV'). a shot which shows the scene from the specific point of view of one of the characters.

Storyboard: a series of drawings and captions (sometimes resembling a comic strip) that shows the planned shot divisions and camera movements of the film, as well as any other information such as sound or other effects, and dialogue.

Tracking shot: when the camera moves along with the action, either on a dolly or in a moving vehicle. Not to be confused with a panning shot in which does not move with the action but follows it from a static position.

Voice-over: The narrator's voice when the narrator is not seen.

Index